The Living Stream

HOLY WELLS
IN HISTORICAL CONTEXT

T0324626

The Living Stream

HOLY WELLS
IN HISTORICAL CONTEXT

James Rattue

THE BOYDELL PRESS

First published 1995
The Boydell Press, Woodbridge
Reprinted in paperback 2001

Transferred to digital printing

ISBN 978-0-85115-601-9 hardback
ISBN 978-0-85115-848-8 paperback

The Boydell Press is an imprint of Boydell & Brewer Ltd
PO Box 9, Woodbridge, Suffolk IP12 3DF, UK
and of Boydell & Brewer Inc.
668 Mt Hope Avenue, Rochester, NY 14620, USA
website: www.boydellandbrewer.com

A catalogue record for this book is available
from the British Library

This publication is printed on acid-free paper

CONTENTS

ILLUSTRATIONS

THIS BOOK IS
DEDICATED TO MY FAMILY

INTRODUCTION

> With the advent of Christian missionaries . . . the worship of gods and goddesses of the wells was gradually discontinued, but their places were taken by Christian saints to whom these wells were then dedicated. (Macintire 1944, 1)

> Holy wells were relatively common in Western Britain, and in the area of Celtic Christianity, and are generally believed to have been places of pagan veneration which were dedicated and perhaps adopted as baptismal foci during the Christian Conversion. (Rodwell 1980, 39)

These, the views of academic authorities, are also presented for public consumption in more popular, uncritical accounts.

> The tradition of worship at wells was deeply embedded in the pagan mind. Christianity redirected these observances and saints presided over the benefits attributed to the waters. (Vince 1978, 31)

> Natural springs were frequently used as pagan shrines; Christianity simply took them over, or moved in so that the shrines became Christian by association. (Lloyd 1988, 89)

We can trace the antecedents of this idea back to the early antiquaries:

> And the fountains of the pagan Cornish, in the vicinity of Churches and hermitages, were walled up . . . and dedicated to the patron saints. (Polwhele 1803, i 65)

Finally the ideas fuse into poetry:

> Throughout the length and breadth of the land, the time-hallowed sites and sacred springs were rededicated to the Christian saints, their latent spiritual properties transferred to the latest in a long line of mystical tenants. (Broadhurst 1988, 36)

And it is at this stage that the image is at its most compelling and most dangerous. Compelling because it dovetails neatly into the modern world's aching need to retreat to a mythical, timeless past. Dangerous because it is a distortion of the real past, an act of mental indiscipline, the preference of the pleasant over the real. The adoption of pagan sites by

1

Christian missionaries is acknowledged as a universal phenomenon, but as regards holy wells the adoption seems to have been by no means as smooth or as total as the popular accounts tend to suggest. Nor do any of the other processes they mention: the assumption of a necessarily Celtic or even earlier origin for these springs, the supposed decline from holy well to spa, the declared uniformity of well-traditions in different regions.

Holy wells have been and continue to be appallingly served by scholarship. As shall be argued in Chapter 9, the public view of them – such as it is – is currently conditioned by a 'mystical consensus' composed of elements of Margaret Murray's *The Witch Cult of Western Europe*, Robert Graves's *The White Goddess* and John Michell's *The View Over Atlantis*, all confused with neurological theories and overlaid by a sort of separatist feminism which turns out to be reactionary and conservative. This has two effects. Firstly it assumes on occasion an almost ideological hostility to rational thought and so tends to dismiss rational criticism of its arguments; secondly, it alienates from the subjects of its attention all those groups who most rely on reason, and those people therefore abandon those subjects to the distortions of the mystics. The extent to which this consensus is affecting public opinion can be witnessed by a trip to Glastonbury, by the popular faith in ley-lines and by the readiness, even eagerness, of many clerics to claim pagan origins for their churches. The church at Beaminster (Dorset) is proud that it stands on 'a mound which may be a pre-Christian sacred site', while the church of St Nicholas, Leicester, boasts of the supposed pagan temple beneath its foundations which was in fact part of the market place. When this is the model adopted by the Anglican Church, corrective action seems desperately needed!

The historiography of holy wells has served them badly too; but since that historiography reflects their history in important ways, we will not discuss it yet. Naturally, before the Reformation and the suppression of all sorts of popular customs, such things were not questioned or investigated; holy wells were reported in this period only by accident. Only afterwards were traditions taken note of and set down by antiquarians. The antiquarian phase lasted, perhaps, until the late 1820s, when the first of Hone's collections of popular customs began to appear, and the systematic study of folklore did not begin until the latter part of the nineteenth century, when that lore was felt to be dying out. Brand's *Observations on Popular Antiquities* (1777) was an early precursor of the field.

It was at this point that tragedy occurred. Not only were the folklorists tabulating popular customs and beliefs at a time when those subjects appeared to be of no historical importance, but their whole approach was alienating to the historians. The folklorists tended to universalize their discoveries, regarding the 'survivals' of ancient custom as the untainted

2

relics of a pure antiquity, and extending the motifs they found still in existence backward to a prehistoric past. This was the assumption of Sir Lawrence Gomme's *The English Village Community*, and it survived into such masterpieces as Sir James Frazer's *The Golden Bough*; and it was exactly the wrong sort of assumption for the intellectual times. Under the unofficial leadership of F.W. Maitland, the historical community was by the 1890s launching into a vast reaction, as they saw it, against the 'Whig History' of Macaulay, Stubbs and Freeman (the last of whom erected a theory of universal 'Aryan institutions' which could be glimpsed across the Europeanized world and which had their roots in the distant past). All universalism had to go, and universalist folklore went with it. Maitland tore Gomme's arguments to shreds, and history and folklore were thereafter severed asunder.

For a long while the folklorists went cheerfully onwards as they had done before, doing the essential but limited work of tabulating traditions, ignoring the societies surrounding those traditions. Equally the historians ignored the value of popular customs to their own studies, relying for their impressions of the Common People of the past on inherited prejudices and economic analyses. The only breaches in this division came in 1941 and 1956, with the publication of G.C. Homans's *English Villagers of the Thirteenth Century* and W.M. Williams's *Sociology of an English Village*, attempts to marry the two disciplines which do seem to have pushed folklore study into a more academic and historical frame of mind (Phythian-Adams 1976, 7–8).

By the 1970s the Folklore Society had become both learned and august, yet there was little reciprocal movement from the opposite side. But an awareness of the inability of pure economic history to touch the real lives of ordinary people – a normal aim for historical enquiry in a democratic age – appears to have been galvanized by the appearance of K.V. Thomas's *Religion and the Decline of Magic*. We have reached the position today at which fine fusions of folklore and history are appearing, such as Bushaway's *By Rite* and Obelkivich's *Religion and Society in South Lindsey*, and where popular tradition is now seen to have a real, legitimate contribution to make to history. Historians are no longer frightened.

But I see reason to be. I would fear that the dominance of the mystical view of holy wells will drive the historians away from them again just as they begin to take an interest. Thus the urgency of staking a claim for history, of making an historical study of the wells of neglected areas, keeping a general chronological framework in mind, and of excavating as many as possible of the surviving fabrics of wells. The signs from France are encouraging: there good historical studies of holy wells have appeared (Hubert 1977; Roblin 1976), but as yet there is nothing comparable for Britain.

3

The poverty of systematic research, particularly in the east and north, presents enormous problems for the development of any intellectually credible general picture; and especially the truth of the common assumption that holy wells are more common in the west of the country than elsewhere (an idea that has its basis in the belief that the well is essentially a Celtic phenomenon) is impossible to judge, as is any possible effect of Scandinavian settlement. Map 1 gives an idea of the current state of play. Documentary and field surveys have been carried out in Scotland, Dorset, Cumbria and Oxfordshire to varying degrees of completeness (Cornwall has been 'done' countless times but only its Christian wells are ever taken account of). A full survey requires a raid of old local or county histories, a scouring of the available place-name evidence, a browse through a suitably large-scale edition of the Ordnance Survey maps, and the questioning of any local people you may come across. It also demands a friendly attitude to the non-holy well, which can give us a great deal of help and record long-forgotten traditions.

Sadly few of these surveys have been carried out. Francis Jones's *Holy Wells of Wales* (1954) is an excellent and historically minded effort, but lacks field-research. Only Taylor-Page's monograph (1990) on Cumbria is especially worthy in that respect. Beyond this, the majority of researchers are careless of sites recorded in place-names, and have concentrated in general on those with impressive folklore. This is shortsighted as there is evidence that many wells began as place-name wells and only later acquired Christian dedications; and besides, such dedications may easily vanish to be replaced by less impressive names. But partial surveys can be topped up by reference to the English Place-Name Society volumes in Cornwall, Gloucestershire, Middlesex, Derbyshire and Cumbria, and West Yorkshire; in Cheshire, Westmorland, Berkshire and Wiltshire those volumes themselves provide the backbone of the available material. Elsewhere, a fullish picture can be constructed for each of Somerset (where Dom. Ethelbert Horne's monograph can be supplemented with a county history and a Geological Survey volume), Herefordshire, Leicestershire and the Isle of Wight. There are also full surveys for County Dublin and County Donegal, and one of unknown usefulness for Suffolk, but I have been unable to locate these.

In these counties we have a good idea of the strength and nature of the well-cult. Nowhere else is this quite the case. The volumes of the EPNS up to that for Wiltshire did not normally include field-names and still had severe limitations long after that. Those before 1939 are almost useless so far as wells are concerned, and of course much of the country has not been covered at all; the publication rate is painfully slow. Investigations of the major sites, as the map shows, have been conducted for several other areas, some of which can be taken as more or less adequate, at least to

4

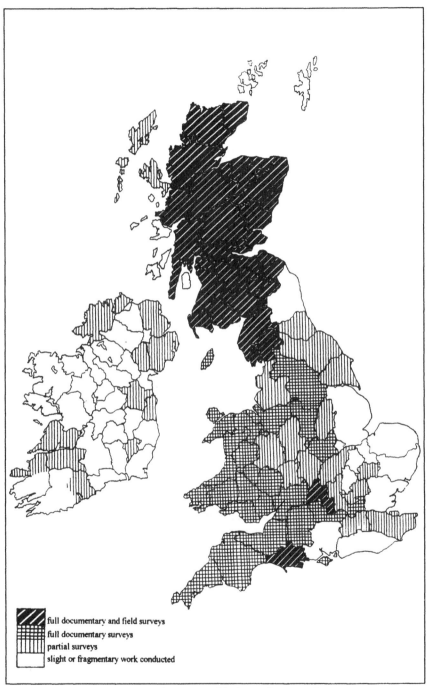

Map 1: The state of holy well research

give us some idea of the importance of the cult. But there are still large swathes of England where no systematic work has been done at all. These distortions inevitably condition the analysis that follows, particularly in terms of distribution maps; concentrations of wells dedicated to a particular saint, or of certain traditions, may then reflect the distribution of research more than a distribution of sites.

Apart from the inadequate scope of the material, there is also its limited nature to consider. Most of it ignores the value of sites recorded in place-names, and the attitude of some researchers to the non-holy well has sometimes been positively condescending, that they are somehow 'illegitimate' in a peculiar way (O'Danachair 1955, 217). Problems also arise from the way in which wells appear in the historical record.

Place-name evidence is very haphazard in the manner of its recording, and is rarely a guide to anything but local conditions (below, pp.14–16). The dates of first record bear no necessary relation to actual fact. We are most likely to come across historical notices of wells when they appear as boundary marks or field names, both of which are especially erratic in appearance; but they can occasionally crop up in episcopal records, usually as a result of conflict. The well of 'St Lawrence' at Peterborough, Holy Well at High Wycombe and the Bisham well are all known only from episcopal condemnations. It is also possible that references will be found in such documents as churchwardens' or guild accounts, but these have never been examined with wells in mind.

Traditions stood a better chance of being recorded only after the Reformation, when they were beginning to die anyway. Thus the early antiquaries, such as John Aubrey, note a large number of beliefs and customs, but this number falls as time goes by. By John Collinson's time (c.1790), wells clearly survive but shorn of much of their traditions, and these men were not overly concerned with hunting down what did survive. Wells were noted down by later collators, Hutchins et al., only by accident, as picturesque morsels. When the study of folklore was born as an independent subject, researchers often hunted in vain for their glimpses of past cultures, finding they had arrived largely too late. Thus we are compelled to scrape through diaries, journals, local histories, for chance references.

This bias has probably contributed as much as anything to the Celto-centrism of modern accounts of holy wells, since traditions lingered longest in Catholic Ireland, Man, the Highlands, and pre-Methodist Wales, long enough to be recorded last century or this. The emphasis on Ireland, so noticeable in, for instance, the Bords' study, is as the map shows especially ironic as so little of it has been properly studied. About half of the holy wells mentioned in *Sacred Waters* hail from Scotland or Wales, with Ireland not far behind. Somewhat less than a third are

English. It is only natural that most investigators have been dazzled by that bias.

This is also intended as a *history* of holy wells. It does not claim to be a compendium of traditional motifs concerned with wells, nor does it analyse them only in relation to themselves. The Bords have already done this admirably. Instead, in the conviction that the holy well stands before a long, if tiny and ill-lit, corridor of history with doors leading off into many unexpected and little-visited rooms, it attempts to portray their development in the context of the society that surrounded and still surrounds them.

Perhaps the core defect of previous research has been that of the primitive folklorists, that of ahistoricalism. Wells have been considered almost in total isolation, divorced from local conditions and subject to all sorts of unlikely generalisations.* But conditions are not everywhere the same. The religious experience of the Celtic fringes is so radically different from that of England (and not just because of the Reformation) that comparisons between the two areas ought not lightly to be made. The Celtocentrism of well-research has left a peculiarly English experience out of the picture. It is time to restate that experience. It is time the holy well became historical.

* This condemnation is not intended as a blanket one. Most local studies make few generalized statements, and the best have eschewed any material outside the immediate area concerned (Logan 1980; Jones 1954; Morris 1981). Possibly the best model for the future is Jim Taylor-Page's study of Cumbria. It is not exhaustive, but involves meticulous field research, and incorporates facts of local history, ecclesiastical organisation and geology in an entirely laudable way.

ONE

Wellsprings of Worship: The Origins of Hydrolatry

> It cannot be stressed too often that everything related to wells, whether in early form or in mangled survival, traces to one source – religion. (Jones 1954, 1)

Surely such an assessment is overstated, as anyone aware of the vast number of well-names in the Middle Ages and later formed by nothing more sacred than the name of the local landowner will agree; yet reverence paid to springs and the debasement of it, from wishing wells to spas, does have deep roots in the soil of religious practice.

The nature of this religion is what is arguable. The idea that hydrolatry originated in the rites surrounding Neolithic megalith-worship has recently gained some degree of currency on the back of orthodox archaeological endorsement. Aubrey Burl has noted the proximity of wells to megalithic monuments, while Colin Burgess has gone so far as to suggest that the water-cult developed as stone circles became useless for astronomical observation after the worsening of the climate at the end of the Bronze Age, c.1000 BCE (Bord 1985, 3).

As the Bords themselves admit, this is unconvincing, but not for the reasons they posit, that the siting of megalithic monuments took place before the shift in climate (Bord 1985, 4). Instead the theory shows far too much reliance on the major sites, the Aveburies, the Stonehenges. Most stone circles were far too small to have been used for astronomical calculations: not for halfway accurate ones, anyway. Besides, at a more fundamental level, it is hardly surprising that water is found near circles, if by 'near' we mean anything below half a mile or so. Firstly circles are commonly placed on prominent sites, above the settlements they were associated with; and it is not unusual to find water halfway down hills. Secondly, wherever there is settlement there has to be water, and the circles could have maintained little sort of function at all without people

8

living nearby. Finally, circles survive in areas of what may have been fairly heavy settlement but which were largely abandoned by the Dark Ages, that is, marginal areas, composed of hard, impermeable soils which retain moisture on the surface, making it more than likely that we will find water nearby. Burgess's idea seems to be a slim base on which to rest the most momentous of theories. What is suggestive is that larger circles in Cumbria do often seem to be sited over underground springs, which hints that there may have been some connection (Taylor Page 1990–91, i 16–22).

Beyond this there is no evidence that water was involved in Neolithic ritual; at Avebury, for instance, another much vaunted example, the so-called Kennet Avenue of stones runs not towards the River Kennet, but to the Sanctuary; and the avenue on the other side of the henge leads to the far from watery Windmill Hill. The only possible glimpses of Neolithic worship survive where megalithic monuments have been incorporated into Christian ceremonies: Carnac, Brittany and Dungiven (Derry), for instance (Jones 1954, 15; Logan 1980, 101–2) and in both cases the relationship is unclear. Such rites are repeated at many locations with no hint of a Neolithic context, so there is no necessary connection.

There are other theories closely related to climate. N.J.G. Pound's is ingenious. Concentrating on Cornwall, he points out that there are several tales of saints creating springs for local people in times of drought, the most well known of these being that of St Meriasek, who performed the service for the inhabitants of Camborne when he arrived there in the sixth century. This is then related to a drying of the climate c.400–700, which would have resulted in water becoming rarer and the consequent worship of those places where it was in abundance (Pound 1942–3, 262–4). This interesting thesis is surely a little limited, as the well-cult clearly pre-dates and extends beyond a period of dry weather in fifth-century Cornwall.

Not all writers submit to the tendency to put religion first in their discussions of the cult. Laurens Otter points out that theories of hydrolatry arising from a 'natural wonder' at the sight of water have one great flaw:

> In hot and dry climates I can fully understand that water would be reverenced . . . But in these islands is water really always desirable? Especially in days when the population was little more than three or four per cent of what it is now? . . . I suspect that by far the greatest number of them contained chemical impurities within their waters. (Otter 1985a, 9)

Meyrick links holiness with healing in a vague manner, but also places the prime emphasis on the medicinal aspects of wells. Or 'man . . . no doubt found some wells were beneficial to his animals and himself and these waters were reverenced as their fame spread' because 'it was inevitable, knowing of the doctrinal connection between religion and healing in Christianity, that some [wells] were regarded as healing springs' (Meyrick 1982, 1–3; Morris 1981, 3; Morrell 1988, 5). Yet the Leggatts, who of all people are most concerned with medicinal wells, stress that in Cornwall 'it is very rare for the water to have any specific mineral content' (1987, 1); but that hardly appears to have put the devotees off. St Mungo's Well, Copgrove (North Yorkshire), continued to have a strong healing reputation into the eighteenth century, but its water contained no minerals (Hartley 1986, 22). So we are left with the puzzle. Which came first – sanctity or medicine? Were holy wells holy by virtue of being healing, or vice versa, with the healing motifs becoming applied to sites to which they are not relevant?

The enormous extension of the cult argues in a different direction. In the context of this single religious motif spanning the whole Eurasian continent and beyond, as shall be discussed later, what is most prominent are not the intrinsic healing properties of water, but its role as the repository or medium of a kind of spiritual power. In Ireland, that gallery of ancient customs, there are plenty of examples of wells being fully reverenced (with circumambulation, prayers and so on) with no specific mention of healing powers. Probably the attitude towards well-worship here was similar to that regarding many other religious practices, that it conferred some sort of spiritual benefit and that it gave practical back-up to the prayers of the supplicant. The well in this context was simply an appropriate place to contact the Deity, to impress Him with your piety, and to communicate your petitions.

In their account of the well-cult, the 'mystic' school of thought probably has the origins best assessed:

> Water is one of the prime necessities of life, and to early man the sight of a spring of crystal liquid bubbling out of the ground, or gushing from some crevice in a rock, must have appeared nothing short of miraculous. (Baker 1985, 25)

This sounds overstated, but in fact it makes good sense. Water is 'other'. Its moods are strange and various. By turns it is quiet, and violent; it can refresh or it can kill. It emerges in a miraculous way from the earth, for it is neither living, nor inanimate; it possesses life, yet is not itself alive, and unlike fire, can never fully be domesticated. Water further comes from below, from darkness, from the place where the dead (in cultures for which that is relevant) are buried, from the brooding presence beneath the feet. We can today best appreciate this feeling when we enter caves from which rivers run. The cave transports even the modern human into a dark and awesome world, reduces her to the status of a child in the night; and this regression is intimately associated with the idea of downward motion, of return to the origin. It is easy to see how rivers with their source in caves – the Axe at Wookey, for instance (Ross 1967, 106–7) – could become reverenced, but the feelings accentuated by the cave can be generalized to the earth as a whole, the same images of darkness, origins, down. The link between the aspect of earth as origin or birthplace, and water, is powerfully expressed by the connection in the words 'spring' and 'fountain' in most western European languages.

> Thou art the well of compassion
> Thou art the root of consolation
> Thou art the living stream of the virgins
> And of them who bear children.   (Carmichael 1958, 179)

The religious imagery of water does not stop here. One of the most powerful of these images, which will recur often in this study, is the miraculous ability of water to cleanse. Fire cleanses with violence, but water with gentleness. This motif occurs in a greatly varied range of religious rituals. Accused of immorality, Sita purified herself in a well at Monghyr (Walters 1928, 118), while the basins of salty water by the doors of Catholic churches testify to the same religious idea. Finally, a flat body of water has the power to reflect. In pools of water the human being first saw his own face, and could see the world mirrored around him: and this is perhaps the most surprising and extraordinary power of water. It transforms the lake or pond into a gateway to another world entirely; an image which can be seen, again, in all religious responses to water from the Celtic lake-hoards to the utterly irrational urge of modern *homo sapiens* to toss coins into fountains in shopping centres.

This lengthy discussion may appear irrelevant. It is certainly 'unhistorical' but none the less necessary, to establish the instinctive roots behind hydrolatry. With a touch of poetry, with an imaginative examination of our own responses to water, we can create a more convincing picture of primitive well-worship than is offered by the climatic or medicinal theories, or any idea that water was considered holy because it was scarce.

Culture and Wells

The implication behind Celtocentrism in the study of holy wells is that race and culture have a large influence on the distribution and nature of the cult. The Celts, it is asserted, had a 'natural' tendency to appreciate the sanctity of water, and this is, in the modern mind, somehow connected with their assumed sensitivity to the Feminine, the earth, the moon, and the intuitive side of the human psyche. The exact details of this will have to wait, but it would be instructive to examine the truth of the idea here.

Certainly holy wells seem to have been more powerful in Celtic areas. At Robertstown (Limerick) and Inismurray (Sligo) in Ireland were springs which had the ability to calm storms, and others were of such sanctity that visitors to them were protected thenceforth from shipwreck (O'Danachair 1955, 215; Logan 1980, 142, 85; Meyrick 1982, 145). Wells in these regions displayed whole personalities of their own. On being insulted they might move from one location to another – this tale is told of over seventy sites, the majority being in Ireland – or might take more drastic action still against those who transgressed against their dignity. Ill fortune followed the farmer who removed the basin from St Cybi's Well, Duloe (Cornwall), while a man who stole the money deposited in St Patrick's Well, Uregare (Limerick) and spent it on drink was struck dead on emerging from the pub (O'Danachair 1955, 217; Meyrick 1982, 39). In the Hebrides there was often a distinction between those wells which were for general use and those for locals only. Fivepennies Well on Eigg was especially chauvinistic: any foreigner who spent the night there seeking a cure would be deformed instead (Martin 1934, 302). English holy wells seldom appear particularly powerful, and traditions of respect for them seem curiously pointless in contrast to the vigorous and vengeful springs of the Celtic areas.

The contrast is commonly ascribed to the fifth and sixth centuries: 'The Anglo-Saxon invasions caused extensive depopulation of the south-eastern district, and few of the wells or streams retained their Celtic names or their supernatural associations' (Anderson 1971, 14–15). Thus the holy well leads us into our first historical minefield, the survival, or otherwise, of the Britons in the centuries following the withdrawal of Roman authority. We are not at the moment concerned with the persistence of the sub-Roman administrative and religious system, or the patchy nature of the conquest itself, but simply with survival at the racial and cultural level.

There was a time when the large-scale survival of a Celtic population in the south-east region of the country would have seemed ludicrous. That this was an impression generated by the biases of documentary evidence has long been recognized: the fire-and-sword image of the English Invasions which, try as we might, is intensely difficult to exorcize, arises largely because Bede's *Ecclesiastical History* is a morality tale, if an historically conscientious one, about the punishment of the ethically lax Britons by God's Own People, while the *Anglo-Saxon Chronicle* appears to have been composed from heroic poetry and other such materials, and is naturally not concerned with the British point of view. The other distorting factor is the historian's great vice, the compression of timescale. Looking back on the foreshortened past, we tend to forget its length. The conquest began with the Saxon revolt c.442 and ended with Egbert's incorporation of Dumnonia within Wessex c.814. If we wish to narrow that picture a little, we can take the capture of eastern Somerset in 658 as the end of the era of rapid English expansion, but this still leaves us with a period of a couple of centuries – that is, from the French Revolution to the present day. A vast amount of political toing and froing can take place in two hundred years. The untidiness of the invasion is now recognized; but the extent of continuity with the past that implies is still a matter of some discussion.

1 Archaeology

After the symbolic withdrawal of Rome the Britons appear to vanish entirely. In his latest summary of the available evidence, Myres writes that their culture after the departure of the legions was 'almost as devoid of durable possessions as any culture can be'. Even making the most generous allowances for the decay of the Roman money economy which was entirely powered by consumer durables, he concludes that no other hypothesis is likely than a 'drastic reduction in the numbers of the native population and an equally drastic reduction in the standard of living of those who remained' (Myres 1989, 21, 23). Where Celtic culture remained vigorous and thriving we do find substantial archaeological remains in the form of memorial stones and so on: in the east of the country there is virtually nothing.

This is powerful argument, and little positive defence has ever actually been raised against it. The usual counter-argument, that because the Celts were Christians we should not expect grave-goods from their side of the cultural divide, barely accounts for the total absence of pottery and the like. Also, as shall be argued later, it is most unlikely that the Britons ever were very Christian below the level of the ruling class. Yet if this is true, then much of the evidence of the English conquest, which relies on plotting maps of 'pagan Saxon sites', is very unreliable, for it becomes impossible to assume that a burial without culturally identifiable grave-goods is English simply by virtue of an orientation (north–south rather than east–west) which is thought to be 'unChristian'; and plenty have been identified solely on that basis.

For example, judging by Jeremy Harte's summary, less than a dozen of the many 'Anglo-Saxon' burials in Dorset can be positively identified as such, because the descriptions of all the rest rely on the assumption that all grave-goods, even mere iron knives, and (so-called) non-Christian grave orientations denote Anglo-Saxon burials. We may guess that the graves we are likely to discover belong to members of the ruling classes, and the British ruling classes were likely to be Christians; because such people would have buried no goods, and these graves have goods, this would reinforce the traditional picture of a great reduction in the numbers of native Britons. But even that is a false argument. These people were rural dwellers; there is no reason why most should have had much contact with the surviving pockets of British Christianity at Wareham or Sherborne, or stayed Christian after being long deprived of priests. Thus the answer to the question 'where are the British?' may be simply 'there they are': in the 'Anglo-Saxon' cemeteries. At least one archaeologist has come to this conclusion (Harke 1990), and besides, invaders did not always wipe out the existing rulers. Gaulish bishops, for instance, were normally Romans for generations after the Franks conquered Gaul (Harte 1986, 9–12; Todd 1987, 249; Haslam 1984, 208–12; Musset 1975, 133–4).

Goods themselves present problems. Ordinary domestic artefacts, designed for practicality rather than for artistic purposes, appear indistinguishable across different cultures (Alcock 1971, 356). Furthermore, it is a commonplace among cautious Eastern European archaeologists that artefacts do not represent the movement of peoples, even if their style is recognizable: they represent the movement of artefacts and that is that. If conspicuously Celtic artefacts can be found at Oving (Buckinghamshire), Hitchin (Hertfordshire) and even at Sutton Hoo itself (Davis 1982, 13), is it inconceivable that English artefacts should have found their way in the opposite direction? A slow, stuttering English conquest is now the accepted model; Bede, copying Gildas, alleges internecine war between the Britons and cross-cultural alliances may well have been made, giving ample opportunity for the exchange of goods. Other prestigious items might, of course, be captured in wartime.

Naturally we cannot dismiss all archaeological evidence as unreliable. Cambridgeshire, Norfolk and Kent were undoubtedly areas of early English settlement, for example, but we simply cannot make any guesses as to the number of settlers the sites represent. Archaeology can give us ideas as to the chronology of the settlement, but not its extent. We must turn elsewhere.

2 Place-names

The Celts have not vanished from the toponymic record as totally as they have from the archaeological one. Jackson's *Language and History in Early Britain* (1953) was the first work to notice the gradual increase in the numbers of Celtic river-names from east to west across the country, and since then scholars have been far readier to accept the notion of the survival of Celtic place-names. Anglo-Saxon *funta* and *eccles* have clearly passed over from the Celtic, while reference to the natives themselves in the forms of the elements *wealas* and *cumbra* 'are the surest and most direct evidence available for the presence of native people in Dark Age England' (Davis 1982, 113; Gelling 1978, 68–74). The list Davis assembles for his area of study is most impressive.

It is also argued that existing place-names may have replaced original British ones in the same way that Wigston (Leicestershire) replaced a lost Saxon name, and Eoforwic/York displaced the ancient Evoragun (Sawyer 1979, 111, 125). Certainly those endless lists of 'so-and-so's *hamms*' attributed, in the want of any more convincing explanation, to unknown Saxon landowners, which so disfigured many of the earlier volumes of the EPNS, may hide Celtic names or Celtic words: no one has ever been minded to look. In modern times names which have appeared inexplicable to locals have been twisted beyond all recognition to make sense of them. A Bullock's Well appears on the Hilton (Dorset) Tithe Map, but derives from the Bollecashe referred to in 1399 – that is, *bulluc aesc*, 'ash-tree', a clear case of local people altering a name after it has been rendered incomprehensible by time (Mills 1989, 212). Surely the invading English were equally able to adopt some elements of names and distort others to forms they recognized?

The imposition of English place-names is more easily explained than the death of the British tongue itself. Davis has considered this too, and argues that the British, deprived of the 'social compactness of a . . . physically isolated community' (which the Cornish and Bretons had) were bound to suffer the destruction of their language, and he points to the comparison of the Danes in eastern England, who were gradually assimilated in the same way. 'Pictish and Etruscan vanished', he claims, 'But not their peoples'. British was doomed to slow attrition (Davis 1982, 122–4).

But this pro-Celtic case is really unable to bear its internal strains. Davis's model of the death of British is one of the control of the social structure by an English aristocracy which gradually wore down the native tongue; but, as Gelling has pointed out, there are no other examples of this process happening, and elsewhere foreign aristocracies are instead themselves worn down by the people they conquer (1979, 110–13). The example of the Danes is misleading, for *thorps* and *bys* are easily recognizable, and the fact that they were coined at a time of widespread record-making while potential Celtic names were not is irrelevant. Better evidence can be gleaned by examining other cultural conquests. The Lombards had conquered northern Italy by c. 616; but by c. 700 they had lost their language, and when their chronicler Paul the Deacon was writing c. 780 they had even abandoned their distinctive styles of dress.

15

'Countless French villages still retain in their . . . names . . . the *nomen* of the Gallo-Roman family to which the estate . . . had belonged', and the case that the British language could not have survived because Britons were cut off from each other is useless: pockets of minority speech persist in abundance in eastern Europe (Wickham 1981, 68; Myres 1989, 31–2).

Large numbers of Slavs were required to change the place-names of western Greece. Gelling's conclusion that 'only a large number of Anglo-Saxon peasant settlers could have caused the Anglicisation of our place-names' therefore seems just (Obolensky 1971, 51–60; Gelling 1979, 113), but until more toponymic work is done we will not know exactly how just. Despite the effects of the Great Plague of the fifth century and the migrations to Brittany (to judge by hagiographical accounts these were probably largely from Wales and Dumnonia anyhow) it is unlikely that by c.450 the lowland British population was substantially reduced from late Roman levels; but at the same time there must have been enough settlers to dominate most villages to change their place-names. Then again, there are possibly Celtic words preserved in the wholly unconsidered field of dialect speech. The experience of the Isle of Lewis shows how difficult any categorical judgement is. 110 of 126 local settlement names are at least partly Scandinavian, though the Gaels can hardly have been wiped out to the extent that might suggest. The spoken language, if not the place-names, had again become Gaelic by the sixteenth century without any massive population shift (Sawyer 1982, 101).

Our conclusions have to be tentative, then, but the weight of the evidence is on the side of a traditionalist picture of the bulk of English settlement being in the south-east, though models of the total destruction of the Celts are surely mistaken. As regards wells, it is not even clear that a large-scale influx of Teutons would make that much difference. They were not as a people averse to well-worship. Tacitus tells us of a sacred lake with an island on which stood 'an inviolate grove'. Nearby was kept a chariot sacred to a goddess, which was washed in the lake by slaves who were then ritually drowned (*Germania*, 40). The god Thor had a well at Thorsas, Norway, while Adam of Bremen reports that a yew tree which overhung the temple at Uppsala stood near a well in which human sacrifices were drowned. In the Icelandic Sagas there is also mention of the *blotkelda* – 'bloody wells' – which may refer to sacrifices (Montelius 1910, 77; Branston 1974, 176; Turville-Petre 1964, 247).

At first glance, Map 2 confirms the Celtocentric model of the well-cult. In general the higher values tend to be in the west and the lower in the east, and it comes as no surprise to find very high values in Wales – 2.6 in Pembrokeshire and 3.4 in Flintshire – and very low ones, such as the 97.7 of Suffolk, in the North Sea coastal counties where there was early Anglo-Saxon penetration. But closer examination reveals great anomalies

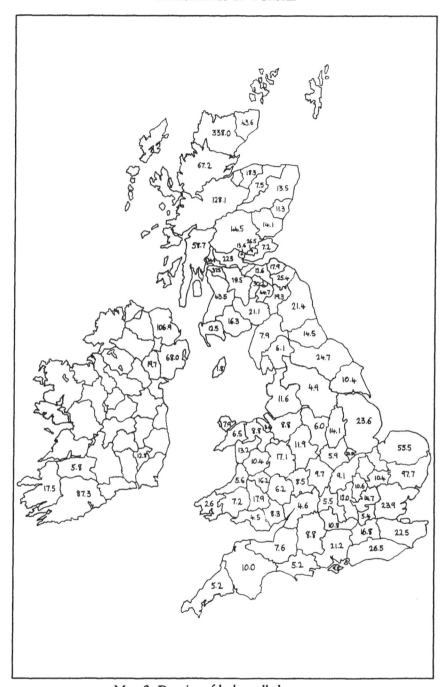

Map 2: Density of holy wells by county
Figures refer to number of square miles per named well

in this simple picture. It does come as a surprise that the figure for Anglicized Oxfordshire is higher than that for Herefordshire in the Welsh Marches – though this may be the effect of uneven research – and surprise is not the right word regarding the figures in Devon and Northamptonshire. Devon has large parts of low population density, but Northamptonshire has not been nearly as well investigated. Cambridgeshire, as yet without an in-depth survey and an area of early Anglo-Saxon settlement to boot, has a figure remarkably high in view of both these facts.

Further, the extraordinarily high figure of West Yorkshire belies its low medieval population and its Danish settlements. The population growth of the eighteenth and nineteenth centuries cannot account for it. Within the ten constituent townships of Leeds, for example, there are twenty-one named wells; of these, only Holme Well, Middleton (first noted in 1841), Tan House Well, Chapel Allerton (a name dependent on a modern feature) and Poverty and Hertford Springs in Temple Newsam (which both occur in 1850 and which may not even be wells) can be so much as half-confidently ascribed to the period of modern growth (Smith 1961–3, ii 140, iv 139, iv 118). Tree-well names (Willow Well, Temple Newsam, 1850) are usually old; and other names – Rising Well, Headingley; Popple and Syke Wells, Middleton – contain old elements and are undated (ibid., iv 118, 143; v 67). All the other wells (thirteen of them) are definitely pre-Industrial Revolution. The supposed strength of the Celtic Church in the north-west, as revealed by the place-name element *eccles* does not help to explain this, as of the eleven *eccles*-townships in Lancashire, Cheshire and West Yorkshire, only four have wells of any kind (Eccles (Lancashire), Ecclesfield, Eccleshall and Eccleshill (West Yorkshire)).

These examples are enough to show that national or racial characteristics are not by themselves sufficient to account for the distribution of wells. Also important is the evidence of towns. Oxford, for instance, is a city without antecedents. Roman activity was confined to the kilns north of the city, and there was no settlement prior to the establishment of St Frideswide's minster about 700. The reliance of the city on Christian insititutions for its very existence makes it highly unlikely that there were pagan settlers, Celtic or English, and consequently no pagan wells. None the less there were a number of holy wells in and around the city. The site at Holywell (cf. p.61) may be pagan, but there is at least no continuity within the walls.

Of course population density played a part. In Wales the lowest densities of wells are those of the mountainous counties; and in Scotland this link is truly spectacular, the empty countryside of Sutherland producing a figure of one well for each 338 square miles. In Scotland generally, only Banffshire and Fife have densities as high as those of

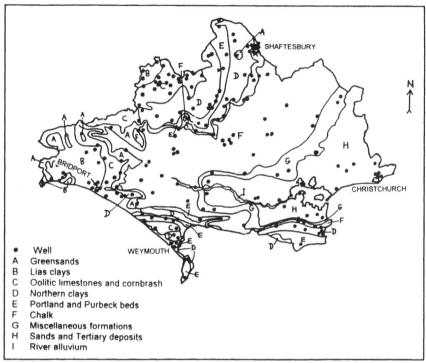

Map 3: Dorset: wells and geology

the western shires of England. It is true that we might expect Somerset and Herefordshire to yield figures as high as Glamorganshire, but the difference can be explained by the social and economic backwardness of Wales and the later collection of its folklore (but cf. p.124).

Population, in the medieval and earlier periods, was dependent on geology, which also affects the water supply. Map 3 shows how Dorset, a county of great geological contrasts, reflects this. Wells are not common on the sands and gravels of the east, and hardly abundant on the central band of hard but porous chalk; by complete contrast, the clays and complex composition of Blackmore Vale in the north, the Weymouth and Bridport areas and the Isle of Purbeck produce higher densities. Yet, assuming that Domesday Book provides at least a schematic idea of population, the density of settlement in Dorset was almost even, apart from the lower concentration in the east where soils were poor (Darby & Welldon Finn 1967, 92); certainly differences in population were not as sharp as those in the distribution of wells. Considering that the whole of eastern England is composed of gravels, chalks and sands – apart from the Kentish Weald, always sparsely inhabited – this, coupled with lower rainfall, must account for some of its scarcity of wells.

Having said all this, densities of population sometimes bear no relation to wells at all. St Kilda (Western Isles) never had a population of many more than two hundred souls, yet possessed no fewer than nine named wells or springs (Martin 1934, 414; Quine 1982, 13–14, 83).

All factors must be taken into account when considering any social custom, not only wells. Emmanuel Le Roy Ladurie was puzzled by the fact that, in Sabarthés in the 1290s, 'God was the master of salvation rather than the power who brought rain or banished typhoid or tempest', and that there appeared to be no public ceremonies of the kind found elsewhere. Even the greatest festival, All Saints' Day, a vital date in the pastoral calendar, was celebrated more with private fasting and public charity, and more conventional vigils – Easter or Christmas, for instance – seem to have been of little importance (Ladurie 1980, 295–6, 310). Many factors must have contributed – notably the constant ideological warfare of Cathars and Catholics forcing the peasants to take a more pious and theological view of religion, and the fact that in Montaillou the *ostal*, the household, seems to have absorbed all the available loyalties of the inhabitants, leaving a community so radically divided that communal ritual was inconceivable. How many such stories, with such a bearing on the history of social custom, lie behind the dots on the distribution map?

TWO

Fons Bandusiae: Wells in the Ancient World

The Universal Cult

The first thing that strikes us when considering the lore of holy wells is the enormous geographical extension of the motif. The example of India is often quoted (e.g., Bord 1985, 2–3), but instances from still further east have been overlooked.

Here, again, the spring or well is the repository of spiritual power. When the 'Great Fifth' Dalai Lama, Lobsang Gyatso, rode to Mongolia to confirm the independence of Tibet, he emphasized his own religious authority by exerting control over that power; with appropriate clanging and chanting he made the streams run backwards. In Tibet the wells were religiously picky. Tibetan Muslims, well established in the country since the sixteenth century, had a sacred spring near the monastery of SeRa.

In the Far East dragons are the controllers of all to do with water, and also live in wells. In the early years of this century, the Korean well-dragons had to be appeased, or thanked, whenever a child was born, by the casting of rice into the water; it was also believed that the spirits of the dead dwelt in wells. Here is an echo of the Russian water demons, the Rusalka-ye, who are the ghosts of drowned women – although specifically drowned in acts of suicide (Gale 1900, 332; Simpson 1987, 56). In Japan the wells had extraordinary powers. Children were protected from small-pox by throwing seven beans into a well and praying to it seven times. A curious ritual is also recorded which jars badly in modern ears. A mother-to-be, wearing her husband's nightclothes or hat, would circumambulate the well three times in the early morning, looked twice at her reflection and, not looking back, repeated the disturbing incantation 'Woman is In, Man is Yo, woman unlucky, man lucky', after which the lid would be replaced on the well for three days. In this way might the sex of an unborn child be changed (Aston 1912, 189–93).

For such an uncompromising faith, Islam seems to have made much accommodation with the hydrolatrous instinct. Mazzam Well is in the

21

precinct of the Kaaba itself; and the sacred fish of Irish holy wells had their counterparts in the fish of the pool at the Mosque in Tripoli, which were believed to be the incarnate souls of Muslim saints. Some of these heroic fish fought in the Crimean War and returned to their pool wounded; and anyone who ate one would die. In 1856, the American Consul consumed the lot, and found them 'coarse and impalatable, but not injurious' (Wakeman 1879–82, 371–2).

In the Consul's own continent wells were sanctified at various times. In the Catholicized regions of Canada native holy springs became Christian ones. In New England, wells could be used for divination much as with those of Europe. The holy springs of the region of Zinacantan, in Mexico, were, at least in the 1960s, still caught between paganism and Christianity. Koral Buro (Donkey Well) and Xul Votl were under the patronage of the Earth Lord; but Tz'uiltasbil Votl, the Blessed Spring, was surmounted by a cross, and the Virgin guarded important salt wells at a Zinacantec church. All springs, pagan and Christian, were blessed on Holy Cross Day (Whitney & Bullock 1925, 120; Laughlin 1977, 141–2, 155–6, 171, 196–200).

Commander Cameron was not impressed by what he regarded as superstitious belief in well-spirits in colonial Africa, and terrified his native servants by refusing to leave the spirits gifts. If guns were fired near springs, or boots worn around them, or even if they were referred to using the word for ordinary water rather than the one for palm wine, the wells would dry up (Cameron 1877, i 144).

Motifs recur and recur: the image of the saint creating a spring by striking a rock is familiar in Britain, but we can also find it in Baluchistan, where the Islamic saint Sakhi Sarwar is the hero, and Japan, where the miracle is wrought either by Saint Kobo Daishi or the monk-emperor Go-Daigo (Dames 1902, 260–61; Blacker 1984, 146–7; Dorson 1962, 33–5). Midsummer visiting of British wells is mirrored by the fact that all water was healing in Morocco at Midsummer; and the common offering of candles or rags at wells occurs at sites as disparate as St Paul's Well, Eresbos (Lesbos), St Chrysostom's Well, Pharasa, and the Well of the Prophet Ali at Kerman, Iran (Rouse 1896, 149; Halliday 1912, 219–20; Sykes 1900, 272).

In view of the universal extension of the well-cult, it is no surprise to find references to it in the Bible. The roadside well on the way to Shur received a sacred name after Hagar was visited by an angel there – possibly an attempt to account for a name which had become corrupted (Gen. 16:7–14), while Moses performed the rock-striking trick at Massah-Meribah (Exod. 17:6–7; Num. 20:7–13). In Christ's time Jacob's Well was still pointed out at Sychar (John 4:5–6) and the miraculous healing powers of the pool of Bethesda, Jerusalem, were attributed to angels (John 5:2–4).

This is not entirely a self-indulgent digression, for we much sketch our canvas before painting it in; and the huge extent of the well-cult demonstrates the truth of our guess that the religious symbolism of water itself is at the root of it.

Britain: *The Celts*

Most accounts of the Celtic well-cult derive from that of Dr Anne Ross in *Pagan Celtic Britain*, and despite quibbles with such unsubstantiated statements as pins being 'invariably associated with childbirth' when used as offerings (1967, 146), it is difficult to see it being superseded. The continental evidence she quotes is incontrovertible. In September 1963 over 140 cult objects, including models of heads and animals in distinctly Celtic styles, were disovered at the source of the Seine, which derives its name from the goddess Sequana. According to Posidinius, 15,000 talents-worth of gold was flung into a sacred pool near Toulouse, while St Gregory of Tours tells us of a three-day festival at Lake Gevaudan in Switzerland with offerings of food and sacrifices being made. The naming of rivers after Celtic deities is commonplace (ibid., 20–22). Also note

lucus erat numquam violatus	There was a grove, immemorially inviolate,
obscurum cingens conexis aera ramis . . .	Hidden from the air above by interlacing branches . . .
Fontibus unda cadit, simulacraque maesta deorum	There fell fountain-streams, there gloomy images of gods
arte cavent caesisque extant in formia truncis.	Stood guard, jutting, human-carven in tree-trunk shape . . .

Lucan, *De Bello Civilis*, iii 399–400, 411–12

This Gaulish grove was in Caesar's way. Superstition prevented his army from cutting it down, so he did it himself.

The Celts in Britain were wont to incorporate monuments of previous cultures within their own. There can be no other explanation behind the rituals at Dungiven, where a well, church and monolith were circumambulated in a rite which the Church would hardly have adopted were it not already part of the established pre-Christian practice (Logan 1980, 110–12). This is also the implication behind the curious rite at Tullybelton (Perthshire), totally unChristianized, where, on Beltane morning, local people drank from a well, circumambulated it three times, and then did the same at a 'Druidic' temple nearby (*Gentleman's Magazine* 1811, 426–7).*

---

* Tobar Chailach, Keith (Banffshire) is not good evidence, however, for pagan Celtic

The three most important sites of Celtic hydrolatry in Britain (for the history of Bath really begins under Rome) are at Llyn Cerrig Bach (Anglesey), Wookey Hole (Somerset) and Milton Keynes (Bedfordshire). At the first, a first-century hoard was discovered in 1943, perhaps deposited as a last desperate attempt to avert the Roman conquest of Anglesey. The second is a most interesting example. The River Axe begins in the depths of Wookey Hole, a cave system which, it was discovered in the 1940s, had been a Celtic burial ground. In particular, the outer caves contained a total of fourteen skulls, with no bodies, thirteen of which appeared to belong to people in their late twenties. The site remained sacred, for William Worcestre spoke of a holy well there in the Fourth Cave – the burial area – in 1470. Third and most important of all, the recently discovered temple at Milton Keynes, dating from the second century but with an Iron Age settlement nearby, was centred on a circular pool in which a 'sun-wheel' was found, along with a votive statuette, sacrificed cockerel (cf. Jones 1954, 104–5; MacPhail 1900, 445–6) and horses' heads close at hand. This is better evidence for Celtic hydrolatry than the much-trumpeted temple of Lydney, which, it is grandly and implausibly suggested, 'makes it clear that the wide estuary of the Severn' was worshipped. (Ross 1967, 22, 24, 107; Worcestre 1981, 290–91; *The Independent* 24.4.1990)

Below this level there were probably innumerable local shrines. A lead figurine found in Bank Well, Giggleswick vicarage (West Yorkshire), 'may date to the La Tene period' (Whelan & Taylor 1989, 56). But clear evidence is hard to find, and traditions of Druids using springs (Morrell 1988, 10), are interesting sidelights but cannot be treated as reliable. The best evidence for Celtic well-worship is that of folkloric motifs, the most common being the connection between wells and heads. This, again, is fully surveyed by Ross: she cites wells and pools with skulls deposited in them in the Celtic period at Caves Inn (Warwickshire) and Heywood (Wiltshire). Tales involving heads in wells pepper the Highlands and Islands, though Ross is honest enough to admit that these are often 'legends and pseudo-historical stories which seek to explain something the local people themselves no longer fully understand' (1967, 106–13). That this connection of heads and wells survived into the Middle Ages to affect the Lives of the Saints – usually but not always Celtic ones – is familiar stuff: SS Cynog, Decuman, Osyth, Sidwell and Urith are enough to remind us. What is often overlooked is that these motifs can become

worship of wells. Certainly the Cailleach ('Old Woman') is one of the aspects of the Mother Goddess (Bord 1985, 15), but the word *nun*, derived from *nonna*, also means 'old woman'; and in the Martyrology of Tallaght, under May 22nd, we find the Three Nuns of Drumnadert – or the Three *Cailleacha*, as the Gaelic has it. Tobar Chailach may simply mean 'Well of the Nun'.

attached to local history, the ingrained image rising to the surface to distort memories of real events. Simon de Montfort was decapitated at Battle Well, Evesham (Worcestershire), and St Thomas's Well, Windlesham (Lancashire) supposedly rose where the head of a Roman Catholic priest martyred while saying Mass fell. It is also likely that the tales of coaches vanishing into pools or wells refer to 'the Celtic notion of pools and springs as the gateway to the Otherworld' (May 1834, 14–15; Taylor 1906, 194–5; Harte 1986, 21).

There was, then, an established native water-cult when the Romans invaded these islands.

Britain: the Romans

Nobody doubts the evidence presented of the Roman takeover of Celtic water-shrines at Bath and Buxton, among others. In contrast, little attention has been paid to those aspects of Classical religion which make this reaction understandable.

For this we need to go back to the Greeks. Greek religion derives its distinctly myth-based bias from the fact that most of what we know about it comes from efforts by Hesiod and Pausanias, among others, to make sense out of chaotic local traditions which developed against a common mythological background but in isolation from each other. In this process the practice of that religion on the ground tended to take second precedence to tales and stories; but even so it is a surprise that we do not find wells often associated with Greek heroes in the way that we find them linked with Christian saints, who often performed a similiar social, if not theological, function.

This is not to say that water, in its aspects as cleanser and purifier, took no role in Greek religious practice. Water containers were placed in all Greek temples, from which visitors had to sprinkle themselves before entering; this was connected with the concept of the temple as a place of supreme purity, from which all potential disturbances of the cool spirit – sex, birth and death – were banished. Where water occurred naturally it was incorporated within the ritual: at the Alea temple in Tegea a door opened on to a stairway to the 'Fountain'. But, as in the Celtic temple at Milton Keynes, where there were no springs artificial wells might be created. The Acropolis, according to Herodotus (8.55), had a pool of salt water in a rock which always had to be kept open to the sky. Where well-temples had dedications they tended to be to major deities – Demeter at Eleusis, for example (Burkert 1985, 77–8, 86; Mylonas 1961, 97–9). When translated into the environment of Rome, these temple wells appear to have been the original inspiration behind the holy wells that were dug in early Christian churches (below, p.43).

One curious aspect of the Greek use of wells, not repeated in other cultures, was their power to inspire prophecy. At Delphi there were two springs, the Cassotis, used for purification, and the Castilian, from which the Sibyl drank before prophesying, according to Oenamaus. There were wells near the temples of the Oracles of Apollo at Ammon in Egypt and at Chryse – the 'Spring of the Nymphs', its function suggested by its proximity to the tomb of the Sibyl Herophile. As at Delphi, the Oracle of Claros, who was male, drew his inspiration from a well to the left of the temple altar (Parke & Wormell 1956, i 27–8; Parke 1967, 198–9; 1985, 177, 139). But there seems to have been little actual offering performed at wells in the Celtic manner. Demeter's/Kallichoron Well at Eleusis, built in the sixth century BCE, was empty of finds when excavated in 1892; although perhaps anything of value had been rifled by the Ottomans long before (Mylonas 1961, 97–9). The Romans were as happy to adopt these sites of hydrolatry as so much else Greek. Tacitus relates the story of Germanicus's visit to the Oracle of Chryse, whose waters prompted the foretelling of his death (*Annales*, 2.54); but the Romans also reinterpreted the prophetic powers of the wells and turned them into inspirers of poetry. Ovid claimed this property for the Castilian Spring itself (*Ars Amatoris*, i 15: 36–8), and the same story was told of the Hippocrene and Aganippe's Springs on Mount Helicon, struck from the earth by the heel of Pegasus. Aganippe was a water-nymph, as were Cassotis and Castilia; Hago, whose well on Mount Lycaeus had the power to halt droughts; Pirene, whose tears formed her well at Corinth; Cyane, who actually became a well in Sicily; and Argyra, patron of an Arcadian well. Arethusa was patron of two wells in Sicily and Boethia (Graves 1961, 383–4; Larousse, 149–40; Pliny 3.7.89, 4.7.25).

Naturally geological oddities attracted the attention of Roman authors as much as they did anybody else. The hot wells of Calirrhoe, which in later centuries were thought to derive their heat from the presence of djinns, came to Pliny's notice, along with ebbing and flowing wells on Cissa and Pallaria, the hundred springs of Mount Talanus, and the Phiala and Panias Springs, sources of the Nile and the Jordan (Spoer 1907, 56; Pliny, 4.7.24, 3.26.151, 4.1.2, 5.10.55, 5.15.71). And in some quarters hydrolatry was still taken seriously. Discussing the North Italian cult of Hercules, Propertius mentions *fontes pianolos*, springs that must be appeased' (4.9.24). Also:

O fons Bandusiae . . .	O Bandusian well . . .
Cras donaberis haedo . . .	Tomorrow you will be presented with a kid . . .
. . . gelidos inficiet tibi	. . . [it will] stain your icy waters
rubro sanguine rivos . . .	With its blushing blood . . .

Horace, *Odes* 3.13

Water might also be important in the mystery religions. Mithraism, in particular, was popular in the later Empire. The Mithraic ritual meal included the consumption of consecrated bread and water; Porphyry, in *De Anto Nympharum*, xviii, says 'in the ritual of Mithras the bowl stands for the spring' and baptism was a crucial sacrament (Hinrells 1975, 302 n84; Vermaseren 1963, 53).

But in general the Roman attitude to wells, at least among the intelligentsia, was devoid of all religious overtones. Persius felt able to treat the powers of the Hippocrene Spring as a subject of the most savage satire (Prologue, lines 1–2); and this is not surprising given the 'secular' feel of the official religion, functional and anaemic as it was. The Goddess Juturna had a well in the Roman forum which was used for public rituals (Cook 1905, 271–2), but we have no instances of private devotion surviving into the Augustan Age. The Romans were, however, capable of extreme superstitiousness, and while not all wells were sacred in an active sense, the motif of the well-shaft as a gateway to the Underworld gave all such places a ritual importance. This may explain the common finds of skulls and arrangements of animals carefully deposited in Roman wells – when a well was abandoned or abused a certain rite had to be performed, as a matter of form (Merrifield 1987, 41–7). But superstition is not devotion.

In their scepticism and rationalism, in their atomized, capitalistic, urban environment, Imperial Romans were in a stage of cultural development familiar to ourselves: relics from the Graeco-Roman past became symbols of a lost morality and innocence. Holy wells were a manifestation of this.

Nunc sacri fontes et delubra locantur Iudaeis . . .	Now the grove of the shrine and fountains is rented out To the Jews . . .
in vallem Egeriae descendimus et speluncas dissimilis veris. Quanto presentius esset numen aquis, viride si margine clauderet herba, nec ingenuum viderent marmora tofum.	Down we go to the valley of Egeria and her pretend, Modernized grotto. What greater sense of sanctity this spring Would have if grass with its green margin were to border The water, and marble didn't violate our innocent limestone.

Juvenal, *Satire 3*, 13–14, 17–20

For Juvenal, the sacred spring was a symbol of the ideal mythical countryside whose modern counterpart he could never quite bring himself to retreat to (3:1–7), a common theme among Roman poets (including

Horace, whose reverence for the Bandusian Spring was another example of anti-modernist romanticism).

This mental connection had great potential significance for the history of the well-cult in Britain. No general account has been offered of Roman wells in Britannia, so let us tabulate the information (see Table 1).

There is a lot of material to dissect here, but first let us dispose of *funta*. Dr Gelling has claimed (1978, 68–74) that this clear Latin loan-word was used by the Saxons to denote a spring sacred in Roman times, but it is odd that four of the nine major sites in which the element is present (Fonthill, Fovant, Teffont, and Urchfont) are within one small tract of Wiltshire countryside whose only sign of Roman habitation is a road five miles or so away from any of the villages. Of all the sites concerned, only Havant (in the table) shows any independent sign of having been important to the Romans, as it is near a second-century crossroads. The Christianization of Roman sites will also be passed over for the time being, though it must be mentioned that two of these wells, Icklingham and Wigginholt, were Christian sites even during the Roman era.

Of course it is not safe to assume that these so-called Roman wells were being used only by Romans. At Camberwell, Corfe, Horton, Low Leyton, Upper Slaughter and Winterborne Kingston the assumption of sanctity rests on the presence of coins and the like, and naturally the native population would have offered these to their own traditional holy wells. At Winterborne Kingston the Britons definitely resorted to the well: a bronze plate inscribed with the image of a hare, a sacred animal to the Celts, was found in it, though the well's masonry is Roman and the site is at a waystation on the Badbury–Dorchester road. This is hardly surprising in view of the number of Celtic wells which were incorporated into the official system of rituals. Bath and Buxton are well enough known, where Sul was assimilated into Minerva and Arnemeta was simply adopted (familiar as the conquerors were with nymphs and naiads). At Little Dean a Celtic shrine was discovered inside a Roman temple-complex in 1985; the Lydney temple followed the same pattern (*Source* 3, 16). The Holy Well of Tadmarton lies near an Iron Age hillfort which was taken over by the Romans, and Camberwell's name (though it foxed the EPNS, Gover et al. 1934, 17), must derive either from the Celti *camber*, 'river bend' , or Saxon *cumbra*, 'Celt'.

Other sites appear to show the initiative lying with the invaders. Mithras had a temple-well at Carrawburgh similar to that of the native nymph Coventina, presumably to cater for the strongly Mithraic army; but dating of the offerings shows that it continued to be used long after the departure of the legions. We will never know whether the impressive Springhead temple, with its mysterious enclosed sacred pool, was a site freshly created or a native shrine, but certainly in some places there was

TABLE 1: ROMAN WELLS IN BRITAIN

	Roman features						Continuity			Traditions			Sources
	villas	forts	settlements	roads	temples	holy	Celtic	Saxon	Christian	Roman use	healing	other	
(a) Roman sites													
Bath (So)			X		X	X	X	X		X	X		Collinson 1791, i 2–7
Bromham (Bd)						X				X			VCH iii 44
Buxton (Db)			X		X	X	X		X	X	X		Cox 1879, ii 72–4
Camberwell (Sy)						X	X	X		X			VCH iv 358
Carrawburgh (Nb)	X				X	X							Ross 1967, 29–30, 105
Chew Stoke (So)						X			X				Rahtz et al. 1957, 104–12
Christleton (Ch)						X			X				Hope 1893, 7
Corfe (Do)			X			X							Hughes 1972, 56
Emberton (Bu)						X							Ross 1967, 29–30
Exeter (Dv):													
St Martin's						X			X				
St Mary's			X		?				X				Fox 1956, 211
Exning (Sf)						X							Johnston 1959, 11–20
Horton (Do)						X							Harte 1986, 21
Housesteads (Nb)		X				X							Bord 1985, 12
Icklingham (Sf)		X	X			X			X				Frere 1976, 444–5
Islip (Ox)					X	X							Goodchild & Kirk 1954, 17
Lincoln (Lc):													
Blind Well			X							X			Adell & Chambers 1971, 19–20
'St Paul's Well'				X			?			X			Rodwell 1989, 144
Little Dean (Gc)					X	X	X						Bord 1985, 12, 14
Litton Cheney (Do)	X									X			Bailey 1982, 46
Lower Slaughter (Gc)						X							Jope 1961, 27–38
Low Leyton (Ex)						X		X	X				RCHM ii 166
Lydney (Gc)					X	X	X						Ross 1967, 22
Morestead (Ha)								?					VCH
Quinton (No)						X							Frere 1976, 399
Seaton (Dv)								?					Brown 1960, 103
Southwark (Sy)						X			?				Hammerson 1978, 206–12
Springhead (Kt)					X	X							Bord 1985, 12–14
Stanton St John (Ox)	X									X	X	X	Manning 1902–3, i 11–12
Stony Middleton (Db)	X								X	X	X		Naylor 1983, 47
Tadmarton (Ox)		X				?	X		X				Beesley 1841, 12
Thatcham (Bk)						X							Ross 1967, 31

	Roman features						Continuity			Traditions			Sources
	villas	forts	settlements	roads	temples	holy	Celtic	Saxon	Christian	Roman use	healing	other	
Upper Slaughter (Gc)						X			?				Walters 1928, 134
Well (NY)						?		X	X				Ross 1967, 31
Welwyn (Ht)						X							Rook , 117–18
Whitestaunton (So)	X					X			X	X	X	X	Horne 1923, 37
Winterborne Kingston (Do)				X	X		X	X					Harte 1986, 21
Wigginholt						X							
(b) Wells at Roman sites													
Binchester (Du)		X								X			Hunt 1987, 14
Burwell (Ca)			X				X						
Charlbury (Ox)	X												Radford 1936, 24–5
Compton Beauchamp (Bk)	X											?	Gelling 1973–4, 360–61
Cranborne (Do)	X								X				Harte 1985, 5
Devizes (Wi)	X											X	Wiltshire 1975, 78; Cunnington 1916, 441
East Brent (So)		X							X				Horne 1922, 23
Fifehead Neville (Do)	X								X				Harte 1985, 5
Havant (Ha)			X	X			X	?		X			Pile 1986, 21–2
Motcombe (Do)					X	?							Harte 1986, 48
Newton (Nt)		X									X		Morrell 1988, 21
Rockbourne (Ha)	X												VCH
Shipham (So)	X						X						Richardson 1928a, 46
Syreford (Gc)		X										X	Walters 1928, 129
Wellow (So)			X				X	X					Horne 1922, 21
West Stour (Do)	X						X						Ross 1984, 118
(c) Traditional Roman wells													
Brantinghamthorpe (EY)										X	X		Smith 1923, 13–14
Flookborough (La)									X	X	X		Taylor 1906, 317–19
Holme on Spaldingmoor (EY)										X	X		Smith 1923, 17
Plaish (Sh)									X	X			Otter 1986a, 27
Wanstead (Ex)										X			RCHM ii 248

Key to Table 1

Bd	Bedfordshire	Ex	Essex	No	Northamptonshire
Bk	Berkshire	EY	East Yorkshire	Nt	Nottinghamshire
Bu	Buckinghamshire	Gc	Gloucestershire	NY	North Yorkshire
Ca	Cambridgeshire	Ha	Hampshire	Ox	Oxfordshire
Ch	Cheshire	Ht	Hertfordshire	Sh	Shropshire
Db	Derbyshire	Kt	Kent	So	Somerset
Do	Dorset	La	Lancashire	Sf	Suffolk
Du	Durham	Lc	Lincolnshire	Sy	Surrey
Dv	Devon	Nb	Northumberland	Wi	Wiltshire

no effort made to integrate with the indigenous religion. The Emberton well-shrine is dedicated to the very Roman and very military Mercury, and the Housesteads well was probably of significance only to the army garrison too.

An illustration may be drawn from further afield. Didyma in modern Turkey was, according to Pausanias, a centre of Milesian culture long before the Greeks arrived; and, when the Temple of Apollo was built, a well to the left of the altar, possibly already long sacred, was incorporated into the oracular rituals. It failed when Didyma was sacked in 493 BCE, but revived in 334 BCE when Alexander the Great arrived there – politically convenient for the Oracle. By the Christian era it had decayed into a common water-supply, but helped the town survive the Gothic seige of 263. At this point, Festus, Governor of Asia 286–93, restored the well and dubbed it Fons Festi in his own honour. The plaque found at the site speaks of the 'spring bubbling with golden-flowing streams'. The Governor had clearly been reading Ovid (Pausanias 5.13.11; Burkert 1985, 86; Parke 1985, 23, 36–7, 94–6).

Festus had reached the point of the eighteenth-century English gentry landscaping their gardens: he was taking an ancient sacred site and using its romantic associations to glorify his own status. Now note the twelve wells in Table 1 which are associated with villas – a fifth of the total. Is it too much to suggest similar processes in operation there? The most useful site to consider is Whitestaunton. Very near the villa site is a warm spring, St Agnes's Well, which has a reputation for the cure of sprains; a Roman shrine was found here in 1882. Let us suppose a Roman gentleman arrives from his town house in Exeter or Ilchester and builds a villa in a secluded valley where he can write bad poetry in peace. He discovers that the locals who work on his farm have a tradition about the spring on the hillside opposite, that it is peculiarly warm and good for the joints. Head a-brim with Ovid, he decides to sanctify it. The invaders might not have to be so active to affect local folklore. In Stanton St John a perfectly ordinary villa bath-house at Wick Farm (an important name, if we believe Dr Gelling) inspired a whole series of stories about ghosts, murdered maids, and healing waters.

Mere traditions of Roman use cannot be used as evidence unsupported, although at Bromham, Little Dean and Litton Cheney archaeology has confirmed local folklore. For the Roman Empire occupies a similar place in popular tradition to the 'lost city' motif (the idea that insignificant places, or even empty fields, were once substantial towns): it symbolized a lost glory, a grander world than the present one which, by implication, might one day be regained.

Thus far we have been picking at established fact. Henceforth, on looking into the water, the scenery we find relected there is uncharted and unknown. Our material becomes more extensive, and our disagreements with the orthodox line more intense.

THREE

The Water of Redemption: Wells and Christianity

In Christian ritual, water is essential. The sacrament that admits people into the Church in the first place, baptism, demands its use, and water, suitably blessed, can be the vehicle for the power of the Holy Ghost when sprinkled on worshipper, building, or – at Haxey, Lincolnshire – on a small roll of leather about to be used in an ancient communal game. The sacred vessels have to washed, too. In these activities water adopts its two traditional religious guises of purifier and transmitter of spiritual power, two roles which could be elided, as when Bede mentions that St Edwin was 'washed in the cleansing water of baptism' (*Ecclesiastical History* ii 14). It would not be a shock, then, if we found that the Christian Churches had widely adopted the holy wells of previous cultures.

Site Continuity

Here we are at the crux of the issue outlined in the Introduction. The Church and the mystic school are in large part convinced that the sacred sites of Christianity have their origins in pagan forebears, but others have resisted this idea. Jeremy Harte lists the churches which he believes fit this picture: Knowlton (Dorset) in its Rings; Rudstone (East Yorkshire) with its megalith; Silchester (Hampshire), a Roman shrine in a graveyard; Stanton Drew (Somerset) and Avebury (Wiltshire), next to stone circles; Old Yeavering (Northumberland) and St Martin's, Leicester, on the sites of possible pagan temples;* and Harrow on the Hill (Middlesex), where the church is built on the presumed site of the temple recorded in the place-name.

---

* St Nicholas's, Leicester, also claims a pagan temple site, but the columns in its graveyard are in truth part of the city Forum.

33

> This brings the total up to eight. As the number of churches and chapels in England must be something like 10,000, those with evidence, good or bad, for the reuse of sites of pagan worship will be seen to account for 0.1% of the whole. It is not an impressive figure. (Harte 1986, 15)

It's a grossly misleading figure, that's what it is. Anyone with a serious interest can sympathize with Harte's irritation at 'sarsen boulders and shapeless mounds' being identified as pagan sites, but his dismissal of 'ancient cemeteries' seems a little unjust, and he later admits that 'the evidence . . . shows continuity of use at these cemeteries.' We may add the unsettling conclusion that a religion based around the worship of rocks, trees, springs, etc., is unlikely to leave much behind for the archaeologists to find. In Ireland objects such as St Senan's Stone, Kilrush (Clare) were reverenced, but we would not know this had not the now-dead tradition been recorded in time (Logan 1980, 103). Less astute investigators than Rahtz and Watts could fail to recognize the true nature of the 'collection of household rubbish' left at an artificial 'cave' near a holy well in Donegal: rags, combs, marbles, pottery, pens, coins, alongside souvenirs from Lourdes and suchlike stuff (Rahtz & Watts 1979, 205–8). The way, perhaps, to shed conclusive light on this matter would be to take a sample of all churches extant at a certain date, and to compare the number known to be built on pagan sites with those most probably not so; but this would be way beyond our present purpose.

There is abundant evidence for the conversion of pagan sites on the Continent; L.V. Grinsell has produced a useful paper on the subject. Pope Boniface IV consecrated the Roman Pantheon to Christ in 609; Syracuse Cathedral stands on the site of temples built successively since the sixth century BCE. At SS Mary and Dionisio churches at Alcobertas (Portugal), subsidiary chapels are formed from dolmens, while at Carnac the Tumulus de St-Michel is surmounted by a church (Grinsell 1986, 29–31).

In Britain, however, it must be admitted that the evidence is ambiguous. Far too much has been made of the transformation of the Irish goddess Brigid into St Bride, the takeover of pagan festival dates, and hilltop dedications to St Michael, and so on. While all these indisputably happened, on their own they are not enough to prove the widespread practice of adopting previously pagan sites of worship. St Agnes, for example, is the patron of lovers, and St Agnes's Eve was a popular time for love-divination (Whitlock 1979, 89), but oddly only one of the twenty wells in the British Isles used for this purpose is dedicated to her. Not much adoption going on in her case.

More useful, perhaps, are the stories of conflict between Church figures and the Devil, especially over the siting of churches. One example will serve to illustrate the somewhat limited genre: at Brentor (Devon) (a hilltop dedication to St Michael, yes) the inhabitants intended to build the church at the hill's foot, but the Devil moved the stones uphill each night; so they eventually gave in and constructed it on its present rocky Dartmoor eyrie (Whitlock 1979, 8). There are innumerable examples of this motif, which is usually taken as the remnant of traditions of the takeover of pagan sites. The Church itself fostered the identification of pagan deities with the Christian Devil: St Gregory's letter to Abbot Mellitus uses this language, as does Archbishop Theodore in his decrees against paganism (*Ecclesiastical History*, i 30; Stenton 1989, 128). But we must still be cautious, as sometimes the motif itself becomes confusing. At Church Eaton (Staffordshire), the church's foundation stones were laid at the most likely pagan site in the parish (St Edith's Well), but then moved away from it to the present location (*VCH Staffs*, iv 91).

Also worth noting are the various applications of the word church. A haunted roundbarrow at Longbridge Deverill (Wiltshire) is known as Gun's Church; a field with a standing stone in Minchinghampton (Gloucestershire) is called Devil's Churchyard; and the site of a Roman basilica at Ickleton (Cambridgeshire) is dubbed Sunken Church (Harte 1986, 19). There was clearly a grey area in the popular mind in which the magical power attributed to the church as a result of what went on in it was transferred to the relics of past cultures.

Yet folklore is of limited help in discovering actual examples of site-continuity, for it is commonly an attempt to explain things the true significance of which the local population has forgotten. Two Dorset examples: in Mappowder church is the tiny effigy of a knight, not, as the local tale asserts, the tomb of a boy Crusader, but a monument to the buried heart of an adult knight whose body remains in the Holy Land. Near Bere Regis is Red Post, whose colour has given rise to rival explanations; one, romantically, speaks of murders and gibbets, while the other argues it was a guide for the guards of prisoners to find their way to Botany Bay Farm, a detention centre for deportees (Osborne 1987, 52, 74–5). Also, beliefs can be transferred to sites to which they are not relevant. In 1973 it was recorded that the Rempstone Stone Circle near Studland (Dorset) was the result of a failed attempt by the Devil to destroy Corfe Castle by throwing rocks at it, but the circle was only discovered this century (Harte 1986, 73). Craziwell is a pool near Princeton (Devon). Possibly because it is 'surrounded on three sides by extremely high banks which make it look black and horrific', it is reputedly bottomless, and on dark nights a voice can be heard announcing the names of those who will die the following year – which is what happens in lychgates on St Mark's Night or New Year's Eve. But Craziwell was formed by seventeenth-century tin-mining activity, and is no more than fifteen feet deep (Brown 1982, 139).

What folklore gives us are instances of the motifs which may record symbolized type-models of historical events. We must recall the context in which folklore was traditionally transmitted – usually from the very old to the very young, which is an excellent environment for garbling, and within the tendency normal among storytellers to romanticize reality according to a set of stock types. Problems also arise when figures with similar names make an impact on popular tradition, such as St George and King George (III), who both appear as heroes of Mumming Plays (Whitlock 1979, 177). Note yet further the related tendency of folktales to cluster. Stories of coaches vanishing into water are common in Dorset, but rarer in Oxfordshire; conversely, legends of ghosts being exorcized in pools or wells are common in Oxfordshire and absent from Dorset. This might extend to orthodox archaeology. Inhumation was the fashion in fifth-century Kent, but cremation was the custom in Norfolk and Lincoln-shire; while in seventh-century Berkshire and Derbyshire there was a fad for being buried in barrows (Morris 1973, 59, 285).

The documentary evidence is contradictory too. Most well known is St Gregory's letter to St Mellitus in 601:

> [we] have come to the conclusion that the temples of the idols among [the English] should on no account be destroyed. The idols are to be destroyed, but the temples themselves should be aspersed with holy water, altars set up in them, and relics deposited there . . . In this way we hope that the people, seeing that their temples are not destroyed, may abandon their error. (*Ecclesiastical History* i 30)

But when the High Priest of Northumbria, Coifi, converted in 627

> . . . he told his companions to set fire to the temple and its enclosures and destroy them. The site where these idols once stood is still shown . . . and is known today as Goodmanham. (ibid. ii 14)

And archaeological opinion has it that the well-temple of Little Dean was destroyed by Christians, and not just ruined but systematically demolished (*Source* 3, 16). Then again, a church appears to have been grafted on to the temple at Lamyatt Beacon (Somerset) (Rahtz & Watts 1979, 187).

Gregory the great Pope was, of course, ignorant of the situation on the ground in England. Stone temples abounded in Italy, ripe for re-dedication, but in Britain no stone building had, so far as anyone could tell, been erected for decades. Even if St Bede's talk of the Goodmanham 'temple' refers to something more substantial than a grove or wooden stockade, it would hardly conform to Gregory's instructions about 'well-built' structures. Additionally, perhaps the fact that until the Synod of Hertford the English Church felt itself to be at war with a Celtic cousin which seemed half-pagan made them more uncompromising towards those relics of paganism that they did uncover.

At several sites which were probably Romano-British holy wells the Christians adopted the iconoclastic model. Broken statues of Roman deities have been found in wells at Emberton (Berkshire), where the god concerned is Mercury, and Carrawburgh (Northumberland), where it is Coventina. The well at Lower Slaughter (Gloucestershire) contained no less than three altars, two beheaded stone figures, and three stone tablets (Jope 1961, 27–38). If, as seems likely, the perpetrators were Christians carrying out the Pope's instructions, they were unwittingly following the pagan model of what the sacred well was: consigning, by way of the dark shaft, the heathen gods to the Underworld where they belonged. But as yet there is no evidence that any well was converted after being so cleansed. A late Roman well under Southwark Cathedral comes closest: it contained a mutilated altar and three statues of gods – one of which had been set on fire after being broken apart (Hammerson 1978, 206–12).

Interestingly the details of the excavation of the thirteenth-century St John's Well in Beverley Minster in 1720 reveal what may be the same behaviour by later generations of Christians. Apart from the usual pins, bones, coins, beads and junk dredged out of the waters, there was also a carving of a monk-figure beneath an ogee-arch, presumably not just casually thrown away (Smith 1923, 176–85), and possibly representing the saint himself.

Christianization of Wells

Below the church of Notre-dame du Port in Clermont-Ferrand – a Druidic cult-centre – is the crypt where the Black Madonna, Our Lady of Clermont, is worshipped in a manner which blatantly derives from the worship of Cybele before her. And here we find a 'well sacred from Gallo-Roman times' (Begg 1985, 181). St Reine's Spring, Alesia, was also originally a Gaulish holy well. St Cornelly's Well, Carnac, stands among the stone avenues; and most openly of all, Thor's Well at Thorsas, Norway, is now known as 'St Thor's'! (Jones 1954, 15; Ross 1967, 109; Montelius 1910, 77).

These foreign examples are all very impressive. But, as with the case of temples or barrows, they only show that continuity was possible, not its extent. Let us examine in detail the British cases of unequivocal pre-medieval conversion of wells. There are few enough of them, for it is not good enough to use paganish ritual as evidence of pagan worship.

St Helen's Well, Burnsall (West Yorkshire). First recorded 1812, and forms a pair with St Margaret's Well a couple of hundred yards away. The rituals appear to centre on the latter, but St Helen's Well itself has the alternative name of Thorskeld. Like Thorskell Well, Hebden (West Yorkshire), however, there is a chance that this may derive from Norse *þyrs*, 'giant', rather than from the Scandinavian thunder god (Whelan & Taylor 1989, 52–3; Whitaker 1878, 499–500; Smith 1961–3, vi 102).

St Augustine's Well, Cerne Abbas (Dorset). The many legends of this spring need not concern us, and we can concentrate on its chronology. Originally known as the Silver Well – a name with possible pagan associations – the spring was the traditional site of the hermitage of St Edwold, reputed brother of St Edmund of East Anglia, who settled here in the ninth century. Late in the eleventh century, however, the Abbey commissioned the quack hagiographer Goscelin to provide it with a more exalted origin, and he came up with a yarn about St Augustine creating the well by striking the earth with his staff (Colley March 1899, 479; Udal 1922, 158–9).

Holy Well, Cranborne (Dorset). A borderline case. The so-called holy well here is near the site of a Roman villa, which may indicate continuity. But the name of the hamlet, Holwell, is clearly derived from *holh wiella*, 'well in the hollow' – though such a distinction may not have worried the early evangelists (Harte 1985, 5; Mills 1986, 89).

Holy Well, Fifehead Neville (Dorset). Another well at a villa site, and so a spurious example (Harte 1985, 5).

Glastonbury (Somerset). We are not yet concerned with the famous Chalice Well, for the older holy well at Glastonbury, now ignored, is St Edmund's Well north-west of the Tor. According to the *Anglo-Saxon Chronicle* King Edmund Ironside was buried at Glastonbury in 1016, but the name may also refer to Edmund I, who made St Dunstan Abbot. The alternative name of the spring is Elder Well. Note further Ashwell Spring south-east of the Tor, commemorated in a lane name. The dates of these wells are yet unknown, but as it stands it is likely that Glastonbury was originally a shrine of springs linked to trees, worth remembering in view of the Holy Thorn (Richardson 1928a, 183–4).

Harrow Well (Middlesex). The place-name indicates that there was a temple here, and a church had been consecrated, on a site probably long sacred, by 1094. There is a large well on the south side of the hill, anciently noted (especially for prodigious catches of fish!) (*VCH Middx*, iv 172).

Low Leyton (Essex). On the north side of the churchyard were discovered in 1718 two Roman wells, full of Roman coins and, of most significance, a plate 'of silver with Saxon characters'. An arched doorway approached by steps was also uncovered, but its function remains unknown. This well was clearly sacred for centuries and also, probably, the crucial factor in the siting of the church, being closed up at a later date (RCHM Essex, ii 166).

St Oswald's Well, Roseberry Topping (North Yorkshire). The king's son Oswy was drowned here by a mysterious flood in the rock cell on the hill, although he had been taken there to avoid just such a fate. An alternative name, Roseberry Well, survives. The name derives from Othenesburg, the Hill of Odin (Turton 1912–13; H.Tr. 1853, 429).

St Martin's Well, Stony Middleton (Derbyshire). The overflow of this warm, healing well flows through the site of a villa (Naylor 1983, 47).

Holy Well, Tadmarton (Oxfordshire). This site, first noted in 1346, is connected with an Iron Age hillfort reused by the Romans: see above, p.28 (Gelling 1953–4, 406).

St Agnes's Well, Whitestaunton (Somerset). (See above, p.31)

Holy Well, Wookey (Somerset). The Celtic water-shrine here has already been mentioned (p.24), though worship here probably goes back much farther, in view of the Neolithic inhabitation of the Caves and the monstrous stone image of a woman there which the middle ages interpreted as the Witch. The caves were abandoned c.400, but it is inconceivable that they would have been forgotten. Perhaps the shrine was never formally Christianized, but Christians certainly frequented it. On his visit in 1470, William Worcestre was taken into the Fourth Cave: 'in the north part of this Parlour is what is called in English a holy-hole, or well, arched over and full of fine water, the depth of which has never been ascertained' (Worcestre 1981, 290–91).

St Hawthorn's Well, the Wrekin (Shropshire). This has been the object of much unlikely philological discussion, but the obvious derivation is the most satisfactory, that it commemorates a sacred tree (Hope 1893, 141; Otter 1985a, 15).

This tiny sample of thirteen sites is woefully inadequate; the appearance of three examples from Dorset alone illustrates this! But mere archaeological continuity can prove continuity of worship no more than folklore can. Two Roman wells in Exeter, for instance, were dedicated to St Martin and St Mary; the former is a popular early dedication with great significance for Dark Age monasticism (*Ecclesiastical History* iii 4), while eventually St Mary's Well, next to the Cathedral, was probably surmounted by a statue of the Virgin (Fox 1956, 210–11). The church of St Paul-in-the-Bail, Lincoln, used a well in the Roman forum for baptisms (Rodwell 1989, 144). But at none of these sites is there any evidence that the wells were actually *sacred* to the Romans as well as the Christians.

The list does not end here, however. There are other considerations,

TABLE 2: ENGLISH WELLS SHOWING POSSIBLE PAGAN CONTINUITY

		Christian (duplicates bracketed)	Non-Christian
sites	wells at barrows	3	3
	wells at caves	2	–
	wells at hillforts/henges	8	10
	wells at megaliths	2	6
folkloric motifs	banshees	1	1
	circumambulation	1 (1)	4
	death (=sacrifice?)	14	26
	the Devil	1	5
	dragons	3	6
	fairies	3 (1)	11
	heads	7 (5)	1
	healing rites with 'pagan features'	1	–
	pin wells	19 (4)	7
	prophetic wells	14 (8)	16
	rag wells	2 (1)	12
	treasure in wells	1	9
	well spirits/guardians	3 (5)	16
	TOTALS	85	133

such as the proximity of pagan sites to wells, and the nature of the folklore connected to them, both of which hint at *possible* pagan origin for such springs. Proximity is important, for whereas there may be no actual evidence of continuity of worship at a well, the Christian evangelists may have looked upon it none the less as a pagan one, and therefore needful of conversion, by virtue of the archaeological features nearby. This seems to be what occurred at Yeavering, where the later structures were super-imposed upon Neolithic or Bronze Age features which probably had no ritual significance (Hope-Taylor 1977). The table includes both sites with and without Christian dedications. Duplicates are taken into account; that is, once they have occurred in the table they are not counted again. So far as Christianized wells go, we have of course no dates of possible conversions, at least for most of the sites. Some, particularly in Cornwall, must be old (below, pp.67–8), but other dedications – to Julian or Anne, for instance – are undoubtedly late. Anyway, we have a context of some kind in which to examine the other side of the equation.

Non-Christianization of Wells

If the number of sites where there is positive evidence of Christianization is tiny, the number where the opposite can be shown to have happened is just as small. The classic example of Wanswell, Hamfallow (Gloucestershire) – as in Bord 1985, 24 – is useless. The belief that the name derives from Woden's Well is an antiquarian fiction, as the true derivation is from *weagn*, 'wagon'; the original form is Weneswella (Smith 1964, ii 230–31, and cf. p.116 below). Let us try again.

Puck's Well, Aynho (Northamptonshire). First recorded 1712 (Gover et al. 1933, 48).

Nicker's Well, Church Holme (Cheshire). A *nicere* is a water-sprite; the name is first noted in 1840 (Dodgson 1970–81, ii 279).

Mab Well, Egton (North Yorkshire). Derivation unclear, but presumably it records the name of the mythical fairy queen (Whelan & Taylor 1989, 22).

Fritwell (Oxfordshire). The village takes its name from the spring at its centre, *fyrht wielle*, 'well of auguries', noted in 1086 (Gelling 1953–4, 211).

Bride's Well, Heavitree (Devon). Suggested as the focus of a pagan Saxon fertility cult, at least from 958 (Brown 1958, 61).

Thor's Well, Holme on Spaldingmoor (East Yorkshire). Cures eczema (Smith 1923, 17).

Nykarspole, Lincoln (Lincolnshire). Recorded 1409 (Hill 1948, 363).

Puck's Well, Rode (Somerset). Cured eye diseases (Horne 1923, 21–2).

Runwell (Essex). 'Well of the runes', noted 1086 (Ekwall 1961, 397).

Saltby (Lincolnshire). Wyville in this parish is Huuelle in 1086, from *weohwiella* – 'well of the shrine', hence pagan Saxon (Ekwall 1961, 541).

Stony Well, Stoneywell (Staffordshire). This village is Stoniwelle in the thirteenth century, named from a pool in which sits a huge boulder. Local people refuse to move it for fear that harm would result to livestock. This would seem a clear instance of pagan reverence (Duignan 1902, 144; Shaw 1798–1801, i 122).

Puck Well, West Knoyle (Wiltshire). First recorded c.1840 (Gover et al. 1939, 177).

Nicker Pool, Wimboldsley (Cheshire). First recorded 1309 (Dodgson 1970–81, ii 258).

This meagre total of thirteen can be added to in various ways. As well as sites roped in as a result of folklore or proximity to other ancient sites, there are also hints of pagan worship recorded in place-names. 'Gold wells' may be 'holy wells where gold objects may have been thrown as a sacrifice to supernatural powers' (Wallenberg 1934, 411); there are nine of these. 'Silver wells' must also have had a similar meaning, though the name may of course refer to the appearance of the water itself. In a couple of cases there are specific legends to confirm the association (Leather 1912, 11; Bord 1985, 57; Hope 1893, 95–6; Morris 1981, 42). There are fourteen examples. The three identified Penny Wells may also have this meaning; the one at Elstree (Hertfordshire) certainly did (*VCH Herts*, ii 349).

Not just money, though, was offered at wells. At two sites the custom of offering pins has died out, but the name Pin Well has lingered. Five Fairy Wells occur without accompanying folklore, and there are eight Maiden Wells. Precedents on the Isle of Man suggest that some tree-wells were originally holy (Chibbyr Unjin at Marown, for instance (Moore 1894, 224)). There are nine Ash Wells, and nine Holly Wells; seven Oak Wells and two apiece for Elder, Elm, Hazel, Maple and Nut; finally there is an isolated single Willow Well. These can also be added to the total.

This covers only those wells which have survived as place-names or in other ways. It is worth casting our minds back to the pits and shafts which are taken to be evidence for Celtic worship of water (Ross 1967, 25–7). Not one seems to have survived into the Roman era. Of the Roman wells in Table 1, most appear to have been ignored by the later Church. The Christleton site is oft-quoted (Hope 1893, 6; Bord 1985, 14); it is true that an altar dedicated to 'the nymphs and fountains' was found nearby, but the modern name Abbot's Well occurs as a result of the water's being led off in a conduit to the Abbey in 1282/3 (Ormerod 1812, ii 778). In 1296 the site was still simply called Wellefeld (Dodgson 1970–81, iv 109). The Abbot may have chosen the well because of its Roman associations, but he can hardly have been intending to convert anyone.

The total figures, then, of both probably converted and definitely not converted wells, amount to 95 against 215. Of course, these figures are, as figures, utterly meaningless. Their importance is schematic; they hint that the extent of the conversion of wells may have been at a far lower level than the established account implies. For this argument to hold, of course, it must be the case that wells lose their folklore if they lose their Christian status, and only at Yattendon (Berkshire) does this rule appear to have been broken (below, p.57). The figures imply that a very substantial number of wells, if not the absolute majority, was in fact left alone by the Church.

The question then arises: which Church did the converting?

The Roman Church

All scholars of sub-Roman Christianity in Britain bewail the lack of sources. The three British bishops at the Council of Arles are famous, but they have few companions in the historical record. Prosper talks of a Pelagian bishop called Agricola, St Patrick refers to bishops in Britain, and there are the churches which met St Germanus in 429. Geoffrey of Monmouth, for what he is worth, litters his (mock?) history with references to sub-Roman clergy, as well as bishops of London and Silchester, and he may have tapped into now-lost records or traditions (Morris 1973, 343, 346; *Ecclesiastical History* i 17; Geoffrey 1966, 125, 145–6, 230, 262).

What is almost completely agreed is the urban bias of Roman Christianity. Verulamium was clearly an important early ecclesiastical centre, but elsewhere only Caerleon and Silchester have produced actual churches, though churches may be hidden among crowds of indistinguishable town-houses. *Eccles*-place-names which may indicate Roman-British churches cluster around Roman roads, and the earliest evidence for Christianity in Britain, a first- or second-century silver cross, has recently been found alongside the Fosse Way (*Western Gazette* 19.7.90). Neither must the odd Christian villa – Frampton, Hinton St Mary, or Lullingstone – be forgotten.

But that, it must be said, is it. There is nothing to suggest that the Roman Church moved into the countryside in a systematic manner. St Patrick denounced its bishops as *dominaticos rhetoricos*: surely not 'learned clerics' (Barley & Hanson 1968, 127), but rather a sneer at their urban, secular sophistication, as public officials rather than preachers of the Gospel. Davies's picture of the Church in Wales *tempore* Gildas as one of 'declining *Romanitas*' is denied by others who point out that it was less a case of survival than a re-invigoration by the monastic emergence of the fifth century (ibid. 140–41; Wilson 1966/7).

Very recently the evidence for rural Roman Christianity has been much stressed, but even Thomas and Morris can only assemble basically what has been summarized above. Identifications of basilicate churches as late Roman are very shaky (though Lydd (Kent) is possible (Fernie 1983, 72)). Even the tiny Icklingham church is close to the Icknield Way. Its cross-inscribed water-tanks do not seem to have been converted Celtic wells, and neither church nor tanks survived the English Invasions (Frere 1976, 444–5).

There is one partial exception. Hubert proposes that the oldest French Christian wells are those near the tombs of early martyrs; these were not converted from pagan wells but deliberately sunk in episcopal basilicas partly to effect healing and partly to emulate the temple-wells of Greece and Rome (Hubert 1977, 262, 265, and above, p.25). The only known English parallel* would be at St Albans, where Bede gives us the legend of the spring welling at the saint's foot as he prayed for water. The shrine, and presumably the well, was still operational in 429 when St Germanus visited it; but because the current Holy Well is not on the hill, where the original legend places it, but at its foot, I believe that the cult had been disrupted by Bede's time. It is also now said that the well rose where St Alban's head fell, an element absent from Bede's account (*Ecclesiastical History* i 7, 17; Haynes 1986, 20). This suggests that the site of the well was lost when Verulamium fell to the Anglo-Saxons, and relocated when the Abbey was founded in the seventh century, with a familiar tale being applied to the new site. It is unsafe to assume any continuity before about 650.

In short, we must look elsewhere for institutions which might have converted the wells.

---

* Though the pretensions of St Andrew's Well, Wells (Somerset), are now being hyped (Blair 1988c).

FOUR

The Saxon Settlement: Wells
and the Conversion of England

The Two Churches

> A religion that was primarily concerned with the relations between
> people, a religion of an isolated rural landscape, in which to meet a
> fellow human being is to hail him. (Toulson 1987, 10–11)

The current fashion is to downrate the idiosyncrasies of the Celtic
Churches. Even Caitlin Matthews ('writer, singer and harpist') claims that
the 'celebration of mass and the regulation of religious life differed little
. . . the Celtic Churches upheld the doctrines common to both Orthodoxy
and Catholicism' (Matthews 1989, 94). But there were real differences in
spirit, differences which had much relevance to the spread of the well-cult
in England.

The tale begins with St Ninian, 'regularly instructed in the mysteries of
the Christian faith in Rome' and presumably inspired by the monastic
example of St Martin, even if he had not actually met him. Yet something
appeared to happen to him in Whithorn. Was it the rain and rocks of
Galloway slowly insinuating themselves into his mind, or simply that
there were no cities of the kind he had known in Britain? Either way
the monasticy that emerged from Candida Casa, his mission church,
and which St Enda carried thence to Aranmore, was different to that of
St Martin's model on the continent (*Ecclesiastical History* iii 4).

Meanwhile in the south of Britain St Germanus's enthusiasm for the
Coptic brand of monasticism had been transmitted, it seems, to his
supposed disciple, St Illtud (Farmer 1987, 217). Illtud's abbey of Llantilltud
Fawr (founded c.450) was one of the legendary Three Perpetual Choirs of
Britain, mentioned in the Welsh Triads and – in tow with the houses of
Illtud's friends SS David and Cadoc – furnished monks for the evangeliza-
tion of the countryside, most famously St Sampson. In the Triad which
mentions Llanilltud is to be believed, Glastonbury and Amesbury were in

existence at the same time. From South Wales the stream flowed into Ireland via St Finnian of Clonard (ibid. 161).

Yet different patterns emerged in England. By the middle of the seventh century Ireland was bursting with big monasteries, and it was this system which would be transported to Scotland and the North. Wales had impressive houses too, if fewer. The distribution of well-dedications indicates the importance of charismatic founders and leaders of monastic culture whose cults were spread by disciples around the area of the foundation (Map 4). St Inghean Baoith has eighteen wells, all in Co. Clare; St David's dedications 'cluster' in south-west Wales, and St Illtud's are all in Glamorganshire. Greater saints (Patrick, Columba, Brigid) have more widely dispersed cults but with clear regional biases. What is most interesting is that the southwest peninsula, Dumnonia, does not reflect these patterns.

The Dumnonian Church has been surveyed by Todd, who concludes that there was only a tiny number of monasteries in the sixth-century south-west; the peninsula may have been scattered with little cells, but these could hardly have been more different from the famous, gigantic colleges of Kildare, Clonmacnoise, or Menevia. 'So far as we know anything about them at all, they were . . . small, isolated communities, often ascetic and inward-looking, having no regard for the lives of other Christians in their neighbourhood. They were not centres of learning or education, nor did they concern themselves with the active propagation of the Christian faith' (Todd 1987, 244). No documents or monuments they produced to our knowledge survive, and of all the saints of the West Country the only one with anything like the status of David or Illtud is Petroc, who has eighteen churches and at least eight wells dedicated to him (Farmer 1987, 351, and Map 4).

How, then, was the west won for Christianity? The clue lies in the large number of sites named after obscure local saints. Todd dismisses the traditional image of 'The Age of the Saints' with its 'powerful and appealing picture of many ascetic monks travelling across the lands of Atlantic Britain and Gaul, promoting the Faith' and he claims that 'too much influence has been attributed to the eremitical movement in the past' (Todd 1987, 240–41). But this seems to ignore the actual existence of individuals, seen as saints, who had wells and churches dedicated to them. Map 5 shows the wells dedicated to local Celtic saints in the West Country (p.50).

Who were these people? Some would have been British, others Irish. None were illustrious, surely, though some were known outside their immediate locality; possibly few were in either monastic or clerical orders. Local traditions present most of them as wandering hermits, likely to be figures of respect in the context of established Celtic society, who taught

46

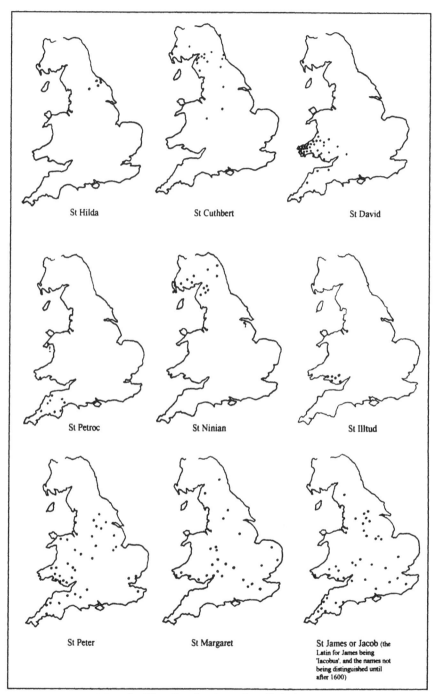

Map 4: The distribution of well-dedications

more by the example of their lives, by mere presence rather than active evangelism. Many West Country wells are explicitly stated by local legend to have been attached to a saint's hermitage, while many more are likely to have been. Though this is largely guesswork, it is most probably to these people that we should ascribe the Christianity of Dumnonia. It was not the work of the Roman Church, nor of the Welsh or Irish monasteries, and certainly not of the Romano-Saxon missionaries.

When St Augustine landed at Ebbsfleet he brought with him not just a new faith but a new culture in some degree. The fact that he created on his arrival a well later dedicated to himself does not alter his Roman identity. Prior of St Andrew Celianus in Rome, Augustine was a thoroughly urban cleric sent by a thoroughly urban Pope to evangelize a wrecked and ruined country. To the warlord-king of Kent he must have appeared an alien figure.

King Ethelbert was not, of course, entirely unfamiliar with Christianity, as his Frankish wife Bertha was a Christian and had a bishop, St Luidhard, as her confessor. She had even restored a church at Canterbury for the use of the small Christian circle about her. But Liudhard was hardly an important person, as Farmer points out, for he played no part in the Christianization, and it was not to him that St Gregory wrote when establishing the mission. Ethelbert clearly found the new Christians strange and frightening, for he refused to meet them indoors lest they bewitch him. It is also clear that Gaulish clerics never visited Britain (Bede, *Ecclesiastical History* i 25–7 (Augustine's Sixth Question); Farmer 1987, 267). What, then, did the cleric say to the king?

'The Catholic bishops had become identified with conservation, with continuity and with [the] tradition of *Romanitas*' (Wallace-Hadrill 1985, 30). The most extreme example is St Severinus of Noricum (not a bishop but occupying an equal if informal position), whose *Life* by Eugippius shows the holy man leading his people from town to town, and negotiating with the Huns; note also the pompous St Sidonius Apollinaris, Bishop of Clermont-Ferrand, whose autobiography records his organization of the city's defence against the Goths. All across Europe, barbarian chieftains were scrambling to inherit the mantle of the Empire. That notable Romano-phile Theodoric wrote as King of Italy to Hermanifrid of Thuringia, granting the hand of his neice Amalberga, 'so that you . . . may now shine more conspicuously by the splendour of Imperial blood' (Cassiodorus, 4.1). The Lombard king Agilulf had his son presented as King in the Circus in Milan (Wickham 1981, 34); and, far, far away in Eastern Europe, Arpad was acclaimed King of the Magyars in about 980 by being raised upon a shield in classic Roman manner. Christianity was the most conspicuous remaining product of the Empire, and consequently was everywhere associated with it in the minds of both conquerors and conquered alike.

St Augustine did not emphasize Christian humility in the face of the English king; that was not the way one dealt with barbarians. Instead he 'approached the king carrying a silver cross as their standard and the likeness of Our Lord painted upon a board' (*Ecclesiastical History* i 27); and he had already told Ethelbert that he had come from Rome, a thing the king, as he had set up his capital in old Durovernum, could appreciate. These priests thus brought with them the mantle of the Eternal City, the Crown of Empire, to which the *bretwalda* of the English, who already thought of himself as a little Emperor, must have been only too keen to attach himself. Gregory, idealist that he was, wished to revive the organization of the Roman Church in the province, with a network of twenty-four sees based on the centres of London and York, which were to have metropolitan bishops. The Canterbury arrangement was clearly intended to terminate when Augustine himself terminated (ibid. i 29). But by the time he write to Ethelbert it is likely that a more realistic attitude had been adopted.

This letter repays attention (ibid. i 32). 'He whose honour you seek and uphold . . . will make your own name glorious to posterity', Gregory promises. There follows a crucial comparison: 'so it was that the devout Emperor Constantine . . . turned the Roman state from its ignorant worship of idols'. The letter concludes with the date thus: 'the nineteenth year of . . . Emperor Maurice Tiberius Augustus'. This is perhaps only what is to be expected from the Pope's *scriptorium* but it is impressive even for form. The Bretwalda was to be the spearhead of the New Faith, to bathe in the reflected glory of the Empire, and blessed by the Pope, steward to the far-off Emperor. An English Clovis, in short.

When in 616 the Kentish nobility reverted to paganism and the pagan Redwald of East Anglia became Bretwalda, the Roman plans for the Church in England lay ruined. Edwin of Northumbria was slain at Hatfield, and when St Oswald came to restore the Church the model he chose was not the Roman one, which had so obviously failed to provide divine protection, but the Irish. This lengthy discussion of the rise of the Two Churches of the isle of Britain is a background to the emotions and institutions which created the quarrel between Roman and Celtic factions and which, it seems, had a considerable impact upon the development of English holy wells.

Regardless of how close the Roman and Celtic churches may have been doctrinally, there was clearly a good deal of mistrust between them, whatever the basis of it, at the Synod of Whitby which that meeting did not put to an end. As P.H. Blair has written, Whitby marked only the first step towards the triumph of Roman forms and manners (1977, 134). In the northern dioceses the conflict was particularly long and bitter.

The Northumbrian diocese was of the Celtic type peculiar in England,

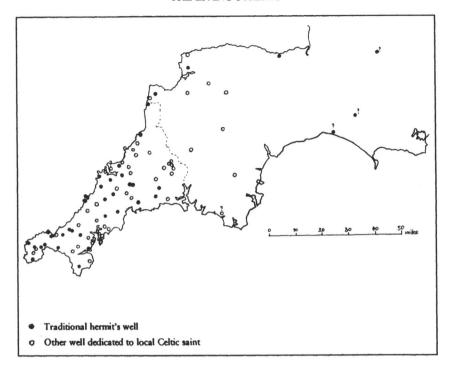

- ● Traditional hermit's well
- ○ Other well dedicated to local Celtic saint

Map 5: Hermits' wells and dedications to local saints in Dumnonia

based on a monastery, Lindisfarne, whose Abbot was also Bishop. This pattern was broken under St Tuda, who was not Abbot (though he had been ordained in Ireland (*Ecclesiastical History* iii 26)), but was resumed under St Eata. Eata was one of the appointees of King Egfrith, along with Bosa, who was sent to the See of York after the expulsion of the obnoxious ultra-Romanist St Wilfrid. This began as a personal and political quarrel between the King and Wilfrid, but swiftly took upon itself the forms of the ecclesiastical disagreement. Both Bosa and Eata had been monks before their elevations to their sees, as had Eadhaed, who Egfrith appointed to his pet see of Lindsey; also, Eadhaed's successor Ethelwin was 'a monk who had travelled to study in Ireland' (ibid. iv 12, iii 27).

Respect for the holy Cuthbert (he was one of Bede's heroes) was so great that he was elected unanimously at 'a great synod' at Twyford attended by both King Egfirth and Archbishop Theodore (ibid. iv 28), though the Chronicle entry for 685 makes it clear that 'King Egfrith had Cuthbert consecrated bishop'. Nothing is known of Cuthbert's immediate successor in the see of Lindisfarne, Eadbert, but St Edfrith (bishop 698–721) and St Ethilwald (721–41) followed in his footsteps: Ethilwald was a noted patron of hermits, for instance (Farmer 1987, 152). Nearby, the diocese of Hexham was the scene of especial conflict. Theodore had obviously attempted moderation and conciliation, agreeing to consecrate Egfrith's client bishops, and, long before, defusing the row over the election of St Chad to the see of York (*Ecclesiastical History* iii 28, iv 12). He certainly was no lover of the aggressive and inflammatory Wilfrid. But his appointee to Hexham, Tumbert, was deposed in 685 for reasons which are not clear, and it is surely no coincidence that the thoroughly Celtic Eata was chosen in his place. After the contest with Wilfrid was over, Celtic personnel remained in the area; Wilfrid II of York, for instance, was trained at Whitby under St Hilda (ibid. iv 23). This may seem to some as reading too much between the lines of the *Ecclesiastical History*. But it appears that there was subsequent competition between the cults of Wilfrid at Hexham and Cuthbert at Lindisfarne which had the Roman-Celtic quarrel as its subtext, and the fact that even different artistic styles are associated with the two houses shows how deep the division ran (Rollason 1988, 214–15; Cramp 1984, 15–19). Besides, there is no hiding the fact that the Northumbrian kings showed decided preference for clerics whose connections were with the Irish Church and its way of doing things. No doubt the argument even at the time was a little vague, which is why the Synod of Whitby concentrated on details such as tonsures and the date of Easter, as a test of ritual submission to Rome whose authority the Celts fully acknowledged in theory. The irrationality of the conflict should not persuade us that it did not happen.

The other diocese under heavy Celtic influence was that of Mercia. The first bishop was St Diuma, a Scot consecrated by St Finan at Lindisfarne; he was succeeded by Ceollach, Trumhere, Jaruman and Chad, all Scottish or Scot-trained. The last in the sequence was Winfrith,* who was one of the signatories of the Synod of Hertford's conclusions in 673; but soon afterwards, to judge by the confused account in the Chronicle entry for 656, he was 'deposed for disobedience' – which, in the absence of a powerful local monarch in opposition, gave Theodore the chance to appoint Sexwulf, Abbot of Peterborough, to the see, and thus to break the (irregular) Celtic succession (*Ecclesiastical History*, iii 21, iv 6).

Elsewhere, the Hwiccan diocese was regularly filled by monks of Whitby. Tatfrid was elected while still resident in the monastery, though he never took office; his successors, Bosel and Oftfor, were also disciples of St Hilda. Possible Celtic influence in the diocese and royal family of Wessex has hitherto been totally overlooked. King Cadwalla has an unequivocally Celtic name, and several others which appear in the Parker Chronicle entry for 688 genealogy bear a similar interpretation. A twelfth-

* Experiment with spelling the name as Wynffrydd!

century interpolation in the same entry claims that King Ina 'built the monastery at Glastonbury', and he, alone among Saxon monarchs, appears in the Welsh saint-lists, indicating some sort of Celtic connection. His daughter St Cuthberga built an Irish-model double house at Wimborne; when Ina became King, Hedda, a monk of Whitby, was bishop, and St Aldhelm, Abbot of the Celtic house at Malmesbury, was chosen as his successor (Aldhelm also had a retreat and holy well at Doulting (Somerset), exactly like Hilda's at Hinderwell (North Yorkshire)). The Wessex nobles also permitted British bishops in their territories, and a Catwali, Abbot of Shaftesbury in the late seventh century, has been uncovered (Baring-Gould & Fisher 1907–13, iii 318; Farmer 1987, 201; *Ecclesiastical History*, iii 28; Haslam 1984, 213).

All this must be seen in the context of Theodore's efforts to unify the various strands of British Christianity. Whitby and the capitulation of such Celtic leaders as Cuthbert and Hilda removed the most acute reasons for conflict, but there were still difficulties; and, while the Primate took control of the Mercian diocese as we saw, in Northumbria there was still utter polarization. Crucial in the process of unity was the Synod of Hertford, whose Conclusions were clearly directed against Celtic practices. Canon 1 concerned the date of Easter; and Canons 2, 4, 5 and 6 curbed itinerancy among bishops, priests and monks. Perhaps Winfrith was deposed for disobeying the rules which he himself had agreed to (*Ecclesiastical History*, iv 5). Gradually the Celtic camp was worn down; Hilda's successors at Whitby, SS Enfleda and Elfleda, were partisans of Wilfrid, and by the time of St Ethilwald the abbacy and bishopric of Lindisfarne had been separated. But west of Severn itinerancy survived into the tenth century, when Cyfeiliog was 'Bishop of Archenfield', a village never a regular see (Farmer 1987, 138, 142; *Ecclesiastical History*, v i; Parker Chronicle for 914).

This is the ecclesiastical background to the spread of the Christian well-cult in early England. We can expect first that Celtic personnel would be more amenable to Christianization of wells than would the English clergy, for consistent denunciation of hydrolatry by the English Church is not matched in the Celtic areas. Secondly, we might expect patterns of dedications to be affected. The Irish model was fully in place only in Northumbria, where there were several very large monasteries whose only parallel in the south was St Ethelburga's abbey at Barking. The monasteries spread the cults of charismatic leader-figures over their immediate areas: Oswald, whose noble life and hideous death made him an obvious model; Cuthbert, the perfect bishop and ascetic, who had himself created a holy well on Inner Farne (Bede, *Life of Cuthbert*, ch. 18); Hilda the foundress of great abbeys and trainer of bishops. Obviously some wells dedicated to these saints are younger, such as St Oswald's on

Roseberry Topping (above, p.39), but the pattern is what is important. What is also important is that these saints are represented in well-dedications more than any other native English saints, with one exceptional exception (pp.71–2), and the pattern of dedications in other regions of the country is totally different.

Wells and the Minster System

Over recent years, local archaeological and historical journals have bristled with talk of the Anglo-Saxon minsters, possibly one of the most important, certainly one of the most shadowy institutions of early England. The device of the minster, the college of missionary priests with the responsibility of spreading the Gospel and administering the Sacraments over a given area, was always known about, but the modern appreciation of its importance appears to have originated with Page. Page pointed out that an undated charter of Wihtred of Kent mentions the 'churches of Kent' as being Rochester, Canterbury, Folkestone, Lyminge, Reculver, Dover, Hoo, Upminster, Southminster and Sheppey; and that the same list was recited in 844. As this list can hardly contain all the religious buildings in Kent, it must refer to 'superior' churches. He also noted that the 'parish' of Evesham in the eleventh century covered the whole of Blackenhurst Hundred (Page 1915, 63–5). Even then, only in the last few years has it come to be seen that the minster was the axial institution of Anglo-Saxon England, playing a crucial role in the development of others.

Often pointed out is the importance St Theodore placed upon the minster. In his *Penitential* he decreed that the minster must remain in place even when the monastery which might constitute a large part of its activities moves; and Blair notes that when a minster was founded close to a royal estate, it was the former that quickly exerted the greater economic pull: this pattern arose at Gloucester (near Kingsholme), Chesterfield (near Newbold), and Aylesbury (near Quarrendon), among others (Haddan & Stubbs 1869–78, iii 195; Blair 1988b, 41). It also seems likely, given Page's observations and more recent work, that the minster's parish was the origin of the unit that later became the Hundred under Edgar (Blair 1987a).

The identification of minster churches themselves presents great problems; minster-spotting has become virtually an historical spectator-sport. On the assumption that each hundred must have its own, Page gives a list identifying them on this basis. This is useless, and I know it is useless because I have tried it. By Domesday, commonly the earliest record of many hundreds, their function had shifted so far towards raising taxes that they are, in many cases, no guide to the original system. In the West Country (the area we shall be considering) the hundreds have been endlessly subdivided, except in Cornwall, where, modern work indicates, Saxon churches were introduced only during the tenth century, when the Church was again hostile to wells (below, pp.79). All counties have hundreds with detached portions, or clearly carved out of one another, an open sign of bureaucratic meddling. Exmoor is spattered with single-manor hundreds, witness to special tax arrangements; in Devon, Somerset, and Dorset the Exon Domesday hundreds differ widely from those of the Tax Returns, while there is no clue to the pattern in Wiltshire at all.

Blair's first attempt to identify minsters used Domesday Book, searching for large landholdings, separate tax returns, or other evidence for 'superior' status of churches (1985). This is a better guide, but appears to include far too many sites, with unlikely concentrations in Berkshire, Wiltshire and Hampshire, while excluding such obvious minsters as Reculver, Minster-in-Sheppey, or Leeds. Hase has based his lists of south Hampshire minsters on royal estate churches, which is probably more satisfactory. Pearce's lists also seem to include too many sites, based on dubious evidence – the inclusion of Halstock (Dorset) for instance, on the grounds of its derivation from *haelige stoc* (Blair 1987a, 46–8; 1988c, ch. 2; Pearce 1978, 98–108). The various attempts to pick out the minsters of south-east Dorset when combined give Wimborne, Bere Regis, two churches in Wareham, Sturminster Marshall, Canford, Winfrith, Kingston and Studland – or nine for 150 square miles. Not a lot for their clergy to do, one might think (Hinton 1987; Pitfield 1981).

The best area to study the minster system is perhaps Oxfordshire. Here the hundreds appear to have been corrupted only in the south of the county, and even there Domesday gives the old names. Elsewhere the large, compact units probably represent the original model, with the exceptions of Dorchester, very small and probably originally united with Benson, and Cropredy, which looks as if it has been carved out of Bloxham-and-Banbury. The chief towns of all the rest were held at Domesday either by the King or the Bishop of Lincoln, indicating the conservatism of the whole system (Oxon. Domesday, i.2–6, 7a; 6.1a–4). The minsters definitely included Bampton, Oxford, Eynsham and Dorchester, all pre-Conquest monasteries or secular houses; and also, probably, Charlbury (the shrine of St Diuma, bishop of Mercia), Bicester (where there may have been a community), Thame, Milton and Banbury, all the central settlements of their hundreds.

This information from Oxfordshire arms us when we turn elsewhere. Given their economic importance, minsters are likely to have been set in what are now towns or at least large villages (though settlements are known to have vanished when the minster did, as at Eiminstre in Atcham parish (Shropshire) (Gelling & Foxall 1990, 123)); they are not likely to have been as numerous as has often been assumed. Since the south-western counties form the largest continuous block of well-research in the country (Map 1) it is they we will examine. Cornwall, as its system of evangelism was very likely completely at odds with the minster model, is included only by way of comparison with other counties. The 'minsters' are the monasteries in Pearce's list, and the pre-Conquest foundations given in Knowles and Hadcock (Pearce 1978, 105–8).

Devon. Pre-Conquest foundations are a good guide to the presence of minsters. The given dates of foundations often conceal long previous histories. For Devon they are: Axminster -940; Braunton, the house of the Celtic St Brannoc, 6th century; Buckfast 1018; Crediton 739; Cullompton -1066; Dartmouth, whose minster is recorded in 1192 but which is apparently far older (Pearce 1978, 104); Exeter c.690; Tavistock 975. Pre-Conquest secular colleges are at Hartland (St Nectan's settlement) -1066, and Plympton -909 (dates Knowles & Hadcock 1971, 52, 57, 143, 413–14, 468, 471). 'Minster' names are rare in Devon – in Dorset they are used indiscriminately – making Exminster a likely site, and parish boundaries indicate minsters at Barnstaple and Lydford (Haslam 1984, 251–6, 259–62).

Somerset. Pre-Conquest houses: Athelney c.888; Banwell c.888; Bath c.676; Bruton c.1005; Cheddar 975; Congresbury, the foundation of St Congar, c.711; Frome 675+; Glastonbury 6th century; Muchelney -673. Secular foundations were at Taunton -904; and Wells c.704. Watchet was the hermitage of St Decuman and an ancient port town which Aston pencils in as a minster, while Crewkerne is more of a guess, a post-Conquest foundation of unknown date, and Saxon royal estate town (Knowles & Hadcock 1971, 52, 54–5, 138, 144, 419, 430, 468, 471; Haslam 1984, 192–3).

Dorset. Regular houses: Cerne, 9th century; Christchurch, -1066; Cranborne c.980; Milton 933; Shaftesbury c.650; Sherborne c.672; Wareham c.672; Wimborne -705. Abbotsbury was a secular college before c.1023 or 1044. In addition we have Bere Regis, centre of an ancient hundred, set below a hillfort, and a Domesday royal estate with a large parish; and Bridport, a Saxon borough with ecclesiastical and parochial minster, given their proximity to each other. Cranborne has been preferred, basically on the grounds of its size as indicative of a greater economic importance, and a legend, recorded in a MS owned by Sir William Dugdale and which Hutchins claimed to have read, that the abbey there had Celtic origins (Knowles & Hadcock 1971, 52–3, 55, 57, 139, 419, 485; Haslam 1984, 213; Hutchins 1861–70, iii 381).

Gloucestershire presents greater problems. It was clearly a pleasant environment for monasteries, given their great profusion! Heighway's list of 'minsters' includes nineteen sites, many of them in very tiny villages and within a few miles of each other, with no corroboratory evidence. Even this list does not include all the post-Conquest foundations. In view of the evidence from Oxfordshire, it seems most unlikely that there were upwards of twenty minsters in this not overly large shire, and so we must be radically selective. I have thus adopted the simple expedient, as in the Cranborne–Horton case, of preferring large sites to small. The dates of the survivors of this process are Berkeley -807; Bristol -1066; Cheltenham -803; Cirencester -839; Gloucester -679; Stow on the Wold c.1010; Tetbury c.680; Tewkesbury c.715; Winchcombe 787; Withington 674; Yate 9th century (Heighway 1987; Knowles & Hadcock 1971, 54, 57–8, 139, 334, 413, 470, 483, 486).

Wiltshire. Pre-Conquest regular houses: Amesbury, one of the Three Perpetual Choirs of the Welsh Triads, but first reliably recorded c.679; Bedwyn 10th century; Bradford on Avon c.705; Calne -1066; Cricklade 10th century; Malmesbury 7th century; Tisbury -710; Wilton 830. Ramsbury was a bishopric for a while in the tenth century and was thus a likely minster site, and the gap in the west is filled by Warminster, a royal estate with a large parish, and the additional indicator of the place-name (ibid. 55, 104, 255, 467–9, 471, 484; Haslam 1984, 118–21).

This list, it must be admitted, no doubt contains, many omissions, unjustified inclusions and distortions, but it can hardly be so inaccurate as not to provide a rough guide (Map 6). Now let us analyse it with regard to holy and ancient wells.

TABLE 3: MINSTERS AND HOLY WELLS IN FIVE SOUTH-WESTERN COUNTIES

county		minsters with					other parishes with					minster : parish ratios	
		named wells		holy wells			named wells		holy wells			named	holy
		no.	%	no.	%		no.	%	no.	%			
Devon	13	12	92.3	9	75.0	414	157	37.9	97	23.4		2.4:1	3.2:1
Dorset	10	10	100.0	10	100.0	283	106	37.5	34	12.0		2.7:1	8.3:1
Somerset	13	10	76.9	8	61.5	388	122	31.4	62	16.0		2.4:1	3.8:1
Wiltshire	11	8	72.7	4	40.0	305	97	31.8	19	6.6		2.3:1	6.1:1
Gloucestershire	11	7	63.6	5	45.5	351	140	39.7	48	13.7		1.6:1	3.3:1
TOTALS	57	47	82.5	36	63.2	1741	622	35.7	261	15.0		2.3:1	4.2:1

(It should be noted that much suppression and reorganization of parish councils has taken place in recent years, and the figures for Gloucestershire, Wiltshire and Devon have been compiled using the EPNS volumes from which so much information was drawn for those counties. This is impossible for Cornwall or Somerset, where the 1990 Municipal Yearbook was used instead, and inappropriate for Dorset, whose total is derived from the Ordnance Survey maps used during the detailed investigation of that county. Former units subsumed within modern boroughs have been resurrected for our purposes.)

Despite these caveats the results are striking. Wells are more likely to occur in minster towns than in other parishes, and if only wells with Christian dedications are taken into account this phenomenon is accentuated. Ratios range from 3.2:1 in Devon to 8.3:1 in Dorset. The figure for wells as a whole in Gloucestershire minster towns may possibly be especially low because of the stringent approach taken above to identifying them. Across the west as a whole, Christian wells are four times as likely to occur in minster settlements as in common parishes. This itself suggests that was some form of link, but what was it?

Some of these western minsters appear to be evidence of a concern to found monastic or other communities on traditionally important sites. Amesbury was a refoundation of a very ancient abbey; Sherborne and Wareham were bastions of the Celtic churches before the conversion of the English, and both were connected with the Irish-trained St Aldhelm. Cerne sits below its famous Giant, Wells was built over a Roman mausoleum (Rodwell 1982, 52); Exeter, Bath, Cirencester and Gloucester were all Roman towns. As regards wells, the evidence is ambiguous. The ancient Congresbury house played host to a May-Day well-cult of clearly pagan nature (Tongue 1967, 185) which was never Christianized; it might be argued that the dedication has dropped off, but the only known parallel of this is at Yattendon (Berkshire), where the Miraculous Well was the scene of annual games on St Peter's Day, and the church is dedicated to SS Peter and Paul (*VCH Berks*, iv 125). Glastonbury's wells may have their origins in a tree-cult (above, p.38), and St Mary's Well at Exeter was probably converted at a very early date.

At Bath the hot springs were also well known at an early point, and became the basis of course for a fashionable and wealthy town in the Roman era. The English captured the city in 577 and the Abbey first appears about a century afterwards. The church was right in the old city centre and mere yards from the sacred springs, and it seems natural that they would have been important in the choice of site. Yet the waters were never formally Christianized. There was a late attempt at Christianization, when the monks put about the tale that they owed their healing powers to being blessed by St David, prior to which they had been thought poisonous; but this was perhaps so demonstrably a lie that nothing ever came of it. It is a puzzle that a site which might have brought the Church so much pecuniary benefit, if nothing else, was never drawn under the Abbey's wing (Collinson 1791, i 7).

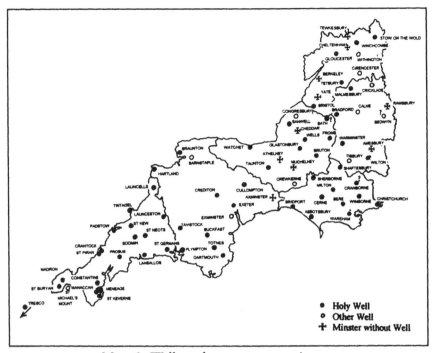

Map 6: Wells and west-country minsters

Nearby Wells is a parallel case. Here the minster seems to have been set up over a Roman mausoleum, with several springs distributed around the site, though there does not appear to have been a great deal of settlement hereabouts. It is quite obvious that the wells were the focal point of the minster settlement; the first record of the place-name is as Fontanelium in 725, and in 766 we hear of 'the minster which is situated next to the great spring which is called Wielea' (Rodwell 1982, 52; Ekwall 1961, 505). Yet there was then no hint of Christianization – no 'halliwella', no 'Seyntandreweswella' – and nor is there any indication that at this time the well was seen as anything more than a notable spring. This was a pagan site of sorts. But perhaps the wells themselves were the creation of a later Christian era? Wells being created by early religious institutions is a phenomenon observed in France. St Martin's Well at Maremoutier was dug by the saint himself, and, in Britain, not only is the Cathedral at Winchester built on ancient wells, but another was sunk in the late tenth-century extensions of the church (Hubert 1977, 266; Biddle 1969, 317–19).

It might be worthwhile to examine a few sites where development can be observed in order to distinguish different models. It will be noticed that

I am not as hostile, in practice, to the notion of pagan holy wells as I am in theory!

Bampton (Oxfordshire). Here the old burial church of St Andrew was imposed, to judge by its name of The Beam, on a pagan tree-cult centre. The Minster of St John the Baptist followed this early site, with other chapels being set up nearby. The place of the Lady Well in this process is not clear, but if Aymer de Valence's castle was built on the site of an Anglo-Saxon royal palace it may be very old, and there certainly seems to be some sort of alignment of religious sites here (Blair 1990).

Bridport (Dorset). The arrangement is similar to that of Bampton. The minster of St Mary is some distance from a St Andrew's chapel, with some other sites in between. If an analogy between these two towns is correct, the presence of a St Andrew's Well at the chapel increases the possibility of its being a pagan site. Sites here also seem to be aligned in some way.

Canterbury (Kent). See Map 7.

Coventry (Warwickshire). The original 'well' of the city was probably St Osburg's Pool, the pond beside the first (now lost) minster. This vanished in the sixteenth century and 'may have been an attempt to Christianize a heathen holy well' – though the odd rites at the Hob's Hole spring, too, may have pagan antecedents (*VCH Warks*, viii 1, 246). St Agnes's Well was probably later and may not even have been a holy well, and St Catherine's Well is definitely fourteenth century.

Exeter (Devon). The Saxon minster rests on a Roman well which (to judge by the presence of a statue-pedestal) was dedicated to the Virgin at least by the thirteenth century, and is very probably much older than that; though there is no positive evidence that this was a pagan site, the early evangelists may have thought it worth their while to convert it anyway (Fox 1956, 210–11). The other old well is St Martin's on the edge of the Cathedral Close, again a Roman well and associated with the pre-Conquest church of St Martin. St Sidwell's Well is a good example of the sacralizing activities of the medieval Church. Some time after 1050, when the city became the see for both Devon and Cornwall, it appears the monks first read the story of St Sativola in the Life of St Paul Aurelian (seeing that she is absent from the early eleventh-century relic-lists, but does appear in the later Exeter Litany), and then applied her name to the pre-existing spring of Sidwell (Pearce 1973). St Anne's Well, on the outskirts of the city, is definitely later medieval, and St Catherine's Well, whose history is lost, is probably more or less contemporary with it.

Lichfield (Staffordshire). It is difficult to work out which is the city's oldest well. St Chad's at Stowe is outside the walls and has long been associated with the saint of the seventh century, but in view of the possible existence of a Celtic monastery before Chad's arrival the original well may have been St Mary's. The *VCH* links this with St Mary's Church, which

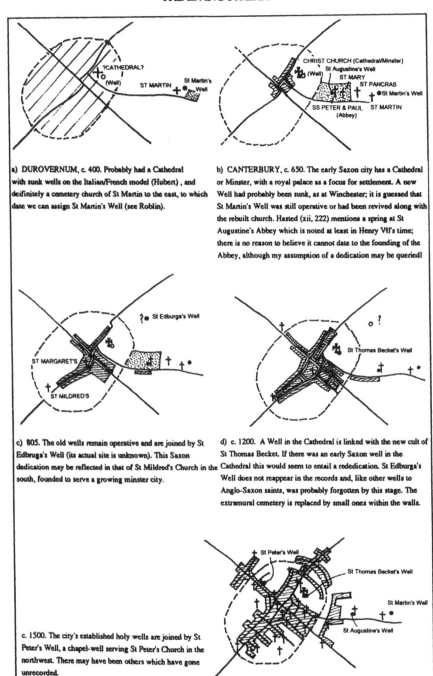

a) DUROVERNUM, c. 400. Probably had a Cathedral with sunk wells on the Italian/French model (Hubert) , and deifinitely a cemetery church of St Martin to the east, to which date we can assign St Martin's Well (see Roblin).

b) CANTERBURY, c. 650. The early Saxon city has a Cathedral or Minster, with a royal palace as a focus for settlement. A new Well had probably been sunk, as at Winchester; it is guessed that St Martin's Well was still operative or had been revived along with the rebuilt church. Hasted (xii, 222) mentions a spring at St Augustine's Abbey which is noted at least in Henry VII's time; there is no reason to believe it cannot date to the founding of the Abbey, although my assumption of a dedication may be queried!

c) 805. The old wells remain operative and are joined by St Edbruga's Well (its actual site is unknown). This Saxon dedication may be reflected in that of St Mildred's Church in the south, founded to serve a growing minster city.

d) c. 1200. A Well in the Cathedral is linked with the new cult of St Thomas Becket. If there was an early Saxon well in the Cathedral this would seem to entail a rededication. St Edburga's Well does not reappear in the records and, like other wells to Anglo-Saxon saints, was probably forgotten by this stage. The extramural cemetery is replaced by small ones within the walls.

c. 1500. The city's established holy wells are joined by St Peter's Well, a chapel-well serving St Peter's Church in the northwest. There may have been others which have gone unrecorded.

Map 7: Hypothetical sequence of sacred topography at Canterbury

only appears in 1293, but the minster was also dedicated to her. Excavations in the chapel of St Peter in the Cathedral have uncovered a deep pit which may have been a well; while there were springs at St Michael's, though they may have been only subterranean (Leland 1913, ii 99; *VCH Staffs*, xiv 4, 49, 99; Plot 1686, 86).

Lincoln (Lincolnshire). The chronology is also difficult here. Lincoln was of course one of the Roman sees, and what is probably the oldest well was the Roman public well in the Forum, used as a baptistry for the church of St Paul which was founded in the old basilica. St Peter's Well sounds early, but is not recorded before 1189; the Holy Well is undatable. Monk's Well is linked with the abbey, while the Fontem Trinitatis of 1318 is clearly later (Rodwell 1989, 144; Cameron 1985, 71, 131, 106; Woodward 1904, 207).

Oxford (Oxfordshire). As at Lichfield the probable oldest well was outside the walls, at Holywell Church, though it is worth remembering that St Margaret's Well at Binsey, with close ties to St Frideswide, is only a couple of miles away. Another well was close by the first but seems to have been younger. St Edmund's and St Mary's Wells are of medieval foundation, and the Holy Well on Holywell Green was set up as late as 1651 (Gelling 1953–4, 36; Wood 1889, i 386, 388, 288–92, 289; Hurst 1899, 120; Rattue 1990, 175).

Shrewsbury (Shropshire). The oldest religious college here was St Chad's, founded sometime before 779, and the well apparently belonging to it was cursorily excavated and filled in again in 1910; a well dedicated to a supposed Welsh king may be even older. A peripheral set, SS Peter and Paul's Wells, seem to have been linked to a later parish church (Knowles & Hadcock 1971, 417; Drinkwater 1910; Baring-Gould & Fisher 1907–13, i 262–4; Hope 1893, 141).

Winchester (Hampshire). The present cathedral is built on wells, one of which is said to have been used by St Birinus for baptisms, but we must note that wells were *deliberately* sunk in the Old Minster, founded in 648, and when the building was extended in the tenth century. St Martin's Well near the city wall is probably very old too (Biddle 1969, 317–19; Keene 1985, ii 982).

York (North Yorkshire). The pattern is like that of Winchester, a baptismal well under the minster (St Peter's) in an old Roman city. The Zouche Chapel well may be of equally ancient date; the Lady Well is probably not, and the Holy Priests' Well takes its name from a late fourteenth-century residence for chantry priests (Hope 1893, 173–4; Raine 1955, 85–7).

Turning away from minsters and back to the specific area of the south-west, we find that patterns of dedications differ from those in other regions. The conclusion to be drawn from Table 4 is unavoidable.

TABLE 4: WELL-DEDICATIONS COMPARED IN THREE REGIONS

	dedications										
	Biblical		local		dispersed *		cluster		B.V.M.		other	
	no.	%	no.	%	no.	%	no.	%	no.	%	no.	%
North*	29	16.4	8	4.5	10	5.6	68	38.4	36	20.3	26	14.7
West	46	21.7	28	13.2	22	10.4	7	3.3	59	27.8	50	23.6
Cornwall	17	13.2	67	51.9	13	10.1	1	0.8	8	6.2	23	17.8

* 'North' here comprises Northumberland, Durham, Cumberland, Westmorland and North Yorkshire. 'Dispersed' dedications are those which yield only a few scattered examples with no clear pattern: e.g. St Dunstan, with two dedications in Somerset, one in Middlesex and another in Sussex.

Patterns of dedications are inextricably related to the methods of evangelization prevailing in the different areas; Irish or Anglo-Celtic saints in clusters in the North, local hermits in Cornwall, and a more general spread of dedications in the Western counties, converted under the minster system.

This chapter has sometimes strayed so far, seemingly, from the topic of holy wells that a concluding paragraph is needed. Hopefully we have done enough to establish that there was a Celtic Church of a kind, distinguished by administrative and hierarchical indiscipline which the Romano-Saxon Church feared and attempted to stamp out. Its influence was widespread in several English dioceses, and to judge by the behaviour of Celtic saints such as St Columba at Invermoriston (Perthshire) (Horstmann 1901, i 201), it was less hostile to hydrolatry than the English Church. But the institutions of the Celtic Church differed from region to region; in the North, great monastic colleges like Whitby and Lindisfarne, and in the Cornish area almost nothing so far as can yet be divined. In the rest of the country the model was conversion by minsters of varying sizes, and these divergences appear to be reflected in the patterns of well-dedications.

This chapter has concentrated exclusively on institutions; from here we turn more to attitudes. When did the English Church conquer its shyness of the Holy Well? How did the Middle Ages become the zenith of English hydrolatry?

FIVE

Unam Ecclesiam: *Wells and the Medieval Church*

Cults and Chronology

The numbers of specifically holy wells recorded before Domesday are very small, though dates are often no guide to antiquity. Wookey's Holy Well (Somerset) is unrecorded before 1470, Tadmarton's (Oxforshire) before 1346, or Roseberry Topping's (North Yorkshire) before about 1600, yet all are obviously much older than this. A list of these pre-Domesday sites, none the less, can tell us something about the chronology of the cult's development. In addition to the Christianized wells outlined above (pp.38–9) the pre-Domesday sites are these:

795 x 805 *Eadburgeswelle, Canterbury (Kent)*. A grant of Archbishop Aethelhard to Christ Church of six *mensurae* next to the well may be a forgery, but in view of the normal degree of redating inflicted on such dubious charters it is still probably pre-Conquest (Urry 1967, 197). The saint is probably St Edburga of Lyminge.

880 *Halgan wylle, Ruisham (Somerset)*. On the south-east boundary of the parish (Grundy 1935, 29).

926 *Cynburge wellan, Chalgrave (Bedfordshire)*. Very probably dedicated to St Cyniburg of Mercia, Abbess of Castor. Perhaps she was born here, in the same way that St Osyth, Abbess of Aylesbury, had a well at her birthplace in Quarrendon (Buckinghamshire), and St Edith, Abbess of Wilton, one at Kemsing (Kent) (Mawer & Stenton 1926, 117; Farmer 1987,107).

931 *Eanswithe wyllas, Cold Ashton (Gloucestershire)*. A dubious example. St Eanswith was Abbess of Folkestone, but there is no apparent connection with Cold Ashton (Smith 1964, iii 64; Farmer 1987, 126).

932 *Halgan welle, Fontmell Magna (Dorset)*. On the parish boundary (Mills 1989, 110).

940 *Abbots wylle, Pewsey (Wiltshire)*. On the boundary of a grant from Edmund to New Minster, Winchester (Grundy 1919, 250–51).

952 *Ceollan wylle, Barkham (Berkshire)*. Named after 'St' Ceolla, sister of St Hean of Helenstow, founder of Abingdon (Stephenson 1858, i 163).

996 *Abban wylle, Bensington (Oxfordshire)*. (Stephenson 1858, i 405)

1026 *Halgan wyl, Portesham (Dorset)*. On the parish boundary (Hutchins 1861–70, ii 774).

Wells recorded for the first time in Domesday Book are: Nun's Well, Brading (Isle of Wight) (Kokeritz 1940, 52–3); Holy Wells at Brixton and Halwill (Devon) (Gover et al. 1936, 250, 141); Holy Well, Radipole (Dorset) (Mills 1977, 242); Holy Wells at Holybourne and Ecchinswell (Hampshire) (Coates 1989, 70, 94); Holy Well, Oxford (Oxfordshire) (Gelling 1953–4, 36); St Hilda's Well, Hinderwell (North Yorkshire) (Smith 1928, 138); and Holy Well, Holywell (Cambridgeshire) (Mawer & Stenton 1926, 209). (There are wells which are referred to even before these, including St Alban's at St Albans, St Cuthbert's at Farne, and St Guthlac's at Croyland (Lincolnshire), but none of them are actually named (*Ecclesiastical History* i 7,17; *Bede's Life of Cuthbert*, 17; Birch 1881, 42).

What we notice from this admittedly small sample of sites is something unaffected by its size. There are three names referring to ecclesiastical personnel, four to fairly obscure Anglo-Saxon saints, and one to a great Anglo-Celtic saint. All the others are simply called 'holy wells', without any firm indication that they were Christianized at all by this stage. There are no dedications to greater saints. There must, of course, have been some of these, particularly to St Martin (of the eight Martin well-dedications in England, six – Canterbury, Exeter, Haresfield (Gloucestershire), Leicester, Stony Middleton (Derbyshire) and Winchester – are at Roman sites). But the point is that none are recorded, and this can only be because there were not many of them about. They simply cannot have been thick on the ground.

There is an even more interesting group of early well-names to consider. These are those cases where a spring name occurs which we know is then Christianized at a later date. There are only a few, but their importance is crucial:

725 *Wells (Somerset)*. See above, p.58.

775 *Wellow (Somerset)*. An ordinary water-source which is now

Julian's Well and which has acquired a banshee and sufficient respect for its water to be used in the church font. The dedication is unlikely to have been coined before the Golden Legend became popular in the late thirteenth century (Ekwall 1961, 505; Horne 1923, 21; Farmer 1987, 243–4).

887   *Brightwell Baldwin (Oxforshire).* There are hints that Bright Wells are perhaps pagan, from the belief that water is especially powerful when the morning sun first shines on it, but this is still extremely dubious. In any case, by 1245 a Holy Well has appeared here, probably at the Bright Well site (Gelling 1953–4, 14, 121).

939   *Willesden (Middlesex).* Willesdune, the well by the hill, is recorded in this year, but there was a shrine of the Virgin with a Black Madonna here at an unspecified date in the Middle Ages (Gover et al. 1942, 160; *VCH Middx*, vii 237).

956   *Cress Well, Abbotskerswell (Devon).* An unassuming spring with cress growing about it, which was converted at an unknown date into a Lady Well (Gover et al. 1936, 504; Brown 1957, 209).

c.1000   *Cress Well, Nymet Tracy (Devon).* An even more perfectly ordinary spring which began its recorded life as a bound mark of Creedy Land. It was later dedicated to the Virgin (Finberg 1962, 50).

1080–86   *Welton (East Yorkshire).* Wealletune, referring to what is now St Anne's Well; St Anne's is a late cult, reaching England only in the twelfth century and taking a long time to achieve popularity (Smith 1937, 219–20; Morris 1989, 89–90).

1086   *Coffinswell (Devon).* Willa in Domesday – the 'Coffin' refers to a later Lord of the manor – now has a Lady Well used before the 1960s for fortune telling by young women (Brown 1963, 132).

1086   *Well (North Yorkshire).* A very doubtful Roman site with no positive evidence for pagan reverence (though it is in Table 1). It later became St Michael's Well (Smith 1928, 229).

It may be objected that several of these names could conceal pagan sites, particularly, in view of their folklore, Wellow and Coffinswell (and indeed I included them in Table 2). But, while it is clear that each of these wells (apart from the Nymet Tracy one, which isn't even at a settlement) were the focal points of their villages, there is no reason to suppose that unadorned Anglo-saxon *wiella* hides pagan worship, since there are other pre-Conquest well-names in which no attempt is made to conceal their pagan nature (above, p.41). Nor is there any precedent for believing that the dedications of these wells were extant at the time the place-name was first noted, place-names in which dedications have been suppressed.

Given these arguments the conclusion is inescapable. Contrary to Morris's guess, what appears to have happened is that some wells were taken over, or created by the English evangelists, who none the less felt ambiguous towards them, understandably. Until the High Middle Ages these wells, regarded as 'holy', were only given patronal dedications to local, obscure saints, and never really became the foci of new cults; and most were left without dedications at all, perhaps in an effort to stamp out what lingered of pagan hydrolatry.

What is crystal clear, at any rate, is that the simplistic model of Christianization is utterly inadequate. There is no way, for instance, that the Nymet Tracy well can be construed as a pagan site, even if more romantic etymologists are correct in their guess that *nymet* refers to a sacred grove, for the well is nowhere near the village and so could have had nothing to do with it. The fact is that the early medieval Church was, at an early date, fully prepared to create its own holy wells, its own well-cults, borrowing elements of popular pagan practice.

We have already mentioned the importance of towns (p.18) and here they can make a similar point. Towns are especially useful for judging the relationship between official and popular religion, for it was in them, presumably, that ecclesiastical authority was most concentrated. Most towns appear to have been abandoned after the fall of the Roman province, and thereafter ecclesiastical institutions were one of the major factors in their revival. Hence public manifestations of religion in towns are likely to be official and Church-sponsored, and there are indeed unlikely to have been any substantial pagan cults in such circumstances in the first place. Thus we might look at St Mary's Well, Oxford, Holy Trinity Well, Lincoln, St Giles's Well, Chester, and All Saints' Well, Norwich, all sites of no great importance and with no traditions remaining, and all closely connected with the church or chapel from which they drew their dedication. The well in these cases seems to have become holy by association, because (presumably) of its use within the church (Wood 1889, i 388n; Cameron 1985, 106; Dodgson 1970–81, v 78–9; Sandred & Lindstrom 1989, 100).

This sort of use was very widespread. Eighty-three wells in England are recorded as having been used for baptisms at one time or another. The practice took longest to die out in the far west, and 37 of these instances occur in Cornwall and Devon; but there are examples from the east of the country, at Holywell and Longstanton (Cambridgeshire), Gainford (Durham), Horsham (Sussex) and Exning (Suffolk) (Wilcox 1985, 12; Brown 1987, 18; Hunt 1987, 11; Hurst 1868, 32–3; Foster 1896–7, 342). In rural areas it is still possible that this practice reflects Christianization of pagan sites, but this is most unlikely in towns, as we have suggested.

Unfortunately for the argument there are very few examples in towns (!), but we can safely extrapolate from elsewhere, there being no good reason why we should not.

The thirteen Chapel Wells in England also no doubt reflect baptismal usage, as may the wells dedicated to St John the Baptist (eleven in England and Cornwall; though of these latter only Bisley (Surrey), Boughton (Northamptonshire) and Morwenstow (Cornwall) have any recorded tradition of this (*VCH Surrey*, iii 398; Valentine 1985a, 3–4; Meyrick 1982, 106–7).* Some of these – Linkinhorne (Cornwall), Boughton, Bisley – unequivocally took their names from the churches, however.

There is in addition an enormous number of named wells within a couple of hundred yards or so of churches; about 370 in England, even with the present partial and uneven state of research, the majority being deemed holy (sixty-six of these are in Cornwall). Some cases are spectacular – the wells beneath Winchester Cathedral for instance, which regularly flood the crypt and one of which is reputed to have been used by St Birinus. But it is in Cornwall that the system can be seen clearest. At Madron an exceedingly ancient chapel stands in a boggy wilderness miles from any settlement near St Madron's Well, the water from which flows through the chapel's font (Hope 1893, 10–11; Camden 1695, 21–2). Table 5 is an analysis of the Cornish baptismal wells (numbers are page-references in Meyrick).

TABLE 5: ANALYSIS OF CORNISH BAPTISMAL WELLS

	used at		
	church and chapel	chapel only	chapel only
same dedication as church	Gwennap (53)	Madron (92–3)	Blisland (19)
	Lesnewth (78–9)	Redruth (129)	Grade Ruan (49)
	North Petherwin (143–4)	St Levan (79)	Laneast (71)
	St Clether (34)		Ludgvan (89–90)
	St Mewan (100–101)		Mylor (108))
			North Hill (119)
			St Wenn (143)
different dedication from church or none	Cardinham (80–81)	Zennor (144)	Illogan (57)
			Landulph (70)
			Morwenstow (106–7)
			Sheviock (132–3)
			Whitstone (144)

* The baptismal church at Canterbury minster was also dedicated to St John the Baptist (Brooks 1970, 38–42).

The arrangement of a well-chapel within a few yards of a church (the left-hand column) is almost universally Celtic and displays once again how thoroughly different Cornwall is from the rest of the country; it is not yet known to occur in more easterly counties. This in turn underlines the point already made, that the Celtic mode of evangelism could not have been extended in any meaningful way east of the Tamar; the dedications to local saints fall off dramatically beyond that point (Map 5). There is evidence that minsters were often, perhaps usually, multiple churches (Canterbury, Jarrow and Wells, for instance (Blair 1977, 148–52; Rodwell 1982, 56), and John Blair believes Bampton followed a similar pattern (Blair 1990, 4)), but only in regions evangelized on the eremitical model do we find the arrangement occurring on the level of ordinary parish churches. And here it is the well that is the focal feature. Certainly the Madron baptistry is older than the parish church, as is the oratory at Cardinham. This can only be explained – although some may find this suggestion rather tendentious – by an incoming system of parish churches adapting itself to a more primitive religious landscape established by hermit-saints and based on chapel-baptistries. This also happened in France: for example at Mortefontaine and Orry-la-Ville in L'Oise and Bomy in Flanders (Roblin 1976, 241–2; Blair 1987b).

We are led here on to a different, but no less vital issue, that of the chronology of well-dedications. Most serious writers assume that dedications to local, obscure saints become prevalent only in the later Middle Ages. Morris declares that wells were most likely to be named after local saints c.1200–1500, 'an age which saw episodes of romantic interest in national origins, and when new outlets for the expression of quasi-devotional superstitions were being sought in reaction to the extension of ecclesiastical officaldom' (1989, 91). But is this really the case? Far more characteristic than investigation of national origins in the late Middle Ages is assertion of national identity: the saints that best expressed this era were George and Louis, not Sulpice and Etheldreda. As for 'quasi-devotional superstitions', these centred on the Virgin or Christ and expressed themselves in beguinage or heresy, not in brooding over the old sarcophagus in the parish church.

No real systematic and modern examination of the medieval cult of saints has to my knowledge been attempted. We have P. Brown's *Cult of the Saints, Its Rise and Function in Latin Christianity* (1988), and Rollason's *Saints and Relics in Anglo-Saxon England* (1988), but the Middle Ages have not been covered. Consequently there is no sign as to where exactly this myth of the late medieval popularity of local saints arose. Nobody could deny that there was a certain amount of interest in them. The minster church at Bampton changed dedication from St John the Baptist to the obscure St Beornwald, whose shrine was in the church, between 1317 and 1370, while the churches of Quenington and Leonard Stanley (Gloucestershire) became dedicated to St Swithun after the twelfth century (*VCH Glos*, vii 127, x 265; Blair 1990, 4). But as the Brookses point out, the cult of local saints 'reflects the growing importance of relics . . . The dedication of churches to other than local saints, the popularity of the Trinity and the Blessed Virgin, all suppose that relics were not essential' (1984, 33–4). Instead devotion to the English local saints was at the very latest High Medieval in origin, beginning with Eadmer and William of Malmesbury (Farmer 1987, xii–xiii).

The enormous majority of church dedications where changes can be observed show that the trend was clearly towards greater saints rather than lesser. The prime case concerns dedications to St Etheldreda in Cambridgeshire. The debased form of the name is Audrey. By the thirteenth century the significance and meaning of the name had been forgotten, and so at Godmanchester and Impington it was displaced by St Andrew, whose name was very similar and who, of course, everybody knew (*VCH Cambs*, v 199, ix 137). According to Miss Arnold-Forster, no less than a fifth of the seventy dedications to St Oswald have been replaced by citations of greater saints: three each to Mary and the Trinity, two each to James and Leonard, and the rest divided between Luke, Peter, Helen and Thomas Becket. In Cornwall, the dedication of Fowey Church appears to have been originally to a shadowy St Orthow to judge by the place-name of Langortha recorded in 1328 (though this may not contain a proper name). But by 1281 the church had become named after St Barry, who was then related by the local clergy to the great St Finbar of Cork; and by 1338 the patronage had passed to St Nicholas, a saint with far more relevance to this fishing community (Pearce 1973). The greater number of shifting dedications move in the same direction.

The evidence from wells, small though it is, is unequivocal. If a well changes dedication, the direction of the change is upwards. In other cases, the well tends to preserve the old dedication when, usually, the church has lost it.

Eltisley (Cambridgeshire). c.1230 the church was dedicated to St Pandonia, a nun of Ely. Now the patronage is shared with St John the Baptist, but the well preserves the previous title, which was clearly in the process of vanishing when it was recorded (*VCH Cambs*, v 55–6; Leland 1869, i 11).

Inchiquin (Clare). A well once named after St Inghean Baoith now bears the name of St Joseph. 'Since about 1850 names of wells have been forgotten locally and a rededication, often to St Joseph, is common' (Westroppe 1911, 209, 213). Not a medieval example, but indicative.

Rousham (Oxfordshire). The church is now dedicated to St Mary. The well, first noted in 1626, preserves the original title of St German's (*VCH Oxon*, xi 159).

St Mabyn (Cornwall). St Mabyn is still dedicatee of the church, but the well is now referred to as St Paul's. Locals, however, remember the old name (Meyrick 1982, 91).

Whitchurch Canonicorum (Dorset). What was St Whyte's church in 1200 was Holy Cross in 1452 and now bears a dual dedication due to local antiquarian consciousness. The well, predictably, records the previous name (Syer 1981, 14–15; Coker 1625, 16–17).

It may be unsafe to draw conclusions from so small a sample. But we simply do not have one example of a major saint being displaced by a local one in a well-name, and instead the opposite process occurs. The well preserves the name of the local saint or is subsumed in that of the greater when the church is rededicated. Naturally, given the date at which most well-names are recorded, we do not hear about it often. But the finding ties in with the fact that there is only one known late-medieval dedication to a lesser saint at all – St Edith's Well, Bristol, set up in 1474 (Walters 1928, 147).

One reason why this may have happened lies again in different patterns of evangelization. The eremitical saints of Cornwall, as the dominant figures of the early Cornish landscape, left their mark in place-names in a way which the minster-system never permitted its saints to do. In time, many of the Saxon saints were no doubt forgotten while the Celtic ones were accordingly, if hazily, remembered. A few, like Whyte or Pandonia, survived in their wells, but others, like Cyniburg at Chalgrave or Eanswith at Cold Ashton, have sunk without trace (above, p.63). Other reasons concern matters of ecclesiastical policy. There may have been some suppression of English dedications owing to the hostility of the Norman incomers. Abbot Paul of St Albans exhumed his blessed predecessors; Athelelm of Abingdon sneered at SS Ethelwold and Edmund as 'English yokels' and even St Cuthbert was dug up to check the legend of his incorruptibility (Knowles 1950, 118–19). In the fourteenth and fifteenth centuries a campaign was waged by the Church to wean people off 'superstition' and on to more 'spiritual' devotions to Christ and the Virgin (Finnucane 1977, 195–6).

There is yet another feature to be considered: the discrepancy between church dedications and those of wells. For the one does not mirror the other (see Table 6).

Among the wells, Helen, Anne, Catherine and Chad are all out of place; All Saints, Nicholas, Peter and Paul, and Lawrence have only a handful of citations and would, if I had shown more than ten rankings, appear way down the bottom alongside such saints as Osyth, Dunstan, or Euny.

TABLE 6: WELL-DEDICATIONS AND CHURCH DEDICATIONS COMPARED

wells				churches			
ranking	ranking in churches	dedication	number	ranking	ranking in wells	dedication	number
1	1	Mary	234	1	1	Mary	2000 +
2	17	Helen	43	2	–	All Saints	1255
3	approx. 40	Anne	42	3	7	Peter	1129
4	7	Jacob/James	34	4	11	Michael	686
5	6	John/John Bapt.	33	5	10	Andrew	637
6	21	Catherine	31	6	5	John Baptist	496
7	3	Peter	26	7	4	James	400 +
8	29	Chad	25	8	–	Nicholas	400
9	11	Margaret	21	9	–	Peter & Paul	283
10	5	Andrew	19	10	–	Lawrence	228

Also not shown is Kentigern, a northern Anglo-Celtic saint with a 'cluster' of wells to the number of twelve – but only nine churches. We might expect upwards of 500 if his representation in churches was to be equivalent to that in wells. Kentigern's, Helen's and Chad's cults are all very old, but those of Anne and Catherine are not. That certain great saints are barely represented is also suggestive: so too is the vast predominance of Mary, which implies an explosive growth in well-dedications in the twelfth and thirteenth centuries. There are two conclusions. First, wells are conservative in dedication and once those 'cluster' saints of the north, Helen and Kentigern, appeared in the hydrolatric record they were not displaced. Second, the majority of wells were dedicated later than has been supposed.

All this ties in with our observation that dedications to major saints may not have begun in earnest until after the Conquest (p.64), and confirms Morris's guess that the 'lateness of the processes . . . would suggest either that the *waeterwyllas* comprised the last class of pagan site to be Christianized, or that the springs so converted were among the least important places within the heathen hierarchy' (1989, 91). This being said, his other deduction, that dedications to great saints preceded those to lesser or local ones, has I hope been exploded.

Dedications to native English saints after the age of conversion are very rare. Edmund of Abingdon, Gilbert of Sempringham, Edward the Confessor, Osmund and Richard of Chichester have one each; Robert of Knaresborough has two; and 'popular' saints such as Sir John Schorne, John Wyclif and Simon de Montfort also have one each. The great exception is St Thomas Becket, who was the subject of a plainly political

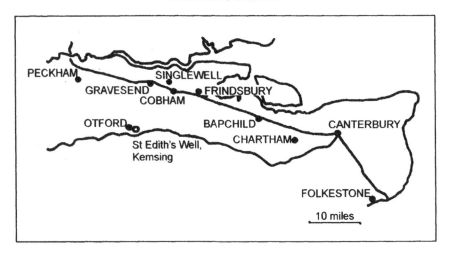

Map 8: Pilgrim routes and wells dedicated to St Thomas Becket

cult if ever there was one. Counting dubious examples, he possessed fifteen wells, ten clustered in Kent (the others were at Boxwell (Wilts), Derby, Northampton, Peckham (Surrey), Plympton (Devon) and Wadsworth (West Yorks)); and Map 4 shows how these were distributed around the main roads. Given that Becket symbolised the Church's resistance to State interference, these holy wells must have been new, like the eponymous 'pebbly spring' at Singlewell recorded in 1240 (Wallenberg 1934: 100-101), or rededications. The Otford well was almost certainly originally dedicated to St Bartholomew, whose miraculous statue stood in the parish church. This was probably because Otford was an archiepiscopal manor, while next-door Kemsing was in secular hands.

One cult worth examining is that of the Virgin. Here the pagan image of the Earth as a goddess is relevant in the development of the cult (for example, as in the odd ceremony at Bampton (Oxfordshire): see *Annual Record of the Oxford & District Folklore Society* 1951, p.8); but its psychological aspects are rarely discussed. The connection with the moon is a popular one, and links her with romantic otherworldliness, as well as being a protection at night; and it must have been easy for medieval men to connect the woman in the heart with the woman in the sky. In the Carmina Burana the Virgin could be addressed thus:

Tu post dominum	You after God
celi agminum	The Empress
magistra	Of Heaven's long march,

Virgo Virginum	Virgin of Virgins,
Lumen Luminum	Tender
ministra . . .	Of the Shining Light . . .
(11*2)	

And a secular lady thus:

Ave formosissima	Hail o most lovely lady
gemma pretiosa	O most precious gemstone
Ave Virgo Virginum	Hail o Virgin of Virgins
virgo gloriosa	(virgin splendrous)
Ave Lumen Luminum	Hail o Light of Lights
Ave Mundi Rosa	Hail o Rose of the World
Blanziflor et Helena	Blanchefleur and Helen in one,
Venus generosa.	O bountiful Venus.
(77.8)	

It was probably this mental connection rather than lingering memories of pagan goddesses that led to the explosion of Mariolatry in the popular literature and liturgy of the High Middle Ages (Southern 1987, 234–43; Graef 1963–5, 229–33, 259–64), and which had its reflection in the number of well-shrines to her honour which appeared in these centuries (Map 10). Map 9 shows the distribution of wells dedicated to the Virgin and also the distribution of various sorts of dedication. What these latter patterns reveal is as yet a mystery.

Topography

The worth of examining holy wells in relation to their surrounding topography is that this can often give insights into the systems of symbolism of which they were part, and the psychological imagery of the sites. Certain patterns emerge that reflect the themes we discussed in ch. 1.

There is little to be said about the usual model of well, the free-standing spring often at some distance from all habitation. Typically the sole embellishment is a small well-house or curbing, for the purely practical purpose of preventing the water from being fouled. Often in towns these coverings could be very grand affairs, the best examples of which are possibly the structures over St Peter's Pump and St Edith's Well in Bristol, now transferred to the gardens at Stourhead (Wiltshire); but rural examples are almost universally more modest.

However, it is the rural holy well that is most commonly linked to other features. Trees associated with springs have already been mentioned in several contexts, but the exact nature of the relationship is problematic. Sacred trees are familiar from Celtic areas, but in England there are only

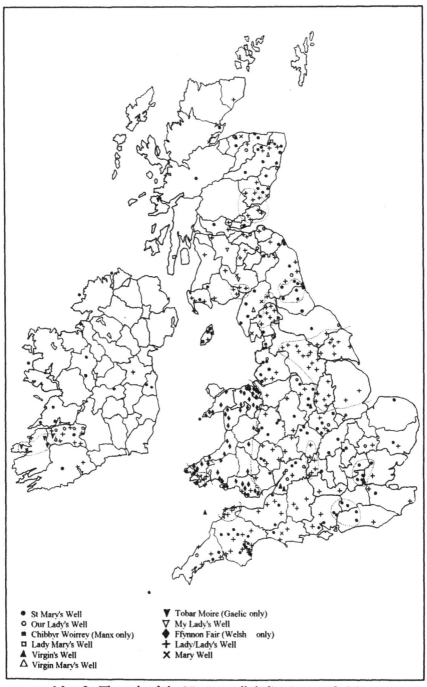

- ● St Mary's Well
- ○ Our Lady's Well
- ■ Chibbyr Woirrey (Manx only)
- ▫ Lady Mary's Well
- ▲ Virgin's Well
- △ Virgin Mary's Well
- ▼ Tobar Moire (Gaelic only)
- ▽ My Lady's Well
- ◆ Ffynnon Fair (Welsh only)
- ✛ Lady/Lady's Well
- ✕ Mary Well

Map 9: The cult of the Virgin: well-dedications to St Mary

a couple of hints. Sites such as St Juthware's Well, Halstock (Dorset), where a spring created in a classic decapitation martyrdom is accompanied by a miraculous oak tree, are very rare indeed (Horstmann 1901, ii 99). Different species of tree have their own folkloric properties, and at one time this was very likely to have had some importance; but the fragments are difficult to assemble into any coherent whole. Oaks do seem to be more prominent than other trees. Not only was St Juthware's Tree an oak, but in 1727 the Rev. Loveday, rector of Caversham, wrote to Thomas Hearne of the 'large ancient oak, just by the Well, which was also held in great veneration' (Margrett 1906, 25–7).

The idea of wells and trees together as boundary-markers, sites of transition from one settlement, set of rights, or precinct to another, is by comparison clear. On the boundary of the parish of Winmarleigh (Lancashire) about the year 1260 was Fons Suani, Swein's Well, and beside it was an oak tree inscribed with a cross (Farrer 1898, 292). We can never know whether these were pagan cult-objects which had been the subject of a cursory attempt at Christianization. What is interesting is the way in which boundaries, margins, edges, are felt to be dangerous places and so need to be defused by the magical power of the Church.

In passing we may mention those pools which have borne Christian dedications, and which really belong in the same class as holy springs – especially when they occur at the heads of rivers and are fed by springs themselves. When at minster towns their status can hardly be doubted. St Osburg's Pool was on the site of the original minster in Coventry (*VCH Warks*, viii 1); St Peter's Pool at Bourne (Lincolnshire) is an embanked, clay-lined pond supposedly fed by seven springs (Birkbeck 1976, 1). At Wimborne (Dorset) the local saint Cuthberga also had a Pool whose waters (if my guess at the site is correct) seem to have been chalybeate (Mills 1977–89, ii 184).

Descriptions of wells as they were in their medieval heyday are unsurprisingly few; fewer still are the sites where the topography has remained sufficiently unchanged for the descriptions still to be useful. Those that are helpful, though, contain certain common elements which we can use to piece together a model of the late-medieval English holy well.

The first of these elements is that of the processional way. Either this led from well-chapel to well, where they were separate, or simply to the well alone. Often the path would have served as the culmination of a long pilgrimage but for less grand occasions the sacred cul-de-sac would still ensure that this particular way could be taken for one purpose only. At Bicester (Oxfordshire) the path was known as St Edburga's Walk; at Caversham, Priest Lane, 'which is supposed to have its name from their going through it from the well' (Camden 1695, 255; Margrett 1906, 25–7). According to Francis Taverner the priests constructed a 'Cawsey

... for the people to passe' at St Faith's Well, Hexton (Hertfordshire); and at Leicester a small bridge over the Soar, leading nowhere but to St Austin's Well, constituted the sacred way (Jones-Baker 1977, 94; Nichols 1795, i 301). At Granchester (Cambridgeshire) documents of 1659 speak of a common way to 'Tardreys Well' (St Audrey/Etheldreda's), and a 'few years' before 1875 a foot-deep path of pebbles was discovered between well and village (Widnall 1875, 27–8; 144–5).

For the medieval Church, sanctity pervaded the world itself, but it had degrees. In some places it was thicker than in others, and those places had to be marked apart. Thus the sanctity of the churchyard was denser than that of the area around; that of the church itself denser still; and inside the church it thickened until you reached the altar. Similarly the holy well was marked off; when it stood in a churchyard or a natural hollow it an enclosure ready-made, but normally one had to be specially constructed. In fact there was a hierarchy of enclosures, reflecting the increasing density of holiness as found in churches, as one approached the water. First was the main enclosure: this might well be a ring of trees, as at Abraham's Well, Shipley (Sussex) (Wimbolt & Arnett 1941, 20–22), or St Austin's, Cerne Abbas (Dorset). Other 'enclosures' lay within: first the chapel enclosing the well, if there was one, and finally the well-housing itself. The Hexton well was 'curbed about' and over it the priests built 'an Howse'. Leland visited St Oswald's Well at Oswestry (Shropshire) and discovered that 'ther is a chapel over it of tymber and the fontein environed with a stone wall' (Leland 1913, iii 175).

Ideally the Christian holy spring flowed out towards the east. There was a sound theological reason behind this: Jerusalem was in that direction, and it was believed Christ would come from there at the Day of Judgement. For similar reasons Christians were buried facing eastwards, and the eastern end of the church is commonly the altar end. But there were also good pagan reasons. East is the direction of the rising sun, and signifies light and growth. A connection between this and the powers of the holy well is often found; thus at Edlesborough (Bedfordshire) an eye well is known as 'sunrising-water', and local belief in the 1920s was that only east-facing springs had healing powers (Gurney 1920, 166–8). The wells at Leicester, Cerne and Oswestry, among others, all face (broadly) east.

Finally we have a motif of descent, coupled with the idea of an entry into darkness. We have already touched on this in the first chapter. The chapel or well-house is symbolically a cave or (possibly) womb, a place of origins, calm and shelter; the movement downwards reinforces this imagery. This applies especially to large bath-wells, as at Otford (Kent), where the fabric of Becket's Well was completed in the fourteenth century; but both the wells at Cerne and Oswestry are set in hollows, and at Sancreed (Cornwall) visitors must actually descend six feet into the

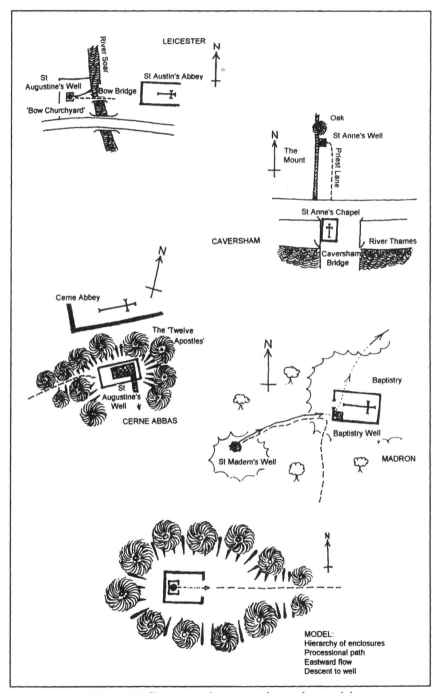

Fig. 1: Well topography: examples and a model

ground, beneath a capstone under a mound, to reach the water. This fabric is clearly very old, though no archaeological work has been conducted to check.

The normal motion in Christianity is upward – towards light, away from darkness, nature, instinct. In a church you ascend towards the altar; the intention is that you overcome your nature, transcend it. Only at the holy well did the Church license downward movement, towards what was natural. It was an appropriate symbol of devotion for a Church which was purging out some of its primitive puritanicalism, and instead developing a religious language which took the holiness of the natural world for granted, and nature as an image of divine love, not a force to be overcome.

Condemnation and Sponsorship

At first the attitude of the Church at the highest level to the water-cult was a completely non-co-operative and uncompromising one. Well-worship was paganism, occult superstition. It was to be stamped out.

c.452   The Second Council of Arles declares that 'if in the territory of a bishop infidels light torches or venerate trees, fountains or stones, and he neglects to abolish this usage, he must know that he is guilty of sacrilege' (Bord 1985, 19).

c.574   A letter of Martin of Braga, chapter 16, states 'to burn candles at stones and trees and springs, and where three roads meet . . . to put bread in a spring, what is that but the worship of the devil? . . . And you do all these things after baptism' (Hillgarth 1986, 62).

561 x 605   The Third Canon of the Council of Auxerre: 'it is forbidden to discharge vows among woods, or at sacred trees or springs' (ibid., 103).

c.640   St Eloi, preaching at Noyon, thunders 'Nor should diabolical phylacteria be used at trees, or springs, or crossroads' (Meaney 1981, 11).

Then, perhaps, a subtle change in attitude:

c.725   The oldest known well-blessing rite is promulgated. It enjoins the Deity to 'drive hence the occult ghosts and demons lying in wait so that purified and faultless this well will remain' (Hope 1893, 211, from Jean Mabillon's *Museum Italicum*, Paris 1724, presumably. Hope says this was in a manuscript from Bobbio 'over a thousand years old' in Mabillon's time, hence my date).

In England at least, the pendulum had swung back towards intransigence by the time of the tenth-century monastic revival:

990–94   Aelfric, in one of the *Catholic Homilies*, 'On Auguries', denounces those of his compatriots who offer gifts to 'some earthfast stone or tree or well-spring' (Fell 1984, 32).

c.1005–8   A Council presided over by St Wulfstan decrees that clerics must 'entirely extinguish every heathen practice; and forbid worship of wells, and necromancy, and worship of trees and worship of stones'. This is the legislation usually referred to as the 'Canons of Edgar' (Whitelock et al. 1981, 320).

c.1008–23 The Laws of the Northumbrian Priests state that 'if there is on anyone's land a sanctuary round a stone or tree or well or any such nonsense, he who made it is then to pay *lahslit*, half to Christ, half to the lord of the manor' (ibid., 463).

1020–22   With the zeal of the newly converted, King Cnut decides that 'it is heathen practice if one worships idols, namely if one worships the heathen gods and the sun or the moon, fire or flood, wells or stones, or any kind of forest trees' (ibid., 489).

Yet there was a final change in attitude. In 1102, the Council of Westminster, under the presidency of St Anselm, passed as part of its twenty-seventh canon the injunction 'ne quis temeraria novitate corporibus mortuorum aut fontibus aut aliis rebus, quod contigisse cognovimus, sine episcopali auctoritate' (Powicke & Cheney 1964, 303). Thus all new cults of wells or small-scale shrines were made subject to the authority of the local bishop. Yet there is, as we have seen, no hint of such an accommodating attitude before 1102. How did it come about? Dr Simon Townley has suggested to me that 'it has a lot to do with the theological shift towards a more hierarchical and authoritarian Church in the twelfth and thirteenth centuries, with the laity seen very much as second-class citizens'; but he sees it more as evidence of conflict than as witness to a softening of attitude to less official forms of devotion, and this does not fit in with the general pattern.

Perhaps the Church was simply no longer frightened? As churches began to spring up in the countryside, as the Christianity of Christendom became a given fact, perhaps the authorities realized that they were no longer living in a sea of sub-paganism? This would be just a guess, but it is difficult to account otherwise for the movement towards qualified acceptance of the holy well, provided it was under episcopal control, than because the Church felt sufficiently confident to be able to control it. Pagan survivals, instead of being threatening, became methods of leading the untutored to the Truth. Itwas surely the same impulse that enabled the Church to adopt a more Crusading spirit, not just towards Islam, but also in terms of the Gregorian

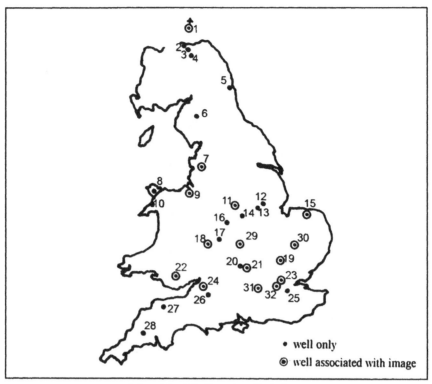

• well only
◉ well associated with image

Map 10: Medieval well-shrines

Key

1	Botriphnie (Fumac)	12	Newark (Catherine)	23	Tottenham (BVM)
2	Restalrig (Triduana)	13	Southwell (Catherine)	24	Brislington (Anne)
3	Musselburgh (BVM)	14	Derby (Alkmund)	25	Bromley (Blaise)
4	Whitekirk (BVM)	15	Walsingham (BVM)	26	Cloford
5	Jesmond (BVM)	16	Ingestre (Erasmus)	27	Painsford (David)
6	Brough (BVM)	17	Clent (Kenelm)	28	Liskeard (BVM)
7	Fernyhalgh (BVM)	18	Stanford on Teme (John the Baptist)	29	Chadshunt (Chad)
8	Llanddwyn (Ddwyn)	19	Hexton (Faith)	30	Woolpit (BVM)
9	Holywell (Winifred)	20	Binsey (Margaret)	31	Caversham (Anne)
10	Clynnog Fawr (Beuno)	21	Cowley (Bartholomew)	32	Willesden (BVM)
11	Buxton (Anne)	22	Ystradyfodwg (BVM)		

crusade against lay control of ecclesiastical affairs and clerical immorality; improving the quality as well as the quantity of conversion. What is clear, anyway, is that by 1102 the Church was no longer afraid of hydrolatry.

The most conspicuous aspect of this fearlessness was the way in which shrines based on wells began to appear in considerable numbers (Map 10). There were at least four in Scotland and the same number in Wales, with a further twenty-five in England and Cornwall. This is very probably an underestimate, as not all of these sites were illustrious: Jesmond, for example, is as yet known only from one reference in Gray's *Chorographia* via Brand (1812, iii 37). For instance, there may have been an unnoticed shrine at Southampton. The old minster of the Anglo-Saxon town, Hamwih, was dedicated to St Mary, and in the thirteenth century we find mention of 'Saintemariwelle' and of Pylgrimesput (also a well), though their sites are not known. On his travels John Leland saw a 'chapelle of our Lady of Grace' where the minster had stood, 'sumtime hauntid with pilgrimes' (Kaye 1976, i 71, ii 43; Leland 1913, i 280).

None of the English examples can confidently be described as pagan survivals. Binsey is a pin well, but this is equivocal evidence; Buxton was certainly a Roman holy well, but was Christianized only late in the fifteenth century, long after it had ceased to function as a sacred site and had become simply a popular place of healing. Nor are the rites practised at Cowley (Oxfordshire) necessarily proof of pagan worship, whatever Anthony Wood might have said: that people came 'to salute the great goddess Flora . . . like the ancient Druids' is just typical antiquarian talk, although the antiquity of the motifs themselves is hardly in doubt. At Tottenham the shrine took over the original 'mossy well' of Muswell Hill (Middlesex), a clear example of a cult being set up on a site not even remotely pagan (Ettlinger 1942–3, 248; above, pp. 23–4; Wood 1889, ii 514–17; Ekwall 1961, 354).

Some of these shrines centred their worship on miraculous images. The most notable, of course, is that of Walsingham (Norfolk) where, traditionally, the Lady of the Manor Richeldis de Favarques had a vision of the Virgin in 1061, whereupon the wells rose at the site of the apparition (though the image does not appear in the earliest stories). Other images of Mary could be found at Tottenham, where one is mentioned in the reign of Henry II, and at Fernyhalgh (Lancashire), whose chapel was built by 1348, though local Roman Catholic tradition ascribes the discovery of the statue to 1471 (Begg 1985, 105–6; Sox 1985, 67–8; Foord 1910, 132–6; Smith 1932, 1–4). The Buxton well was Christianized when an image of St Anne was found there; it has been speculated that this would really have been a statue of Arnemeta, the Roman nymph of the spring. St Anne had another image at Brislington (Somerset) (Hope 1893, 49–52; Horne 1923, 13). Other patrons of well-shrines with miraculous images were St Faith at Hexton (Hertfordshire), St Bartholomew at Cowley, and St John the Baptist at Stanford on Teme (Worcestershire) (*VCH Herts*, ii 352; Nash 1781–2, ii 336). The image was usually far more important than the well. This was the case at Botriphnie (Perthshire), where the well had been used by St Fumac for bathing and where, upon his feast-day, the statue of him kept in the shrine-chapel was washed before being processed through the village (Morris 1981, 68). The well of St Sidwell, Morebath (Devon), although not at a shrine, stood in similarly subordinate relationship to the statue in the church (Whiting 1988, 272; Brown 1975, 144).

The wealth brought in by these shrines was of course a powerful motive in keeping them going. There need have been nothing hypocritical in this, though Protestants naturally viewed it all as an horrific racket. In a society in which gifts made to the Church are meritous (in the Buddhist sense) there was nothing odd in this idea save to those sceptics who did not believe in any case. After all, clerics themselves were capable of generosity: when one Bishop of Worcester left his entire relic collection to Walsingham it was no small gift for a religious.

St Anne's Well at Brislington, as a traditional sailors' chapel, received gifts of tiny silver boats, and in 1502 Elizabeth of York gave it 11s 6d. The Virgin's well-shrine at Whitekirk (East Lothian) received 15,653 pilgrims and offerings totalling 1,422 merks in 1413, while St Faith's and St Erasmus's Wells, Hexton and Ingestre (Staffordshire), both produced enough to support the lucky incumbents in high style (Morris 1981, 142–3; Plot 1686, 99). Wells did not only bring prosperity to portions of the Church, but also to the surrounding communities. Jesmond's well supported an inn in Newcastle, and though stories of the twenty-two inns of Seacourt (Berkshire) catering for the pilgrims to Binsey are exaggerated, there is probably a grain of truth there; and Binsey was where the clergy of St Frideswide's Shrine in Oxford sent pilgrims suffering from less serious afflictions, as if it were a second-class site (Wood 1889, i 328–9; info. from Dr H.M.R.E. Mayr-Harting). Nor were shrines even necessary provided the flow of pilgrims was sufficient. Llaneilian church (Anglesey) owned two farms bought with the proceeds from St Eilian's Well, and ten public houses in Bedfordshire, Huntingdonshire and Buckinghamshire bore the name of The Boot in reference to their role in catering for the travellers to Sir John Schorne's Well at North Marston (Buckinghamshire), the boot being his symbol (Jones 1954, 50; Valentine 1985a, 25). The pretensions of other wells were more modest. St John the Baptist's at Stanford on Teme, where services in the chapel were followed by ritual drinking at the well, produced a mere 40 shillings in 1535.

Occasionally the Church went so far as to fuel the pilgrimages with formal indulgences. Note these comments on St Blaise's Well, Bromley (Kent), which

> . . . having great resort of it antiently, on account of its medicinal virtues, had an oratory attached to it, dedicated to that Saint. It was frequented particularly at Whitsuntide, on account of a remission of forty days' enjoined penance, to such as would visit this chapel, and offer up their orisons in it, on the three holy days of Pentecost. (Hasted 1797–1801, i 551)

The Cowley well also had an indulgence of forty days granted by Bishop Burgwash of Lincoln in 1336.

The original impulse behind the formation of the shrines probably varied. Some were clearly 'popular' in origin and, at Bromley, Buxton and Whitekirk (where the shrine was built as a result of popular patronization in 1309, twelve years after its miraculous properties had been discovered by Agnes of Dunbar), these popular traditions were taken over by the Church, anxious to use any means to raise the merely practical into the religious and no doubt to make some cash as well. In this they stand in direct contrast to the great shrines – Becket's at Canterbury, the Blood of Hailes and so on – which were largely 'clerical' in inspiration.

There are naturally instances of 'clerical' wells which were probably designed as money-spinners. In Wavertree (Lancashire) was a well owned by the local abbey, to whom its revenues passed, surmounted by a cross inscribed

Qui non dat quod habet   If full-pursed you try to go
daemon infra videt.   A demon you will see below!

A terrifying prospect (Hope 1893, 83). Note also St Edmund's Well at Oxford, the site at which the saint, a master at the University 1195–1222, had a vision of Christ. The well's fame coincided with the rise of St Edmund Hall as an independent establishment, and the two facts can hardly be unconnected (Wood 1889, i 288–91; Farmer 1987, 132).

Monasteries were also crucial in the development of the well-cult in certain areas; it has been suggested that the lack of wells in the Salford Hundred of Lancashire is related to the low density of religious houses (Taylor 1902–4, ii 5). Certainly the convent at Nunburnholme (East Yorkshire) was the origin of both the village and its Lady Well, as was the Austin Friary at Hermitage (Dorset) with its Lady Well (Whelan & Taylor 1989, 71; Harte 1985, 6). When the Austin Friars arrived at West Bromwich (Staffordshire) c.1190, they discovered a spring on sandy soil, the Sandwell (though the name first appears only in the thirteenth century) and promptly dedicated it to St Augustine (Knowles & Hadcock

1971, 76; Hope 1893, 158; Duignan 1902, 131). Farnham Abbey (Surrey), founded in 1128, was watered by a spring on a hill called Ludwell ('loud well'?). This failed in 1216, but a Brother Simon conduited a new spring from just below the Ludwell, which new source was then dubbed St Mary's after the Abbey's patron saint (*VCH Surrey*, ii 20). The monks of Chertsey sanctified a spring at Bisley (Surrey) which they had used (Cater 1892, 50–51).

There are occasional examples of Christianization by religious houses too. The fair at, and visiting of, Barnwell, Cambridge, by the town's youth on St John the Baptist's Eve, clearly derives from pagan models, though the ecclesiastical authorities must have taken a sanguine view of it. Sometime after 1092 a local monastery moved its premises to this site (Pennick 1985, 9).

The later Middle Ages bristled with hospitals and almshouses, and it is no surprise to find that these, too, were responsible for the creation or conversion of more holy wells. Cowley was one such case. Some clearly had a practical basis, where the chemical composition of the water would have had a beneficial effect upon the inhabitants of the hospital. The lazar house at Lyme Regis (Dorset) stood by a well in the chapel of St Mary and the Holy Spirit, apparently of sulphuric attributes. St Mary's Well was a chalybeate spring near a lazar house at Lubenham (Leicestershire), while the leper-hospital of Burton Lazars (Leicestershire) was founded in 1135 near healing springs (Rattue 1986a, 16; Nichols 1795, ii 272). St James's, Berkhamsted (Hertfordshire), St Peter's, Windsor (Berkshire), St Elizabeth's, Crediton (Devon) and St George's, Wilton (Somerset) were all wells owing their dedications to hospitals; St Peter's was known by 1719 as Elias's Spittle (*VCH Herts*, ii 163; *VCH Berks*, ii 101–2; Brown 1957, 211; Collinson 1791, iii 294; Gelling 1973–4, i 35).

It must be remembered, as well-researchers seldom do, that many of these sites did not commemorate popular traditions. Abbot's, Nun's, Priest's and Monk's Wells occur in large numbers and are easily explained by the ownership of the sites on which they stood by religious institutions.* Some of these would possibly have earned the respect of local people as a result, but they did not originate in folk custom or pagan survivals. The Abbot's Well at Ellon (Aberdeenshire) was on land owned by Kinloss Abbey; Torpichen (West Lothian), headquarters of the Scottish Hospitallers, had a St John's Well named after the Order's patron saint; the Monk Kelds at Kettlewell (West Yorkshire) were owned by Fountains Abbey, and at Beaulieu (Hampshire) there are both Monk's and Abbot's Wells (Morris 1981, 31, 145; Smith 1961–3, vi 110; Rattue 1987a, 18). Norton, Sheffield (West Yorkshire) has a more interesting example

---

* Abbot's Wells, 6; Bishop's, 6; Friar's, 4; Monk's, 12; Nun's, 10; Priest's, 6; Prior's, 2.

of the influence of religious houses. Beauchief Abbey here was a Premonstratensian house owing allegiance to St-Quintin near Premontré itself. Under Edward I, a spring near the manor boundary was known as Quintinewell, which by 1808 had assumed its modern form of Twenty-wells (Cameron 1959, 285). Ownership leading to sanctity might cause confusion, though, as in the case of Park de Haliwelle, recorded in 1327 in Ash (Kent): it was so-called not from a well but because the owner was Holywell convent, Shoreditch (Wallenberg 1934, 37).

Similar points might be made concerning wells and chantries. There is no discussion needed over Chantry Well, Huyton (Lancashire), where the well was near a free-standing chantry chapel, but other examples are more curious. In Wokingham Without parish (Berkshire) a Lady Well seems to have no religious inspiration, for this was a suburban parish with no church of its own. This is until we discover the endowment of a St Mary's Chantry in the parish church of All Saints in 1443; the well probably stood on land donated for the support of the chantry (Taylor 1902–4, i 66–7; Gelling 1973–4, i 145; *VCH Berks*, iii 232). This was the pattern at Aberdeen, where St Mary's and St John's Wells stood on land whose rents supported the chantry-altars of those saints in the church of St Nicholas, and at Churchover (Warwickshire), where the chantry possessed two virgates of land at Holywell (Morris 1981, 25; *VCH Warks*, vi 64). The enormous variety of processes which gave rise to holy wells is totally ignored by the simplistic account outlined in the Introduction.*

That being said, the opposite process seems to have occurred at Ebony (Kent), where the well was the origin of the chantry; the Hogwell Light received legacies in the sixteenth century (Winnifrith 1984, 160).

Holy wells might even be created by accident. There are several cases of local place-names being reinterpreted in such a way as to give them sacred connotations which they did not previously have. Holwell (Oxfordshire) changed its name from Holewella ('well in the hollow') to Haliwelle ('holy well') between 1189 and 1222, and though Dr Gelling still derives the name from *haelige* this would be unparalleled (Gelling 1953–4, 325). Lady Well, Turvey (Bedfordshire), was Landimareswell in 1279, the 'land boundary spring', though the date when the change occurred is unknown. In Burbage (Wiltshire) is Lady Well Copse, first so called in 1626; but in 1264 it was Ladelwlle, 'spring drawn with a ladle'. This change is unlikely to have occurred after the Reformation. A similar shift is said to have taken place at Lady Well, Burley (Hampshire) (Mawer & Stenton 1926, 49; Gover et al. 1939, 338; Rattue 1987a, 17).

St Chad's is another cult in which etymological errors have played a large part. At Dagenham, Birdbrook and Chadwell (Essex) there are all

---

* Cf. parallel uses in Field, 1972, 1, 21, 41, 44–5, 84, 120, 121, 141, 153, 173–4, 190.

St Chad's Wells, though the derivation in each case is clearly from *cealdwiella*, 'cold well' (Reaney 1935, 92, 150, 412–13). Some of these mistakes were modern (see Table 7 below) but the most notable example could not have been. At Chadshunt (Warwickshire), Camden's editors found that 'in the chapel yard was an ancient oratory, and in it (as the inhabitants report) was the image of St Chadde; by reason of the resort of pilgrims worth 16*l* per Annum to the Priest (*Inquis. Cart.* 4 Elizabeth). Here also is a well or spring, that still retains the name of Chad's-well'. So there is. But the original (949) name of the village was Caedelesfuntan; Chad first appears only in c.1023 when the name was Chaddeleshunt and the identification with him seems to have occurred at this point. It was an identification which was obviously endorsed with clerical gusto (Camden 1695, 510; Gover et al. 1936, 249–50).

Despite this abundant evidence of the clerical sponsorship of wells, the exact details of the pattern in individual localities is still mysterious. Hull, a prosperous port-town, was built on salt flats and has no wells within its walls. Nor has Salisbury, the marshy cathedral city created new in the thirteenth century. The new town of Winchelsea (Sussex), though, was established at the same time, yet it has a flock of wells – St Leonard's, St Katherine's, Friar's, and three non-Christian wells (*VCH Sussex*, ix 64–5).

Nor was the Church's attitude to hydrolatry wholly favourable; the pagan origins of the cult could never quite be swept under the carpet. Thus a dichotomy was set up: wells authorized by the Church were healthy, for by this authorization the pilgrims had access to the source of spiritual grace; wells not so approved were pure superstition. St Hugh of Lincoln denounced the worship of a well at High Wycombe (Buckinghamshire) supposed to have been used by St Wulfstan in a miraculous cure. A successor of Hugh's, Oliver Sutton, bishop 1280–99 and fierce in his campaign against unofficial cults, condemned St Edmund's Well, Oxford (as the scene of 'pretended holy miracles'), and St Laurence's Well, Peterborough (Northamptonshire), in 1291; he also closed down a holy well at Linslade (Buckinghamshire) in 1299, ordering the Archdeacon of Buckingham to have the ban announced every Sunday until August 15th in every church in the Archdeaconry, and the Vicar to account before the Consistory Court (*VCH Bucks*, iii 113; Wood 1889, i 288–91; Hill 1969, 186) No bishop, though, was as 'thorough' as Ralph Erghum of Salisbury (1375–88). In 1385 Erghum heard of a well at Bisham (Berkshire) where a tame bird dwelt atop a tree, in whose nest offerings were left in return for the cure of sore eyes at the well. The Bishop retorted that this was the perfectly natural effect of cold water, had the well filled in and the tree torn out and publicly burned (*VCH Berks*, ii 14). Puritanism did not originate with the Puritans.

Clashes between higher and lower clergy are evident in these exchanges;

it was natural that local cults should be promoted by local clerics for both religious and pecuniary reasons. The Oxford well was probably, we have argued, connected with the rise of St Edmund Hall; the Vicar of Linslade encouraged the pilgrimage to his well; and the Bisham well – reported to Erghum as 'new-found' – was owned by the Augustinian house founded there in 1337 (*VCH Berks*, iii 139). There were continued difficulties at Oxford; Bishop John Dalderby (1300–20) had to condemn the offering of candles at the well in 1305; but elswhere the endorsement of the Church was often eventually granted. The Diocese of Worcester condemned the well at North Cerney (Gloucestershire), among others, in 1240, and Bishop Robert Mascall of Hereford one at Turnastone, a pagan megalithic site, in 1410, for 'without the authority of the Church [they] wrongfully worship the said stone and well'. Both sites were later formally adopted: at Turnastone we find a Lady Well, and at North Cerney is a well surmounted by a cross (Boase 1887, 57; Powicke & Cheney 1964, 303 can. 30; Dew 1932, 97; Richardson 1935, 45). Bishop Beckington of Bath and Wells (1443–65) was more cautious than outraged when in 1464 a well at Wembdon (Somerset) was reported to him 'to which an immense concourse of people had resorted within a few days, and not before resorted': he simply ordered an investigation into the veracity of the cures. The well now bears the name of St John the Baptist, whom the first visitors had invoked (Maxwell-Lyte & Dawes 1934, i 414). More general condemnations of unauthorized worship were issued for the dioceses of Wells c.1258, Winchester 1262–5 and Exeter 1287, all in the same, stock language: 'not stones nor woods, trees nor wells . . . should be worshipped as if they were holy' (Powicke & Cheney 1964, 622, 722, 1044).

The problems of hydrolatry were mirrored elsewhere.The 'saint' Laurence whose well was at Peterborough was a felon 'who had been hung on account of his evil crimes', and for some reason the monks were encouraging pilgrimages to his grave in St Thomas's Hospital. In 1298 Oliver Sutton – a glance through his registers reveals him as paranoid about the supposed threats of paganism – despatched the Dean of Newport Pagnell to investigate possible superstitious pilgrimages at North Crawley (Buckinghamshire), and in 1351 Bishop Grandisson of Exeter had to reprimand the Prior of Frithelstock for building a chapel near the village full of pagan and sexual imagery: the statues 'reminded one more of the proud and disobedient Eve, or the shameless Diana, than of the humble and most submissive Blessed Virgin Mary' (*VCH Northants*, ii 89; Hagerty 1985, 70; Hingeston-Randolph, fols. 169–70). The most curious survival was the cult of St Guinefort. About 1250 the Inquisitor for the Lyons area, Stephen of Bourbon, was summoned to investigate an unofficial shrine in a wood near a ruined castle. When he arrived he was stunned to discover that the saint was in fact a dog. A 'sinister old woman' administered healing rites at a well where Guinefort was supposed to have been drowned. The horrified Inquisitor ordered that the shrine be destroyed and the wood be cut down (Schmitt 1985).

The well-cult reached its zenith in England in the late Middle Ages. If we are correct, the first rank of wells, at minsters and dedicated to English saints (if at all) began to be renamed in the twelfth century as a result of Norman hostility, popular ignorance and Church self-confidence, and then exploded outwards into the countryside, where some pagan wells were converted, others suppressed, and yet more sites created afresh – especially, perhaps, those dedicated to the Virgin. Holy wells became an accepted, established part of the Church's spiritual weaponry. The cult continued undisturbed by the social disruption of the fourteenth century, that rise of the individual that was fostered by the breakdown in villeinage, because it, like all medieval religious practice, was at one level deeply individualistic. The well was one of the places where the soul might enter into individual communion with God.

But not just with God. All religious ritual was also neutral: there were cases when the power transmitted through it could be put to baleful use. 'Black fasts' encouraged the death of an enemy; initiation into Cornish witchcraft consisted of repeating the Lord's Prayer three times backwards at Mass and giving the Host to a toad (Thomas 1978, 49; *Cornish Charms*, 7). The most fearful of these rites was the Black Mass of St Secaire (Summers 1925, 157). The Mass was said backwards on a desecrated altar, timed to end at the stroke of midnight; the Host was black and triangular, and the wine was replaced with water drawn, note, from a well into which had been cast the body of an unbaptized baby. 'And the man for whom that Mass is said will slowly pine away, nor doctor's skill nor physic will avail him aught, but he will suffer, and dwindle, and shall surely drop into the grave.'

SIX

At the Heart of the Community: Wells and Medieval Society

A dependable source of water is essential to any community. (Morrell 1988, 5)

Place-names

The truth of Morrell's statement is witnessed by the large number of settlements which contain the element 'well' in their names. The issue is endlessly clouded by the possibility of the translation of Old English *wiella* as 'stream', and in many cases the word clearly does mean this. At Littlehampton (Gloucestershire) a field-name, Stock Well, appears as Stokkesbrok in 986; in Ledston (West Yorkshire) there was a *Linewelle rivuli* c.1180, but a *fontem Linewelle* c.1188 (Smith 1964, iii 119; 1961–3, iv 51–2). In Dorset there are five parishes which clearly derive their names from springs, with possibly up to thirty lesser settlements with similar origins; in Oxfordshire the corresponding figures are eleven and eighteen (Rattue 1990). In the east of the country these figures are lower but still occur in reasonable numbers, as far as the state of research allows us to judge.

Some of these settlements are obviously very old. The oldest of all is Ewell (Surrey), first recorded in 675 (Gover et al. 1934, 75), and after this they occur with some frequency. Secular pre-Domesday confirmed spring names presently total twenty-eight, and there are many more whose exact status can only be decided by detailed map and field research. There is little remarkable that can be said about them that is not obvious. Some names are topographical or descriptive: Colwell (Northumberland) ('cold'); Burwell (Cambridgeshire) ('by the burgh'); Blashenwell, Corfe (Dorset) ('bleaching'). Others, such as Wells and Wellow (Somerset), are entirely unadorned. A couple are folkloric (the bride's well, Heavitree (Devon); treasure well, Compton Beauchamp (Berkshire)), while eight refer to ownership.

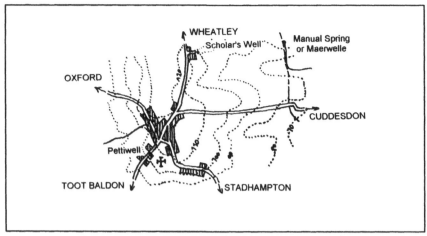

Map 11: Garsington, Oxfordshire, and its wells

There are two main types among these early well-names; wells at the centre of settlements and wells on the peripheries, as boundary-markers. Garsington (Oxfordshire) seems to have both types. The actual age of the Pettiwell, the spring at the village centre, is unknown, but the site suggests antiquity, and there is a well on the boundary of the parish with Cuddesdon noted in 956 as Maerwelle, the 'boundary spring' (Gelling 1953–4, 9; Rattue 1990, 174).

It is obvious that well-names were among the very earliest coined. The second oldest name, from 681, occurs at Tetbury (Gloucestershire): Cucwanwellan, the Cuckoo Spring. It is not even the name of a settlement, and is just a humble boundary-marker (Grundy 1919, ii 10); and if even tiny sites such as this were receiving names by this date, how much older are those prominent sites whose names we know? After the Conquest, the numbers naturally rocket, and become a little hard to handle in the process. They contain no surprises in any case.

One point is worth making: it has not hitherto been noticed that wells in place-names may be hidden behind the word 'pit'. Latin for both these concepts is *puteum*, and converted into Old English as *putte* or *pytte* a word emerging into modern English as 'pit' could conceivably mean either. We begin with such sites as Powke Putte i at Malvern (1540) and Pylgrimesput in Southampton (1346), both thought to be wells. Next come to sites like Seint Marypot at Glasson (Lancashire), a boundary-mark of the fishing rights of Furness Abbey, called by the middle of the nineteenth century St Mary's Well. Finally we arrive at Fullerespits, King's Lynn, which was definitely a well, reported as being cleaned out in 1372–3. In the light of this sort of philological crossover, place-names like the Lady Pitt at Newbold Pacey (Warwickshire) take on a new appearance (Smith 1964, 173; Kaye 1976, i 43; Taylor 1906, 359; Owen 1984, 213; Barratt 1971, 18).

Social Control

Again, the contrasts between the English experience and that of the Celtic fringes cast a long shadow. It will be argued shortly that most of the religious ritual of the well was shorn off at the Reformation in England (ch. 7), but traditions were generally recorded long after this date. Thus our glimpse at the role of the holy well in medieval England is slight and skance, mainly by extension from the few rituals that did survive in remote regions (close as this may be to traditional folklore methodology!). There is no reason to believe that the local holy well had not been as important as it continued to be in, for instance, the Irish patterns, however little direct evidence we have of it.

Excluding Cornwall for a change, the number of English wells at which 'patterns' – meaning public rituals with some religious content, held on a particular date and with accompanying popular festivities – took place is twenty-four. They functioned, presumably, as a reinforcement of the social unity of the community, largely under the legitimizing aegis of the Church, though there were wells where the Church played no active part in the rituals, as at Skimmington Well, Curry Mallett (Somerset), East Well, Baschurch (Shropshire), and Old Brine, Nantwich (Cheshire). Even so, at Baschurch the pattern was still held on Palm Sunday (Tongue 1967, 22–3; Burne 1888, 68; Aubrey 1881, 58).

A mixture of frivolity and solemnity prevailed at these gatherings. Many accounts mention the holding of 'games', while the pattern at St Edmund's Well, Oxford, was the occasion for the swearing of vows. To judge by the Irish parallels they were not frequently the resort of the genteel or polite society; and while the only records are post-Reformation, the upper classes have always had their own amusements. The pattern at Warrenstown (Meath) was specifically prohibited by an Act of the Irish Parliament under Anne as 'a popish gathering . . . detrimental to the public peace and safety of the realm', and it finally died out after a girl was killed in a faction-fight. The pattern at Kilreedy Major was halted after the murder of the local priest, Father Mulqueen, in the revel in 1819. Critical observers of the early nineteenth-century Irish pattern speak of fantastic drunkenness and brawling (Thunder 1885–6, 657–8; O'Danachair 1955, 208; Logan 1980, 133–9). In a society in which the facts of life were equally hard and the individual's hold on existence no less precarious, it would be odd if the medieval English pattern were any different. Rowdyism, for example, was the cause of the rites at Penrith

(Cumberland) being suppressed in the nineteenth century (Hope 1893, 42–3). Nottingham evangelicals condemned St Anne's Well about 1830 as 'a resort of loose characters, who spend the Sabbath Day in drunkenness and tumult', while brawling was a characteristic component of the pattern at Roan Well, Hurst (North Yorkshire) (Morrell 1987, 10; G.A.W. 1830). Diversion from a hard life in riot and revel was only natural. Fairs, of course, which occur in conjunction with patterns at all eighteen sites in one way or another, were a strong motive for keeping the pattern going, and the ritual at Droitwich (Worcestershire) was a celebration of the benefits brought by St Richard's Well, the salt spring which fuelled the whole economy of the town (Aubrey 1881, 33).

Different layers of tradition mingle in these rituals. An unnamed spring at Donisthorpe (Leicestershire), almost on the county boundary, was 'long frequented by country people, who resort here in great numbers every Sunday morning during the summer season', for, among other purposes, the cure of scorbutic complaints. A farmer was able in 1795 to point out a ring close by, worn by generations of circumambulating feet (Nichols 1795, iii 998). It is unclear whether we should call this a 'pattern' or not, but there are no such doubts about the Roan Well of Hurst (North Yorkshire). Its guardian killed a traveller whose blood polluted the water. The Virgin cleansed the spring by dipping her foot in it, whereafter it became medicinal, and this event was celebrated by a pattern on Trinity Sunday (G.A.W. 1830).

On a lower level than the full pattern was the visiting of springs at a certain time of the year, which in general seems to have performed a different function. Very few of these occasions were social affairs; instead the majority were simply traditional times when the healing or wishing powers of the well were deemed to be at their strongest. May was the commonest season, either May Day itself or the successive Sundays, wells being visited then at St Buryan, Madron and St Neots (Cornwall), Aikton and Edenhall (Cumberland), Wootton Bassett (Wiltshire), Ashill (Somerset), Green's Norton (Northamptonshire), Wooler (Northumberland), Milton (Staffordshire) and East Dean (Gloucestershire) (Meyrick 1982, 25, 110, 92–3; McIntire 1944, 4; Hope 1893, 42, 102–3, 154; Parsons 1895, 252; Valentine 1985a, 7; Walters 1928, 76–80). The root of this custom must be the Celtic Beltane festival of May 1st, and the visiting of wells at Midsummer also reflects Celtic models. Christian feasts which coincide with patterns or visits occur mainly in the spring and summer also: Easter, Good Friday, Palm Sunday, Ascension Day. Exceptions tend to be feasts-days of saints, such as St Tibba at Ryhall (Rutland), St Edward at Stow on the Wold (Gloucestershire) (Potter 1985b, 15; Walters 1928, 15–20). The basis of this tendency, even deeper than the Celtic roots of the practice, is no doubt an archetypal connection between the waxing sun, the waxing year, and the powers of the well. All water was healing in Morocco at Midsummer (Westermarch 1905, 31–2), while in 1912 the parishioners of the Rev. W.E. Frost at Avening (Gloucestershire) thought that all water which had been lit by the dawn sun was good for the eyes (Partridge 1912, 335).

Some customs were so idiosyncratic that they must have performed the social-cohesion role of the full pattern; that is, they were social occasions and not merely on the level of individuals simply visiting wells at certain times of the year. The explanation of the peculiar rituals at Newton-on-the-Moor (Northumberland) on St Mark's Day was that King John had fallen in a well while travelling, and enjoined the freemen of Alnwick to dam the spring each year and walk through the water as a punishment for failing to maintain the roads properly. Thus the spring became known as Freeman's Well (Hope 1893, 101–2). Each year on Good Friday the mysterious effigy of Molly Grime in the church of Glentham (Lincolnshire) was washed in water brought from New Well by seven old ladies for a shilling fee to the amusement of locals (*Lincs. Notes and Queries*, 2 (1888–9), 125).

The most famous and widespread single custom, famous because it not only survives but is becoming more popular (see Map 13) was the dressing of wells. In contrast to the patterns that survived to be recorded, well-dressings were always polite and decorous affairs. Perhaps any rowdier elements were actively suppressed after the Reformation, but there is no direct evidence of this. Only the dressing of St Bartholomew's Well, Cowley (Oxfordshire), which appears to be the origin of the Oxford May Day customs, was possibly the scene of riotous behaviour; unlike the pattern, the well-dressing seems to have been completely under the control of the Church.

> The texts of Scripture, and other religious sentiments, that are placed among the greens and flowers about these wells, together with the service solemnized at the Church, shew the grandeur and sublimity of a Christian worship. (Rawlins 1823, 293–5)

This was Tissington (Derbyshire) in 1823, but the assumption is safe that the condemnations of Puritans show that the form of the custom is very old. The high textual content of the ritual was perhaps a later development, but its social importance is clear. Sociologists often have extreme estimations of the power of religious ritual to control social groups; well-dressings hardly could, or did, stop riots or enforce unity of opinion, but they could symbolize and intensify the continuity of the community, and do the same for the Church in its role as provider of a common language, mental imagery and experience for the society that surrounded it. The well-dressing was the rural equivalent, almost, of the mystery play. As Porteous points out, the elaborate flower-pictures that have become so prominent in modern dressings are no older than the late eighteenth century (Porteous 1973, 1); but 'garlands' are mentioned in the oldest accounts, Leland uses the word 'tapestry' to describe the hangings about the salt well at Droitwich (1913, ii 93), and such objects always seem to have been fashioned to adorn wells; in the same way that Corn Dollies, which the Church also blessed, did, such activities would have given ordinary people a sense of involvement in producing ritual.

The healing aspects of wells have been fully dealt with elsewhere (Bord 1985, 34–54), and there is no reason to repeat that work. There is time (lest anyone be tempted to accept it) to mention John Wilcock's preposterous thesis that 'the sacred wells clearly divided into geographical zones . . . this argues a detailed system of ritual planning on a countrywide basis located in the mineral properties of various areas' (Wilcock 1976). This supposes a powerful overarching authority and an efficient communication network in remote antiquity (Neolithic people have not been 'rehabilitated' that far), and also comes up against the minor detail that it is totally at odds with the true patterns of distribution, which are completely random. As to the enormous number of eye-wells, Thomas notes that the lack of vitamin A in the diet of all classes in the Middle Ages would have rendered them liable to xerophthalmia; thus the 388 wells in the British Isles said to cure this disorder (Thomas 1978, 7).*

In several cases wells were visited specifically by younger people. Naturally this also occurred in towns, as at St Nicholas's Well, Carlisle (Cumberland), but the majority of examples are rural (McIntire 1944, 7). The normal pattern was the use of the occasion for love-divination, with pins or pebbles dropped into the water to discover the enquirer's amorous prospects, at, for instance, St Buryan, Madron and Roche (Cornwall), Bovey Tracy (Devon) and Wooler (Northumberland) (Meyrick 1982, 25, 92–3, 129; Brown 1957, 209; Hope 1893, 102–3). This may possibly have had its roots in a pre-Christian period when marriage was not

* Cornwall 15; England 200; Ireland 102; Man 5; Wales 53; Scotland 13 (what was peculiar about the Scottish diet?). But there are odd features in the connection between eyes and wells. Ffynnon Gwenlais, Llanfihangel Aberbythych (Carmarthenshire) 'has two eyes, they say'; the well at Easter Rarichie (Ross and Cromarty) is Sul Na Ba, the 'Cow's Eye'; St Siamus's Well, St-Cieux (Brittany) is referred to as the 'tears' of the saint; St Chrysostom's Well, Pharasa, flows from the saint's eyes, according to tradition (Jones 1954, 44; Morris 1981, 170; Baring-Gould & Fisher 1907–13, iv 197; Halliday 1912, 219–20). Binnall's theories on the motif, relating it to baptism, the myth of Odin's eye, and the Egyptian creation legend, are, as usual, unconvincing (1944–5, 362–4), but I have no better ideas. Carey noted the archetypal poetic connection between eyes and pools, which is also unexplained (1983 214–17).

solemnized by Church ritual but simply by communal declaration, but, as usual, origins are less interesting than the motivation behind a custom's continuing. Where wells were deemed the particular resort of the young, that motivation was probably a mixture of initiation, romantic titillation, and generational as opposed to social cohesion – the chance for the young to assert their identity independent of the rest of the community.

Similar remarks might be made regarding wells visited solely by women. We have the well at Shottery (Warwickshire) which cured 'women's complaints'; twenty wells whose responsibility was over the diseases of childhood; and another nine bringing fertility. All of these would have been mainly a woman's preserve. In addition there are curious oddities, such as the South Well, Congresbury (Somerset), which on May or Midsummer's Day was circumambulated by the women of the parish, 'howling like dogs' (Tongue 1967, 185). Wells thus provided women, too, with an opportunity to assert an independent – if limited – identity. Certainly the wells of Honiley (Warwickshire) underlined the differentiation of the sexes, although the witness for this custom is late and gives no source. It is, however, so without parallel that it rings of truth. There were two holy wells here; before Confession, men bathed in St John's Well, women in St Mary's (Harris & Huggins 1924, 78).

The Beating of the Bounds was a very different ceremony. Originally it was deeply respected, but must also have been feared; for though some writers make it sound a little sanguine (the function was 'partly to make clear to parish officers their boundaries for poor-law and burial purposes', says Margaret Baker (1988, 158)), in actual fact 'young people had [the bound-marks'] situation impressed upon their memories by painful physical experience', including ducking in ponds, dragging through hedges, and being thrashed (Hole 1978, 252; Whitlock 1979, 148). While some Puritans objected to the ritual (Thomas 1978, 73) even the Puritan Church of England never abandoned it; it was too useful socially, for it reinforced the village as the primary unit of society. Beating the bounds was also an urban custom, though it must have made less sense in towns (particularly in Oxford, where it oddly survives), where parish boundaries ran down the sides of streets or across them. In adulthood, all male parishioners would have been able to point out the line, drilled into them years before, where their village interfaced with the outside world. Nobody would claim that this world was unknown, of course, but the effect of communal rites was to keep it 'other', to emphasize the primacy of the parish.

Wells were obvious bound-marks. A total of 72 named wells in England and Cornwall can be show to lie on parish or manor boundaries, while very many more nameless springs occupy a similar position. Eald Gemot Wyll, Baverstock (Wiltshire), recorded under Edgar, shows that some of these bound-wells, at least, were used as moots (Grundy 1919, ii 268–9). The control of the ceremony by the Church, the reading of Scripture at the bound-marks, was a further element in the acculturation process of which bound-beating was the very epitome, and so we might expect to find wells being considered holy by virtue of being included in the ritual. There is no specific example, only a general feeling in this direction:

> In Cheshire, in Mr M. Kent's grandmother's time, when they went in Perambulation, they did Blesse the Springes, they did read a Ghospell at them, and did believe the water was the better. (Aubrey 1881, 58)

The problem of whether named wells are formed on boundaries or boundaries shaped around pre-existing wells is also relevant to other sorts of sites – barrows, for instance (Bonney 1979).

The grandeur to which boundary-wells could ascend is shown by the description of the full rituals of Freeman's Well, Alnwick (Northumberland), which we have already mentioned, written in 1845. The Leaping of the Well was part of a boundary perambulation by the Freemen, but it was no sedate and gentle affair, even in early Victorian Northumberland. 'Men who were seldom if ever before on horseback dash onward, fearless of consequences' – the witness saw at least four or five men fall, and indeed fell himself. The 'Leaping' – wading through the dammed Well – was just as violent, as participants fought with each other to be first across. This was only halfway round the boundaries, too: miles more of riding, bruised and drenched, awaited the perambulators. It was 'an important era in a freeman's life. It publicly marks the period when the youth shoots into the independence of manhood; it is, therefore, looked forward to with high expectation by every freeman's son and freeman's apprentice'. When this rough ancestor of the modern Common Ridings, which survive only in the Scottish Borders, came to an end is not known; but something of the kind must have happened at Lancaster, where St Patrick's and Wolf's Wells were also visited in boundary riding ceremonies (Tate 1866, ii 241–51; Taylor 1906, 347).

Perhaps the most practical of all wells in a rural environment were those which predicted changes in the price of corn. There were fourteen of these, plus an isolated example in Gloucestershire; a full eight of them are in Staffordshire. At Seighford (Staffordshire), Broad Chalke and Fonthill Episcopi (Wiltshire) the waters rose to predict dearth (Plot 1686, 47; Aubrey 1847, 23, 32); at Langley (Kent) and Rushton Spencer (Staffordshire) they dried up to do the same thing (Hope 1893, 81; Plot 1686, 49–50). the most puzzling aspect is that not one is known – yet – from the bread-basket of East Anglia.

Historians ought to take careful note of the role of folklore in social control, the employment of childhood terrorism to generate a disposition to accept the standards of the surrounding community. Ferocious infantile demons were the first manifestation of this. The foul Rawhead and Bloody Bones – 'fear'd by children', says Aubrey laconically (1881, 59) – sat in cupboards on piles of bad children's bones and survived long enough to stalk Ruth Tongue's Somerset childhood in 1904–12 (Tongue 1967, 123). Black Annis would grab and eat Leicester children who wandered too far from home; Jenny Greenteeth was an evil spirit of pools who also devoured small children, and localized examples of such creatures abounded, such as Cutty Dyer in south Devon (Brown 1982, 141–2). Again, 'pagan survivals' are not the point. The point is that these screaming childhood fiends, of whom 'God' all too easily became one, were methods of keeping children in their place and ensuring that the instinct survived into adult life. These legends also often performed the practical function of warding children away from dangerous pools, rivers, or wells, or simply from the strange world outside the parish boundaries, where it has been noticed that ghosts tend to cluster (Legg 1987, 62).

Wells were part of this battery of social control and protection mechanisms. Some were haunted, others bottomless, all were awesome for the reasons already given (pp.10–11) and a little fearsome. The rituals in which they played a prominent part helped reinforce communal and group unity, and the position of the Church as the prime medium of cultural expression.

Towns and Water Supply

In the divided environment of the town, public rituals, whether Corpus Christi processions or Passion Plays, were even more important than in rural areas for rubbing the sharp edges from social conflict. Sometimes wells featured in Beating of the Bounds ceremonies, such as the eight wells in Lichfield (Staffordshire) which still mark parish boundaries (Hole 1978, 250), but more important still in the urban context was the provision of the public water supply.

In very many towns the initiative appears to have lain with the Church. Many of the springs conduited by local abbeys or priories into towns were simply ordinary ones: the Colwell at Southampton (Hampshire) was granted by Nicholas de Barbflete to the Franciscans in 1190; in 1234 the spring was given a dome and culverted to a tank on today's Commercial Road. The Franciscans also used a Houndwell Spring for the town's supply (Rance 1986, 37–8, 52). In Winchester, two of the public springs, Segrim's Well and Fons Trintram, were owned by the Bishop in 1208/9 and 1283/4; the New Well at Sherborne (Dorset) was culverted into the public conduit by the Abbey c.1510; and the Three Wells at Northampton were led into the town by the Dominicans in 1291 (Keene 1985, ii 1071, 1084–5; Penn 1980, 93–4; Woodward & Thompson 1909, 125). Other water-supply wells were holy before being employed in this way: St Edmund's Well, Glastonbury (Somerset), fed the public conduit, while Bishop Beckington of Bath and Wells licensed a culvert from St Andrew's Well, Wells (Somerset) through the High Cross itself in 1451 (Richardson 1928a, 183–4; Maxwell-Lyte & Dawes 1934, i 170). Throughout the 1390s the churchwardens of Ripon were buying equipment for St Wilfrid's Well which demonstrates its importance simply as a source of water: buckets in 1391/2 and 1393/4, and a new windlass arrangement in 1396/7 (Fowler 1882, 106, 120, 123). There are three wells, used for the public supply, recorded in Kentish wills and to which money was bequeathed for their upkeep: St Nicholas's, Strood, in 1444; St Ethelburga's, Lyminge, in 1490; and St Margaret's at Broomfield in 1507 (Duncan & Hussey 1906–7; i 75; ii 39, 204).

Naturally the model might also be one of conflict between civil and religious authorities. Hull, situated on salt flats, had to bring in its fresh water from outside: that is, from estates owned by Haltemprice Priory. It was in 1376 that it was first proposed that the Julian Wells in Anlaby should be included in the supply, but this was not done until 1402; and even then repeated sabotage of the culvert-pipes by the Priory's tenants forced the Pope to intervene on Hull's behalf in 1412. Priory and Corporation fought a legal battle over the East Wells in Anlaby between 1447 and 1517 (*VCH E. Yorks*, i 371). It was understandable that the Corporation of Newport (Shropshire) chose to act purely on its own initiative in renting Wodewalle spring from Richard Attebruggehend in 1309 (Jones 1885, 248–9). At Cambridge the normal process was reversed in 1350; the Corporation gave Hoker's Well, named after a tenth-century landowner, to the local Carmelite convent to supply their manse in Milne Street. However, the intention may have been for the monks to do the work of improving the supply. This was certainly the case when the canons of Waltham Abbey were given the Chaldewelle of Little Amwell (Hertfordshire) in 1214 and 1223, for in this instance the terms of the lease actually enjoined them to do so (Gray 1925, 74; Ransford, 216).

Most interesting of all were the wells which were obviously regarded as holy because they had been used by the Church for the water-supply. Again, this was logical given the method of distributing the water; with the Church as the most prominent urban institution it made sense for churches to be the points of distribution. At Bristol and Bath, St John's and St Mary's Conduits took their names from adjacent churches, and the well-house over the Carswell in Abingdon (Berkshire), provided by the Abbey, was crowned with a cross. Abbot's Well, Christleton (Cheshire), was so called from being led off for the abbey of Chester in 1282–3 (Smith & Ralph 1972, 38; Collinson 1791, i 29; Preston 1941; Ormerod 1812, ii 778). The town's market cross was also a natural focal point, and here we commonly find public wells, as at Winchester (Keene 1985, ii 594–5). Lichfield had Crucifix Conduit in 1301, Stone Cross Conduit in the fifteenth century, and Market Cross Conduit by 1540 (*VCH Staffs*, xiv 96).

The systems of Bristol and Bath are best-recorded, and both repay examination. In the former, as well as St Mary's Conduit, there was also SS Peter and Paul's, on the site of the old High Cross and with a cross-shaped tank. It was supplied, like St Mary's, from St Swithun's Well in Walcote parish, named after the church. St Michael's Conduit stood beside its church in the north of the city (Collinson 1791, i 31, 73). In Bristol there was a large number of sites. Jacob's Well on Brandon Hill, where there had been a Jewish cemetery, was culverted and cared for by the Austin Friars; the Templars conduited Raven's Well, Totterdown Hill, through Temple Pipe; Huge Well's water was distributed from St Mary Redcliffe church. St Peter's Pump and St Edith's Well were built in 1474 by Mayor William Spencer, and finally there were St Thomas's Pump and St Nicholas's Pipe (Walters 1928, 146–50). In both these places the wells were the subject of public ceremonies. Collinson writes of St Mary's Conduit, Bath:

> To this conduit the mayor and citizens of Bath, borrowing their practice from days of old, when wells and fountains had their particular honours, usually made their grand processions, and here they generally halted.

The pipes and pumps in Bristol, too, were annually inspected with ceremony.

There were echoes of this everywhere. A strange ritual at Shaftesbury (Dorset) marked the recognition by the town of the suburb-parish of Enmore Green's rights over the water-supply, when an extraordinary object known as the Byzant was handed over. This rite is first heard of as far back as 1304 (Udal 1922, 125–6; Legg 1987, 120). The parish clerks of Finsbury (Middlesex) visited the Skinner's Well, which was owned by St James's Clerkenwell, to perform plays and rituals, at least in 1309 and 1409; while at Coventry (Warwickshire) the district of the spring known as Hob's Hole annually elected its own 'mayor' or 'king' who was then dunked in the water. The Patchells, who note that the conduit license for Coventry actually precedes the founding of the Corporation, even ask 'may we claim that democratic local government has its roots in the administration of the water-supply, and in well-ritual?' There are hints that something similar took place at Abingdon (Berkshire), where Ock Street, site of the Carswell, elected its own 'mayor' too (Hone 1826–7, ii 559; Fretton n.d., 8–9; Patchell 1987, 11–12). Leicester's public wells, including several Christian ones, were guarded from 1584 by two well-reeves in each ward, appointed by the Aldermen (Nichols 1795, i 404).

Certainly the decorous processions at Bath and Bristol, and the more rowdy entertainments at Shaftesbury and Coventry, instilled a respect for the water-supply which was underlined by legislation, and which had a good practical basis. St James's Well, Berkhamsted (Hertfordshire), had its own wardens who were officials of the Portmote Court; in 1400 charges were brought against people who had polluted the water. The people of fourteenth-century South Shields (Durham) were warned not to wash clothes in Caldwell, or steep flax in Denis (probably St Denis's) Well (Hodgson 1903, 56). The normal concern of officialdom was that pollution by the washing of clothes or animals, or the overuse of wells for private purposes, such as brewing, should be prohibited. The Statutes of Lancaster provide a good example (*VCH Herts*, ii 168; *VCH Lancs*, viii 44 n.180). At Bakewell (Derbyshire) the penalty for washing 'cloathes, beasts or swine or filthy things' was 3s 4d; the manor court of Spelsbury (Oxfordshire) charged 3s 6d in 1552, with a further 4d fine for each duck allowed to foul Cirver Well (Naylor 1983, 28; Corbett 1962, 77). A danger for public wells was that they might become places of death in ways which were both more prosaic and more threatening to their function than those of the folktales we have already discussed. In 1269, Richard son of Robert the Reeve of Staplock (Bedfordshire) was found guilty of murdering his wife Ivette at the Witewell in Eaton Scoton, and throwing her body in it. From 1265 to 1380 the Bedfordshire coroners' rolls record eleven examples of people dying from falls into wells (Hunniset 1961, 11). Medieval people clearly understood the connection between disease and 'bad water', regardless of what might commonly be thought, and the demands of the community were, as ever, impressed and enforced by ritual and by the everpresent Church.

SEVEN

Christ is Truth, not Custom: Wells and the Reformation

In these words, Thomas Hall summarized the entire Protestant Reformation in Britain. Reason was not invented by the rise of mechanistic science which was ushered into the parlour of the European mind by Galileo and Descartes; instead it was the mid-sixteenth century which turned the rational power of the human mind upon the Church's traditions and institutions, unaffected by sentiment, and the psychology of rebellion and disgust was just the same.

Compliance and Resistance

Following Professor Dickens there is still a tendency to interpret the Reformation as an outbreak of reason against the palpable unreason-ability of Catholicism, an outbreak predestined by the invention of the printing press, the growth in trade, and the rise of literacy; Dr Anne Hudson's use of the term 'premature Reformation' to describe the Lollards epitomizes this. It is not only outrageously Protestant but also wrong. The history of heresy shows it is wrong, that the unfettered action of pure human reason is possible in all times and places. Henry the Monk, the heretic of Le Mans (fl. 1116–45), rejected the Old Testament as part of the Bible, and, using the New Testament as his base, denied the Church's power to administer sacraments, burned church ornamenta-tion and preached Pelagianism. The followers of Peter de Bruys burned crucifixes, forced monks to marry (no, not each other), and ate meat on Friday, even Good Friday. Landulf, one of the leaders of the mid-eleventh century Pataria reform movement in Milan, declared that churches were cattle-sheds, and the Host, dog-dirt (Lambert 1977, 50–57).

If these views sound uncannily close to many of those espoused by 'Lollards', that is because they are. All Lollards were equivocal on the subject of the Mass; Wyclif denied transubstantiation, and the Lollard

Vicar of Manuden (Essex) claimed in 1431 that the Host was 'not the body of Christ in His nature'. Other ideas show the same sort of continuity with earlier heresies – rejection of images and Masses for the dead, and a strain of Donatism – but it would be folly to judge that there was any institutional continuity (Hudson, 1988). The truth is that much of Catholic practice was irrational and unBiblical, and anyone with a yen for thought might appreciate this, whether in the late eleventh century or the sixteenth.

Christ was born 'through the coitus of a man and a woman, just like the rest of us', sneered Raymond de l'Aire, the village atheist of fourteenth-century Tignac, who also believed that Heaven was when one was happy and Hell when one was unhappy, a position characteristic too of Ranters in the English Civil War. His contemporary Guillaume Austatz doubted how the dead could be resurrected with their own bones when those bones were heaped indiscriminately together in graves. The Lollard William Colyn in 1428 declared that human beings owed greater allegiance to the Son than to the Father, since the Father created Adam, the originator of sin, and should have known better (Ladurie 1980, 320–21; Hill 1975, 228; Hudson 1988, 384). The unaided exercise of reason led William of Ockham to the Schopenhauerian doctrine of morality as will, and Christian morality as submission to the Will of God; and it led Uthred of Baldon to declare that religions adopted on earth were irrelevant to the final salvation of the soul (Knowles 1951). All ideas, perhaps, exist in all periods. Materialistic Lollards, according to Dickens, 'feel appreciably nearer to the Age of Voltaire than is normal in the sixteenth century' (1959, 13). Perhaps; but then perhaps we ought not to be too surprised either.

The mere existence of 'Lollards', therefore, is not enough to demonstrate widespread disaffection from the national religion at a local level. Indeed there is remarkably little evidence that the Church in England felt on the defensive, or that people felt it to be distant from them. Oxley judged that 'an examination of the Church in Essex at the beginning of the sixteenth century reveals that many people were passionately devoted to religion'. Donation to the great shrines was indeed in severe decline: even the Shrine of Becket at Canterbury raised only £36 in 1535. But at parish level religion flourished. Brightlingsea Church (Essex) was completely rebuilt c.1490–1510, and the parishioners of Probus (Cornwall) paid for their church to be rebuilt 'of their good minds and devotions'. Great Dunmow's (Essex) Corpus Christi feast made a profit of 23 shillings in 1522–3, and by 1533–4 this had actually risen to 30s 3d. Tiny West Country villages such as Winkleigh or North Petherwin supported a dozen guilds each. The Earl of Shrewsbury, who suppressed the Pilgrimage of Grace, that great upsurge of Catholic militancy, in 1536, left in his will the following year enough money to pay for a thousand priests to say Mass for his soul on his death, and for three to say it daily for twenty years, a total of 22,900 masses (Oxley 1965, 1, 25; Whiting 1988, 90, 107; Finnucane 1977, 193; Scarisbrick 1984, 8).

No attempt has been made to assess quantitatively how widespread enthusiastic Protestantism actually was in early sixteenth-century England, but there is no reason to suppose it should have been increasing apart from the wider dissemination of ideas that followed the invention of the printing press. The Papacy was indeed venal and corrupt, but at least it was both distant and irrelevant save as a final appeal court, as it had been since the Captivity in Avignon. The higher clergy were corrupt pluralists, but this was nothing new and they had the excuse of being locked immovably into a corrupt system: in 1499 Thomas Jane had to fork out 7,300 florins for his investiture as Bishop of Norwich, which largely accounted for the necessity of pluralism for him and clerics like him (Oxley 1965, 38). Nowhere is there evidence that Catholicism was on its last legs. That huge, grand machine of devotion, despite the distortions brought by long power, was in perfect operational order until the demands of an hereditary monarchy jammed a spanner into the gears. Henry VIII himself lit a candle before the statue of Our Lady of Walsingham as late as March 1538 (Finnucane 1977, 202).

Holy wells slot perfectly into this more general picture. Not only is the continuity of worship undisturbed at many sites – St Winifred's, Holywell (Flintshire) being the best-known example – but other, less noted sites reveal the same pattern. The Chapel of St Anne, Caversham (Berkshire), was first recorded 1551/2 and was probably not very much older than that; the well stood near it. The shrine at Southwell (Nottinghamshire) was only founded in 1482, and maintained its popularity until the Reformation (Gelling 1973–4, 179; Morrell 1988, 28). The Christianization of new sites also continued until the very last minute. St Anne's Well at Nottingham, previously Robin Hood's Well, was converted after a chapel was built next to it by the Cluniac Priory of Lenton some time in the fifteenth century, while it was as late as 1519 that a chapel to SS Mary and John the Baptist was licensed beside the Maiden Well in Great Brickhill (Buckinghamshire), in the same year that Bishop Longland was burning Lollards at Salisbury. In Bakewell (Derbyshire) we hear of 'Cappwell or St Maries Well' in 1606; the former name dates back to the time of Henry III, and it is probably the case that the Christianization here, too, was very late and that accordingly the old name was still remembered (Morrell 1988, 22; *VCH Bucks*, iv 298; Cameron 1959, 37).

The wells, like the rest of Catholic paraphernalia, do not, then, appear to have been suffering any decline until the changes of 1538–58. Heretical outbursts were nothing new, and to judge by the standards of Boccaccio and the Carmina Burana anticlericalism was as old as the clergy itself. But, as Raymond de Laburat of Sabarthes/Quie remarked in the early 1300s, 'the church and its bells belong to us [the ordinary people]. We built it, we bought and put in it everything that was necessary' (Ladurie 1980, 261–2). To argue whether the Pilgrimage of Grace was begun by priests or nobles or was spontaneous is to miss the point, the point being that the people were defending their churches. As rumours flew about the northeast that the treasures of churches were about to be seized and the old religion assailed, so in many places they rebelled to safeguard what was theirs, that part of their Church that they felt was closest to them and most involved with their spiritual lives.

Naturally there were plenty of manifestations of sentiment in the opposite direction. Henry VIII complained in his last speech to Parliament in 1545 that the Bible was being discussed in taverns and alehouses, and we might wonder what, given that he had ordered it translated, he expected would happen. On the occasion of the marriage of Mary to Philip II of Spain in 1554 a cat dressed and tonsured as a priest was hanged at Cheapside; in 1547 churchwardens in one London parish and in Portsmouth jumped the legislative gun and tore down their images and lights, while the guilds, despite their old vigour, collapsed almost at once, and never revived (Hutton 1987, 118–19).

But, as is increasingly becoming clear, the characteristic response at local level was conformity. It almost seems as if the less well-educated parish priests and ordinary parishioners do not understand what is going on. The Mass sung and bells rung for Edward VI's accession at Melton Mowbray (Leicestershire) – we can guess he would not have been grateful – have the air of innocence rather than rebellion. At Woodbury (Devon) the parishioners carted their Latin texts to Exeter to be burned under Edward, and bought new ones under Mary. The Protestant Carew Rising of 1554 was a complete non-starter in Devon, but the churchwardens of Ashburton still had to pay to have Protestant inscriptions in the church whitewashed out when Mary's government ordered it (Whiting 1988, 192). There was no recorded resistance to the destruction of local shrines. By 1549 all of the 198 parishes with surviving accounts had abandoned their images; by 1550 all had also given up the festivals banned in the injunctions of 1548 (Hutton 1987, 121–2). They revived under the Marian injunctions and vanished again under Elizabeth.

Wells were not high in the hierarchy of catholic 'ritualia' and nor, it seems, in the attentions of the puritan reformers. This cannot have been because the visiting of holy wells was a custom of the ordinary people and not of the ruling classes, for Henry VIII himself patronized both Walsingham and Binsey (Oxfordshire) (Brand 1812, ii 370–71); Wood 1889, i 328–9). The injunctions of 1538, condemning lights, relics and images, made no mention of wells. Even in Wales, Bishop Robinson in 1563

> . . . found since I came to this country images and aulters standing in churches undefaced, lewde and indecent vigils and watches observed, much pilgrimage goying, many candells sett up to the honour of saintes, some reliques yet carried about, . . . besides diverse other monuments of willfull serving of God. (Walker 1976, 68)

– but no wells. The exception is Edward Downlee, MP for Carmarthen in 1588, who told Parliament of adulteries committed 'in the solitary and closeness of the place' where idols were worshipped 'and of the superstition they use to a spring-well, in casting it over their shoulders and head' (Neale 1957, 153).

In England specific attacks on wells were few. They were confined to the more famous shrine-wells, and even then attention was focused more on the images and the fabric of the shrine than on the worship of the water. The statue of St Anne at Buxton (Derbyshire) was sent to London on the order of Thomas Cromwell and burned (Naylor 1983, 39); at Fernyhalgh the chapel was demolished but the pilgrimage continued – though the authority for that is an eighteenth-century Roman Catholic priest (Smith 1932, 1–4). St Bartholomew's image at Cowley (Oxfordshire) was burned and the pilgrimage stopped under Elizabeth (Wood 1889, ii 517–18). At Caversham (Berkshire) the force of the assault was directed against the motley collection of relics in the chapel, as one of Cromwell's commissioners, Dr London, reported: not only 'the image of Our Ladye at Caversham whereunto wasse greate pilgremage', but also 'the Holy dager that kylled Kinge Henrye, and the holy knyfe that kylled Seynt Edwarde' (Margrett 1906, 25–7).

Only at Hexton (Hertfordshire) was the well the most offensive item; it was filled in (*VCH Herts*, ii 352). In Wales, too, only two wells were attacked, at least during the period of reform; in 1592 the chapel of Pistyll Meugan, Llanfair Nantgwym (Pembrokeshire), was torn down, and in 1538 Cromwell ordered that the statue of the Virgin and Child at Ffynnon Fair, Ystradyfodwg (Glamorganshire) be brought to London for burning in secret for fear that the action might provoke a riot (Jones 1954, 59–60). In Scotland wells were condemned in a total of nineteen parishes, most of them not at all prominent except in the immediate vicinity.

This is all the stranger in view of the ferocious denunciation by puritans of 'paganism', by which they meant all the ritual of Catholic piety. Thomas Hall, who declared that 'antiquity without verity is of no validity. Christ is Truth, not Custome' claimed that May Games derived from 'one Flora a notable Harlot which had got much riches by whoring, [who] at her death bequeathed her substance to the people of Rome' and that May Day – Floralia – was established in her memory: 'all the whores were called to the sports, where they danced naked about the streets'. In an inadvertently appropriate metaphor, he goes on ''tis a forsaking of God, who is the Fountain of living waters, to go a broken Cistern'. John Perry claimed that Catholicism constituted a pact with the Devil, and the Puritan Francis Taverner reveals how radicals of his ilk regarded the great well-shrines:

> The people that came to offer did cast some thing into the Well, which if it swamme above they were accepted and theire petition granted, but if it suncke, then rejected, which the experienced Prieste had arts enowe to cause to swymme or sincke according as himselfe was pleased with the Partye, or rather with the offring made by the partie . . . (Jones-Baker 1977, 94)

Equally there are no examples of popular attacks on wells until much later. The earliest yet known was the Rev. Palmer of Etlisley's (Cambridge-shire) assault on St Pandonia's Well, which stood in his churchyard, in 1575, but he was a 'scandalous parson' and not especially pious, so his motives may not have been holy outrage (*VCH Cambs*, v 57).

It is the well at Buxton about which we know most. Sir William Bassett wrote to Cromwell that he had not only sent on the statue of St Anne, but also removed 'crutches shirts and shifts . . . which were offered being things that entice and allure the ignorant to the said offering'. The 'baths and wells' were sealed so that 'none shall enter to wash there till your Lordship's pleasure be further known'. Thereafter the site passed into the ownership of one Roger Cottrell, who cut back all the religious activities but retained the therapeutic ones. In 1553 Cottrell was bound over for the very great sum of £100 for allowing 'youthful persons to wash and bathe them in the well called St Anne's Well, not only to get tipple and drink within the said chapel on the Sundays and holydays, but also to pipe, dance, hop and sing within the same to the great disturbance of the inhabitants'. This, too, was accordingly reined in and activities were restricted to selling the water (Cox 1879, ii 72–4; Langham & Wells 1986, 33–4).

Not only were wells under attack, but all sorts of popular customs. In Coventry, the abolition of guilds meant the collapse of a system of 'exaggerated social precedence of ceremonial occasions' by way of reward for muncipal service; the two great guilds of Corpus Christi and the Holy Trinity amalgamated in 1535 and were dissolved in 1547. In 1579 the Corpus Christi Day procession was abolished; in 1591 the maypole was taken down and the midsummer procession was abolished too, and even football came beneath the puritan axe four years later. Women suffered a loss of status; the restriction of guilds to those involved with trade was exclusive of women as there were no female journeymen, and by the early 1600s wives of civic dignitaries were not even taking the civic oaths as they had always done before. 'A whole vigorous and variegated popular culture, the matrix of everyday life, was eroded and began to perish' (Phythian-Adams 1972, 57, 62, 79).

While Camden assigned the prime responsibility for the decline of the wells to the Reformation, John Aubrey was inclined to blame the Revolution. Certainly instances of positive repression became more frequent after the structures of the Church were officially Protestant and Puritans began turning their attention to the actual practices of the ordinary people. The chapel of St Wenn's Well at St Wenn (Cornwall) is said to have been torn down by soldiers stationed nearby in the Civil War. In 1639 Alderman Sayle of Oxford destroyed the structure of St Margaret's Well, Binsey (Oxfordshire), and attacks on the whole economy around St Winifred's Well, Holywell (Flintshire) were launched in 1637. Moor Well, a boundary spring at Dodleston (Cheshire) was visited annually by priest and people until they were challenged by soldiers in 1642 (Meyrick 1982, 143; Wood 1889, i 328–9; Jones 1954, 59; Richards 1947, 147–8). In Droitwich (Worcestershire)

> . . . on the day of St Richard the tutelar saint/patron of ye well (i.e.) salt-well, they keepe Holydaye, dresse the well with green boughes and flowers. One yeare . . . in the Presbyterian times it was discontinued in the Civil Warres. (Aubrey 1881, 33)

St Edmund's Well in Oxford was still operative in 1630, when it was restored, but after the closure of Millham Bridge during the conflict 'by degrees for want of recourse in summertime was stopped up' (Wood 1889, ii 291). Nearby, Thomas Hearne visited St Begga's Well, Begbrooke (Oxfordshire), on December 17th, 1726; he says it 'was in Old Time much resorted to, as other Wells of the same nature were' (Hearne 1914, ix 238).

The Derbyshire antiquary William Woolley died in 1719; and by his time the St Alkmund's and Becket's Wells in Derby were 'formerly esteemed' holy wells (Woolley 1981, 25, 33). St Catharine's Well at Barton (Lincolnshire) appears to have been a very notable site, for the Rev. de la Pryme found that it 'had the image of that St well cut in white marble standing by it within the memory of several men now liveing', which was in 1697, but 'it was all broke in pieces in Cromwell's time' (de la Pryme 1870, 142).

Save for a few prominent examples, then, the wells were ignored by the puritan reformers, who had other concerns. Yet something had obviously happened to them; there had been some sort of disruption which affected numbers of sites. Certainly around Oxford there was a significant decline in many very notable cults; thus the great well of St Margaret at Binsey, which had once been so important to the local economy, was by the 1660s 'overgrowne with nettles and other weeds, harbouring froggs, snails and vermin, [it] scarce owneth the name of a well' (Wood 1889, i 328–9). That something had happened to disrupt the continuity of worship is further evidenced at Stamford. The antiquary Richard Butcher wrote in 1646 an account of how he had gone hunting for St Thomas's Well, one of no fewer than six in the medieval town. Butcher's father had told him it was east of the town on the road to Uffington; but nobody whom he asked had ever heard of it. That even a holy well's memory could vanish within three generations of the Reformation indicates how disastrous it had been (Butcher 1660, 15). What wells survived, survived as part of the shreds of the Catholic substructure almost unnoticed beneath the veneer of Protestant conformity.

Pointing out that the guilds did not revive under Mary, Hutton writes that the people 'lost faith in precisely those aspects of the pre-Reformation Church which had been most dynamic, most personal, and most localized' (1987, 138). Most dynamic, perhaps, but most personal or localized, no. The elements of the Old Church that survived were exactly those most personal and furthest beyond the control of the authorities. The York Commission to 'search out certain monuments of superstition' in 1562–77 resulted in the discovery of widespread Catholic popular customs such as the lighting of candles for the dead. In 1626 a firm Puritan minister arrived at Eccleston (Lancashire) after it had suffered decades of ecclesiastical neglect, and discovered the lighting of candles, the placing of corpses by crosses, blessing of sick cattle, and the invocation of the saints (Halley 1869, 271–2). Two years later Sir Benjamin Rudyerd told the House of Commons of 'divers parts of Wales' and 'the uttermost skirts of the North, where the prayers of the people are more like spells and charms than devotions' (Hill 1963, 96).

In this context the Civil Wars seem to have altered very little in some parts of the country. Erasmus Saunders's *State of Religion in the Diocese of St Davids* (1721) revealed widespread crossing and praying on graves, 'not only to the Deity, but to the Holy Virgin, and other saints; for Mair Wen, Jago, Teilaw Mawr, Celer, Celynog and the others are often thus remembered as if they had hardly yet forgotten the use of praying to them'; and this was in a fairly Anglicized part of Wales, where in the 1790s communion was celebrated far less frequently than elsewhere (Jones 1976, 104–5; Mather 1985, 274). In 1725 Bourne, the curate of Newcastle, noted that 'the generality of old people among the commonality' bowed or genuflected on entering church (Brand 1812).

Such people would no doubt have been horrified had they been told they were all-but-Catholics. They were still living in the ritual landscape the medieval Church had created for them. It provided them with a sense of 'context', a method of bringing to themselves vague, ill-defined magical benefits, and nothing had changed in their lives to persuade them to leave it. If the Church itself had ceased to perform this function for them, that was its affair and not theirs. This was, however, the sub-structure of debased ritual and superstition that kept the well-cult in operation. What had vanished was the official backup, the superstructure. The great well-shrines had all gone, and the public rituals of the blessing of the water-supply and the Corpus Christi processions had been dispensed with. Even the innocent bound-beating came in for criticism. The common people were more or less on their own so far as ritual was concerned.

Except in especial circumstances. Oxford in the early 1600s was a centre of the Arminian resistance to Puritanism – Laud had become President of St John's in 1611 – and it must have been in this favourable environment that New College, into whose hands the old chapel at Cowley had passed, decided to revive the pattern and dressing of St Bartholomew's Well, without the offensive aspects of image-worship and indulgences, of course; and transferred these observances from St Bartholomew's Day to May Day and Holy Thursday. Has this happened elsewhere, we may wonder (Tyacke 1986, 58–86; Wood 1889, ii 514–17).

Formal Roman Catholicism was of particular importance in maintaining the well-cult in Lancashire. St Thomas's Well, Windleshaw, arose where a Catholic priest was decapitated in time of persecution, and Roman Catholics visited St Helen's Well, Brindle, in the 1680s. It was especially the Irish who frequented St Mary's Well, Penwortham (Taylor 1906, 54–5; Baines 1836, iii 497; Darwen 1988b, 27). Elsewhere Roman Catholics made a difference too. A Holy Well at Newent (Gloucester-shire) was visited by Irish labourers, and St Helen's Well, Stainland (West Yorkshire) was sustained by Catholic pilgrims (Walters 1928, 81; Haigh 1986). None the less folk did not have to be Roman Catholics to participate, even in heavily sub-Catholic ritual. As late as the early twentieth century, all springs in Somerset would grant wishes at night if you whispered the wish three times and signed a cross over the water; and even in divided religious environments this was often just as true. At Fortanne (Clare) the Protestant landowner signed a cross over St Mochulla's Well, said the Lord's Prayer, made a hollow with her left heel, and left a gift of milk for the 'fairies' in order to aid the production of butter (Tongue 1967, 25; Westroppe 1910, 195–6). And at Tullybeltane (Perthshire)

... on Beltane morning, superstitious people go to this well and drink of it; then they make a procession round it, as I am informed, nine times; after this they in like manner go round the Temple. So deep-rooted is this superstition in the minds of many who reckon themselves good Protestants, that they will not neglect these rites, even when Beltane falls on Sabbath. (*Gentleman's Magazine*, 1811, 426–7)

But the Catholic gentry apparently took a far less enthusiastic view of holy wells than their lower-class co-religionists. Only at North Lees (Derbyshire) did they show any gusto: the Trinity Well there stood by the Trinity Chapel erected courageously by the Eyres in 1683. This was despite the use of wells' healing powers in Roman Catholic propaganda, as was the case at Holywell (Flintshire) in the eighteenth century (Binnall 1940, 62; Thomas 1978, 80–81 and n.74).

Those very people who could be found crossing themselves on entering churches could, on occasion, also be found attacking holy wells as a manifestation of militant Papism. By 1688 a century of indoctrination had equated Catholicism with foreign domination and tyranny in the minds of all classes, and had produced mob assaults on St Winifred's Well, Holywell, in which the crucifix was torn from the altar and burned in the market place. Ten years later Celia Fiennes discovered crowds of worshippers there 'deluded by an ignorant blind zeal and are to be pitied by us that have the advantage of knowing better'; but in 1718 there was a further attack on the chapel (Hole 1966, 96). Fernyhalgh (Lancashire), also a potent symbol of Roman Catholicism – 1099 people were confirmed there in 1687 – was the scene of repeated persecution. The Corporation of Preston ordered that the penal laws be enforced against the chapel in 1714; and in 1715, while devotions were not actually suppressed, the chapel was sacked and the priests driven away. The shrine was plundered again in 1719, and although the worshippers were left in peace from the 1720s onwards, the fabric was actually burned down in 1745 as a reaction to the Jacobite Rebellion (Smith 1932, 1–4).

In Scotland persecution of wells was a little more prominent if not much more effective. This is probably to be explained by the democratic structures of the Presbyterian Kirk which enabled a closer scrutiny by the authorities of what the people were actually doing. The Virgin's Well at the Chapel of Seggatt (Aberdeenshire) was ordered to be filled in by the Presbytery of Turriff; but on two occasions the local people cleared it out again. The Aberdeen Sessions regarded those who resorted to St Fittack's Well, Nigg (Ross and Cromarty) in 1630 as to be 'censured in penaltie and repentance in such degre as fornicatouris' (Morris 1981, 27, 38–9). The Morrises note condemnations at nineteen separate sites, with more general injunctions swelling this number. This is far more interest in wells than the English Church ever showed.

The great difference between Catholic and Protestant areas was of course the active aid given by the Church to wells in the former. The use of Rosaries, Paters and Aves in Irish well-rituals is obviously post-Reformation, while the Roman Catholic Church could easily be persuaded to create new wells of its own. In the parish of Cuail Eira (Sligo) in 1750, an invalid was cured at a well in a dream, and on waking discovered the site with the aid of the parish priest. As visitors began to flock to the spring – on Saturday nights, imitating the practice at older wells – the parish clergy foretold that there would be a 'lockruinn, or heavenly illumination' which only increased the volume of pilgrims. Eventually the clergy wrote to the Vatican asking for a suggestion for the name of the well. Uncovering in the records, so he said, a 'Tobar na Ttrinoid' in the vicinity, the Pope decided on a dedication to the Trinity (*Gentleman's Magazine* 1766, 172–3). At Marmalane (Cork) in 1795 a priest dreamed of a healing spring and, on finding the site next morning, dedicated it to SS Peter and Paul, whose feast it happened to be. By 1836 it had actually cured people and was attracting pilgrims (Hardy 1836, 36).

With the removal of such clerical sponsorship, the process of conversion of wells in England halted. In some places it even went into reverse. The healing St Agnes le Clear Pool in London (Middlesex) was supposed to bear the name of Annis Clare, a rich widow who drowned herself here in Edward I's reign. It had gained the saint's dignity at some later point and lost it again as early as 1567. St Agnes's Well, Crook (Westmorland) was merely called Anna's by 1614 (Foord 1910, 108–12; Smith 1967–8, i 182). Often the occasion for the decline was the use of the well for the public water supply: St Giles's Well, Chester, became Barrell Well after 1575; St Lawrence's Well, Norwich, became Gybson's Well in 1578; and Trinity Well, Gloucester, was reincarnated as Scriven's Conduit in 1684 (Dodgson 1970–81, v 78–9; Hope 1893, 98; Walters 1928, 60). At Utkinton (Cheshire), the Newe Found Well of 1600, a healing spring, was not as new as its name implied, for it had been St Stephen's Well only a few years before (Dodgson 1970–81, v 78–9; Ormerod 1812, ii 252). This process went on far into the future; Holy Well, Middle Aston (Oxfordshire) degenerated into Horse Well some time between 1686 and 1896, and what was Patrick's Well, Burton in Wirral (Cheshire) in 1609 had by 1847 decayed into Hampstone's Well. Other wells, while retaining their names, were in all other respects forgotten: thus the Rev. Bedwell bemoaned the state of St Dunstan's Well, Tottenham (Middlesex) in 1631 (Brookes 1929, 22; Booth 1984, 55; Foord 1910, 128).

Reformation and Revolution were not fatal to hydrolatry in England, but they did it no favours. Further threats to its survival and attempts at its rescue are the subject of the next chapter.

EIGHT

The Two Cultures: Wells, Class and the Great Change

The Gentry and Nobility

Great social changes are always difficult to pin down and express, for commonly they are simply too vast for the mind to grasp with ease. In this way, that some mighty crisis overtook the English social system in the middle of the sixteenth century is undoubted, but what actually happened and why are far more difficult questions to answer.

The first element in this change has already been touched upon: the division of religions opened up by the Reformation, a division of society into a Protestantized gentry and upper class and a set of lower classes whose religious instincts were sub-Catholic and 'superstitious', the destruction of the old common language of imagery and experience. Although of course the division was hardly that clear-cut, in broad terms it will serve.

The nobility seems to have altered its entire character, the old chivalric ethic undergoing a subtle change. There was nothing new about the sort of service nobility working in the court bureaucracy that appears to have become so prominent in the Tudor period, but in some way aspirations were changing; the old military social ideal was shifting. The past became a fantastic rag-box to be pillaged that the service nobility might dress themselves up in military garb. Burghley, Elizabeth's minister, concocted a mythical lineage descending from a supposed Saxon noble from Cornwall for himself, while the Wellesbourne family not only drew up fake documents to 'prove' their descent from the Montforts, but even had fake effigies made and deposited them in the village church (Stone 1976, 23–4). By 1622 Sir Charles Cavendish was building a fake castle to add medieval lustre to his estate. When Clarkson, the Percys' agent, toured the family's Northumbrian estates in the 1560s he discovered that, even in this oft-debated border country, military service had lapsed in half the thirty villages, and that the Knights' Court of Alnwick, the core of Percy authority, was disused and ignored. Faced with this disintegration in the military system, central control, in the form of Lords Lieutenant (made permanent in 1585), trained bands (1573) and corn commissioners (1577), and central patronage began to push its way into the localities, intensifying the processes of change whose effects it was intended to remedy.

The third strand was the sudden availability and conformity of education. Again, educated nobles or even gentry (the Pastons of the 1450s are the obvious case) were hardly a new phenomenon. What was new was the form and content of the education. No longer were the sons (and sons they largely were) of the ruling classes packed off into service in a lord's court as the sum of their schooling; instead they went to the new grammar schools, which were blossoming everywhere, and thence to the Universities or the Inns of Court, with the whole process rounded off by foreign travel. This would, as Stone points out, be an opportunity to learn languages – a matter of necessity with the rupture in the universality of Latin, which now became an antiquarian pursuit at best. New technologies made warfare ever more complex, a matter for study as much as for experience. 'The sixteenth-century transition from elementary education by private tutors', says Wrightson, 'to formal education in the grammar schools and . . . attendance at . . . central educational institutions . . . contributed markedly to the growth of a homogenous national culture among the English ruling class' (1982, 191).

This culture was based on romance. The Reformation had left a countryside littered with ruins, with the visible relics of a wholly lost world which, even in Shakespeare's time, was passing into the mists of nostalgia; on the other hand, the basis of the New Education in the classical canon of Roman poets and authors created a common language for these gentrified romantics to speak. The Roman authors had been in a similar position to themselves; that of a sophisticated, semi-sceptical upper-class which felt an awkward anxiety that it had lost something worth having. It was little wonder that this kind of literature had an appeal (above, pp.27–8).

And so they attempted to recapture that loss. The antiquarian instinct comprised the whole of the lost world. The great *Monasticon Anglicanum* of Sir William Dugdale and Roger Dodsworth was first published 1655–73 and aimed to collect documents and drawings relating to the destroyed religious houses; the title-page of the 1682 edition bore a representation of Henry VIII pointing to a ruin and declaring 'Sic Volo' – Thus I Will. This was the time when Sir Thomas Cotton was collecting his Library, and when John Tradescant was gathering his Ark, a 'closet of rareties' stored at Lambeth. Until the middle of the eighteenth century the gentry evoked their chosen past by shutting themselves away from their tenants on the vast estates they had bought from the pillage of the Dissolution and erecting Palladian mansions, Grecian temples, Gothic follies, romantic grottos, and surrounding themselves with libraries-full of antiquarian literature. The poor, now 'not merely poor, but to a significant degree culturally different' (Wrightson 1982, 221), with their amusing, peculiar customs and beliefs, were still, to an extent, in touch with the old world from which the gentry had isolated themselves. The antiquarian instinct encompassed them, too.

From the very start the touring antiquarians found the lore of ancient wells a rich resource for this trans-cultural pillaging, and regarded them with a mixture of fascination, amusement and astonishment. John Leland, though often called an 'antiquarian', has nothing of the wide-eyed gawper at the past about him, and so we really ought to turn elsewhere, from the travel-journal of Leland's *Itinerary* to William Camden's *Britannia*, which first appeared in 1586 and is a true example of the antiquarian genre – a rag-bag of traditions and oddities. He begins the work with an account of the Roman and Saxon past of the kingdom, and then launches on a topographical description of the entire country, including such things as ebbing-and-flowing wells, petrifying wells, and notable holy wells – such as St Madron's, Madron (Cornwall), St Edburga's, Lyminge (Kent), Barnwell, Cambridge, and St Winifred's, Holywell (Flintshire). His comments on the well at Pitchford (Shropshire) epitomize the sort of mental environment in which he was operating:

> There is a well in a poor man's yard, upon which there floats a sort of liquid bitumen, although it be continually scumm'd off; after the same manner as it doth on the lake Asphaltites in Judaea, and on a standing pool about Samosata, and on a spring by Agrigentum in Sicily; but the inhabitants make no other use of it than as pitch. Whether it be a preservative against the Falling-Sickness, or be good for the draining and healing of wounds (as that in Judaea is) I known no one yet that hath made the experiment. (1695, 545)

Camden's comments on St Richard's Well at Droitwich (Worcestershire) (whose salt springs were popularly attributed to the Saint) exhibit the divided attitudes of these antiquarians:

> I am afraid that some would censure me as very injurious to the Divine Providence, and over-credulous of old wives' fables. Nevertheless, so great was the pious credulity of our ancestors, that they did not only believe it firmly themselves, and transit it in writing to us, but also upon that account paid him honours in a manner divine. (1695, 518)

Joseph Childrey was another sceptic even if his reasoning was not always entirely sound. The supposed effect of 'St Kaines Well' at St Keyne (Cornwall) on the marital relations of a couple was 'a fit fable for the vulgar to believe'. Springs which predicted dearth by their rising were easily explained away: the gluts of rain which brought them on also ruined the crops. As for Cornwall, 'that the springs should be so frequent in a barren countrey, I do not wonder; for where the vegetables are but few and small, to spend the stock of rain that falls, there must needs be the more left to soak into the earth, and make springs' (Childrey 1661, 24, 45–6, 16).

Other objections were more religious than intellectual. In his manuscripts of Oxford's antiquities, Anthony Wood described the activities at St Edmund's Well as 'horrible superstitions and prophane', and a scribbled note in the margin of the MS by a later owner accused Wood of 'popery' for speaking so much of wells (1889, 289 n.3, 386 n.3). In 1725 the Rev. Henry Bourne wrote that the custom of dedicating wells to saints was purely a practice of 'the dark Ages of Popery' (Brand 1777, 82). Old wells were clearly suspicious in some quarters for some time.

Accounts of local antiquaries, as well as national surveys, also showed the same combination of concerns: customs, medicine, oddities. The Rev. William Bedwell's *Brief Description of the Towne of Tottenham High Crosse* was one of the first, appearing in 1631, and mentioned St Eligius's, St Dunstan's and Bishop's Wells. Dr Robert Plot's *Natural Histories* of Oxfordshire and Staffordshire (1676 and 1686) are invaluable records not only of local wells but also of the attitudes of a class. Plot toured the counties, examining holy wells, healing wells, prophetic and petrifying wells, 'testing' their waters with syrup of violets and tinctures of lime and gall ('try it with syrup of violetts', advises Aubrey of Holy Well, Chippenham (Wiltshire), and not to improve the taste (1847, 20)). He also toured the gardens and houses of his gentry friends, often having engravings made of them. He even inspected their springs for them: Dr Lane of Banbury, Dr Rawlinson of Chadlington, Dr Thomas Taylor of Osney, Sir Thomas Penystone of Cornwell (Plot 1705, 26, 39, 44, 365). According to Plot, the perennial well at Cleydon (Oxfordshire), which ran most plentifully in the driest weather, 'resembled the Scatebrae of Pliny'.

John Aubrey was possibly the most assiduous collector of folklore among the early antiquarians, particularly with regard to his native Wiltshire. The Holy Well of Chippenham, he found, produced nitrous 'particles as bige as grosse sand', and from the Holy Well at Bitteston 'five-pointed stones doe bubble up . . . which do move in vinegar'. Antedock's Well at Lydiard Tregoze was 'famous heretofore in the old time' for its healing powers; in this quotation, the feeling of the passing of an old world so prevalent in all these antiquarian writings is made explicit in precisely the same phrase used by Thomas Hearne (above, p.107). Aubrey visited John Evelyn's Eye Well at Upper Deptford, and his quizzings of other gentry friends made up his folkloristic compilation *Remaines of Gentilisme and Judaisme*. Like Plot, Aubrey was prone to drawing classical comparisons. He described St Edmund's Well, Oxford, as the site where the saint 'did sometimes meet and converse with an Angel or Nymph; as Numa Pompilius did with Egeria' (1847, 20, 21, 23, 45; 1881, 34).

As the attentions of the antiquaries came to focus more on manorial history and parochial architecture than topography and primitive chemistry, the popular customs of the people, including their wells, were still matters of fascination. 'Fountains were certainly in the earliest ages superstitiously frequented, and loaded with unusual honours by our good forefathers', wrote Collinson; he discovered, for instance, a spring at Ellworthy (Somerset) which was bottomless 'according to vulgar report' (1791, iii 104, 525). The megalithic surveys of Aubrey (*Templa Druidum*, c.1690) and Stukeley (*Stonehenge, a Temple Restored to the British Druids*, 1740) created the necessary conditions for the soon-to-be commonplace connection between popish wells and pagan wells by generating the image of an indigenous paganism based around the figures of the Druids. Via not only their books, but also organs such as the Society of Antiquaries and the *Gentleman's Magazine* investigators such as Stukeley added the Druids to the already-heady brew of upper-class mythology. The first emergence of this idea of continuity, however, occurs very early in the seventeenth century, and it is so outrageously wrong and yet has been so influential that it has to be quoted in full. It refers to the Wanswell in Hamfallow (Gloucestershire).

> . . . a fresh springe arisinge not farre of nowe called Holy well, held to bee of vertue and medicinable; Anciently called Woden well or Wodenswell, from the Goddesse [sic] Woden the Idoll of our old Ancestors the paynim Saxons, of whom we have the name of Wednesday . . . ffrom which goddesse and this her well, strange cures there wrought, that from the concurrence and confluence of all ages and sexes, meetinge at this un-holy well, The proverb arose, which yet continueth; That all the maids in Wanswell, may dance in an egshell: (Smyth 1892, iii 371)

To which there is no adequate reply. The real derivation of Wanswell has already been discussed above (p.41).

By the later part of the eighteenth century the romanticism was getting out of hand. The Dilletante Society, founded in 1736, promoted the knowledge of and taste for Grecian architectural styles which resulted in a rash of porticos and temples in upper-class gardens; Sanderson Millar's

Gothic folly on the Edgehill estate in 1746 brought him a torrent of commissions for sham castles – all of which, in the words of Mrs Delaney and Mrs Montague, were intended to 'raise the imagination to sublime enthusiasm, and soften the heart to poetic melancholy' (Clarke 1962, 67). At Old Wardour (Wiltshire) a ruined castle combined forces with a Grecian mansion across an artificial lake, a romantic grotto and a summerhouse of indeterminate but vaguely Gothic style to achieve the aims so ably expressed by these Society ladies.

This was the context of numerous instances of the restoration of wells by the gentry after the Reformation. One of the earliest was the forty shillings paid by Lady Forster in 1630 to repair St Edmund's Well, Oxford, but the majority occur in the somewhat safer environment for such 'popish' activities after the restoration of 1660. St Cuthbert's Well, Durham, was rebuilt and given the title Fons Cuthberti in 1660 (or this is at least the most probable date), and St Philip's Well, Keyingham (East Yorkshire) was rebuilt by the mysterious 'WH', 'WD' and 'WR' in 1667, to judge by the inscription which could be seen on the well in 1923. The most likely date for the restoration of the Holy Well at King's Newton (Derbyshire) is 1688, but its Latin inscription – 'Fons Sacer Hic Struitor Robertus Nominis Hardinge' – seems to suggest it was not to celebrate the Glorious Revolution (Hunt 1987, 10; Smith 1923, 43–8; Usher 1986).

More spectacular a gesture than merely restoring your local holy well was to incorporate it into your romantic landscaped (or, come to that, formal) garden. At the heart of this activity was the educational background of the upper-classes, drenched in images of nymphs and springs derived from classical literature. The connection began very early. John Skelton, Henry VIII's poet laureate, wrote of a spring noted by the Roman authors:

> But for I am a mayde
> Tymerous, halfe afrayde
> That never yet asayde
> Of Elyconys well
> Where the Muses dwell ('Phyllyp Sparowe', lines 607–11)

Sir John Stradling wrote an ode to his ebbing-and-flowing well at Newton (Glamorganshire), imagining it pursued by the sea, a poem which he communicated to Camden:

> Nympha fluit proprius; Fons
>   defluit. Illa recedit,
> Iste rediit. Sic livor inest at pugna
>   pereniis.

> The nymph flows nearer; the
>   Fountain flees. She flies
> And he returns. Thus desire
>   lingers, the war endures.

> (Camden 1695, 612)

The earliest example of this phenomenon is at Woodstock (Oxfordshire), where Henry II made the Everswell – derived perhaps from *eofor*, 'wild boar' – the focal point of his ornamental gardens, but the mentality is obviously different from the backward-looking romanticism which transformed Everswell further into Fair Rosamund's Well, after the King's mistress, by 1577. The other likely very early instance is at Eastwell Park (Kent), where the grounds contain Duke's Well and Plantagenet's Spring; these take their name from a bricklayer on the estate of Sir Thomas Moyle, who built the House in 1545, who claimed to be the illegitimate son of Richard III and whose claim was believed locally to the extent that his name was entered in the burial register in the church as 'Richard Plantagenet' (Bond & Tillar 1987, 46–7; *Reader's Digest* 1973, 199).

One might, if one was sufficiently lucky to have one handy, adopt a local holy well into one's garden. Astrop Park in King's Sutton (Northamptonshire) includes St Rumbald's Well, which was 'discovered' as a spa in 1664; the Holy Well at St Albans (at the foot of the hill, see p.44) was the focal point of John Churchill's gardens created in the late seventeenth century. The whole village of Burton Dassett was pulled down by Sir Edward Bealknap and its church and Holy Well incorporated within his Park (Valentine 1985a, 7–8; Haynes 1987, 21; Bord 1985, 175). A healing well on the site of a medieval hospital chapel at Lyme Regis (Dorset) was described as 'the grotto' in a garden perambulation of the eighteenth century, indicating that it had by then been put to a less exalted use (Wanklyn 1927, 218), and the Nun's Well at Gokewell (Lincolnshire) was diverted to supply the ornamental gardens and fountains (de la Pryme 1870, 127).

It was not necessary for the well so incorporated to be a Holy one. Thomas Bushell employed the Gold Well, Enstone (Oxfordshire) to create the 'famous wells, natural and artificial, Grotts and Fountains, called Bushell's Wells' which John Evelyn visited in 1664; and Evelyn's own father-in-law, Sir Richard Bourne, restored the Eye Well in the garden of his house at Upper Deptford (Wiltshire) (Jordan 1857, 18–20; Aubrey 1847, 21). On his late eighteenth-century *Tours* Arthur Young visited the house of the Halswells at Goathurst (Somerset) and found, in a wood, 'a spot beautifully wild and sequestered, where a limpid spring rises at the foot of a rock overhung in a fine manner by wood growing from its clefts. The water winds away through the grove in a proper manner'. A marble tablet nearby called attention to the legend of Moses creating springs in the desert (Exod. 17: 6–7). The Halswells had probably romanticized the spring which gave their manor, and themselves, their name. For good measure the gardens also contained Robin Hood's and Druid's Temples (Collinson 1791, i 80–81).

But a generation which felt able to employ people to act the role of hermits in fake hermitages was hardly above creating its own wells from scratch. The Earl of Aylesbury built, or at least rebuilt, 'Diana's Well', East Witton (North Yorkshire) in 1821 with stones and a gargoyle probably taken from Jervaulx Abbey, and constructed a drive from it to his house; it was a favourite picnic spot for guests. There was another Dinnes Temple Well at Doncaster (West Yorkshire) in 1581 which may have been the same sort of edifice, for the 'name is . . . one usually given by early antiquaries to ancient or artificial ruins' (we have already seen that, to medieval clerics, Diana was simply the type-model of a pagan goddess (p.87)). Near Doncaster, Stukeley visited a Robin Hood's Well at Burghwallis (West Yorkshire) built for Lord Carlisle and designed by Vanburgh. According to Mr Gent, 'passengers from the coach frequently drink of the fair water, and give their charity to two people who attend there' (Whelan & Thompson 1989, 40; Smith 1961–3, i 34; Smith 1967–8, 1 93; Hope 1893, 171; Lukis 1883, iii 373; Gent 1730, 334).

Eyford Gardens (Gloucestershire) were laid out in the 1710s and some time between then and c.1775 the old village well was dubbed Milton's Well, the tale being that the poet had written much of Paradise Lost at its side. There is no evidence for this, of course (*VCH Glos*, vi 73). Carshalton (Surrey) had a Grotto Spring in its Park, while Leigh Place at Godstone (Surrey) contained a Diana's Well as the centrepiece of formal gardens and ponds (Whitaker 1912, 44–5; *VCH Surrey*, iv 288). Most extreme of all the landscaping gentry was Henry Hoare of Stourton (Wiltshire). Stourhead, his estate, includes Seven Wells Bottom, the site where King Alfred supposedly prayed for water for his army and was rewarded with the bursting forth of seven springs. In 1768 the St Peter's Pump in Bristol was ripped up and transferred to the highest of these springs, to top a romantic grotto-like structure, and the Cross which had stood over St Edith's Well in the city was transplanted to its present position near Stourton Church. Hoare dubbed the source of the Wiltshire–Dorset Stour 'Ariadne's Well', placed a statue of the nymph in the centre of the waters, surrounded it by marble-carved verses by Alexander Pope, and built a grotto over the whole thing. Paradise Well stood behind Hoare's Temple of Apollo, and Dyer's Well, on the edge of the park, was named from a certain Thomas Dyer in 1566 (Bord 1985, 97; *The Western Gazette*, 15.6.90; Gover et al. 1939, 182). As counter-evidence to all this it is as well to remember that when Lord Damer built his house at Milton Abbas (Dorset) in the 1770s he submerged the medieval Lady Well under his picturesque ponds.

Antiquarianism *per se* also had a powerful influence on some old wells by raising their status, often to the extent of giving them a Christian dignity which they did not previously possess, as a result of the misinterpretation of place-names. The table shows the examples uncovered to date:

TABLE 7: WELLS AFFECTED BY ANTIQUARIAN SPECULATION AFTER
THE REFORMATION

site	first name	later names	source
Ashover (Db)	Sir William's Well, 1671	St William's Well, 20th cent.	Cameron 1959, 194
Bristol (Gc)	Hotwell, 15th cent.	St Vincent's Spring, 1702	Waite 1972
Cerne Abbas (Do)	?	Hel Well, 1897	Colley March 1899, 479
Chadwell (Ex)	Chawdwell, 1578	St Chad's Well, 20th cent.	Reaney 1935, 150
Cranborne (Do)	Holewella, 1194	Holy Well, 1929*	Harte 1985,5; Mills 1986, 89
Finchampstead (Bk)	Dozells, 1638	St Oswald's Well,1895	Gelling 1973–4, 96 & Lyon 1895, 16–18
Gleaston (La)	Sir Michael's Well, c.1700	St Michael's Well, late 19th cent.	Taylor 1906, 312–13
Hamfallow (Gc)	Weneswella, 1170 x 90	Woden's Well, c.1610	Smith 1964, iv 230–31; Smyth 1892, iii 371
Houghton Regis (Bd)	Bidwell, ?	St Bride's Well, –1912	VCH Beds, iii 390
Ibberton (Do)	Stachy's Well, c.1340	St Eustace's Well, 1771	Hutchins 1861–70, iv 361–2
Melbury Bubb (Do)	Oilenwell/Ailwell 1771	Holy Well 19th cent.	Hutchins 1861–70, ii 645, 655
Middleham (EY)	Alkeld, ?	St Arild's Well, ?	Whelan 1986, 4
Newton by Chester (Ch)	Newtoneswell, 1278	Aganippe's Well, ? St Aganippe's Well, 1878	Dodgson 1970–81, iv 147–8
Painswick (Gc)	Tony's Well, temp. Hen. VIII	Tobyes Well, temp. Eliz. I Tybbye Well, 1617 St Tabitha's Well, 1928	Walters 1928, 89–94
Wigginton (Ox)	Hollowell, 1685	Holywell, 19th cent.	Gelling 1953–4, 408

* This name may have been changed before the Reformation, but it is not the most likely hypothesis.

Key

Bd	Bedfordshire	Bk	Berkshire	Ch	Cheshire	Db	Derbyshire	Do	Dorset
Ex	Essex	EY	East Yorkshire	Gc	Gloucestershire	La	Lancashire	Ox	Oxfordshire

Some of these wells are obviously the result of speculation about place-names. Hamfallow has already been dealt with (p.44). At Ibberton, the dedication of the church had been lost by the later 1700s and once the local Stachy's Well, named after a family of medieval landowners, had been interpreted as 'St Eustachius's' it was an easy step to transfer the pseudo-dedication to the church. Newton-by-Chester looks like a cross-class effort. Newton's Well was originally led off to feed Chester Abbey, and the antiquarians named it Aganippe's after the pure well on Mount Helicon; the saint's title was probably the effort of local and less learned people.

Naturally it was not only holy wells which were the object of this process. Aristotle's and Plato's Wells at Oxford were Brooman's Well in 1382 and Stock Well c.1205; the former had gained its modern name at least by 1615, and later was the focus of a number of rituals. Sugar was mixed with the water and drunk until about 1880; in 1718, the victors of student games left their trophies there; and it also had a reputation as a wishing well (Rattue 1990, 174–5).

One of the subsets of this sort of antiquarianism was the rise of interest in spas, prompted not only by a fascination with topographical oddities, such as healing springs, but also by the incorporation of the Royal College of Physicians in 1518 and the rapid growth in the numbers of doctors and surgeons (Thomas 1978, 11–14). It has been stated that

> The Spas began as holy wells . . . At the Reformation . . . the Holy Wells became wishing wells . . . Consequently there were fewer cures, and by Cromwell's time, when most of the wells were neglected, the saints were despised and the cures forgotten. (Addison 1951, 3)

For which the only excuse is ignorance. Shakespeare certainly knew of the healing powers of wells long after the Reformation:

> This brand she quenched in a cool well by
> Which from Love's fire took heat perpetual
> Growing a bath and healthful remedy
> For men diseas'd . . . (Sonnets, CLIV, lines 9–12)

Besides, while some healing springs certainly gained a new lease of life in this period, most spas were founded new and only fourteen can be shown to have degenerated from holy wells. These include St Catherine's, Southwell (Nottinghamshire); Lady Well, Birmingham (Warwickshire); and St Anne's Wells at Buxton (Derbyshire) and Brighton (Sussex). The oldest spa was probably the Bristol Hotwell, discovered in the late fifteenth century and the focus of attention until the later 1830s (Waite 1972). There was continued creation of spas throughout the 1600s and an upsurge of interest c.1780–1830.

The fashion for making up *de novo* spas was obviously well-known as early as 1631, as testified by this useful piece of advice:

> Let them find out some strange Water, some unheard-of Spring. It is an easie matter to discolour or alter the Taste of it in some measure (it makes no matter how little). Report strange Cures that it hath done.

Beget a superstitious opinion of it. Good Fellowship shall uphold it, and the neighbouring Townes shall al sweare for it. (Powell 1661, 31)

At Glastonbury this advice was enthusiastically followed. The Chilk Well began life as an innocent chalybeate spring built into a well to supply the Abbey reredorter after the fire of 1184. It did this equally innocent job until its services were no longer required for the purpose. Then, in 1750, Matthew Chancellor of North Wootton, an asthmatic, dreamed of being cured at a spring in Glastonbury; a figure told him to drink of the water which 'comes out of the holy ground where many saints and martyrs are buried' secretly for seven Sunday mornings (for the Seven Days of Creation) and then announce the miracle to the world. By May 1751 the spring was receiving 10,000 visitors, though it was 'no more than a spring of common fair water, possessing no medical properties whatever; . . . the whole story was designedly trumped up with a view of bringing custom to the town'. The original well soon became kitted out with a subterranean bath-chamber. It is, of course, the Chalice Well (Collinson 1791, ii 266; Rahtz 1964).

The interest in the phenomenon of spas for the consideration of holy wells also lies in how far these new centres of healing undermined the old ones. There is as yet no evidence to suggest this. At Northaw (Hertfordshire) for instance, the popularity of King's Well, a spring noted in the locality since the middle ages, did not eclipse belief in the powers of John's Hole, a hermit's well in Berevenue Forest, which survived beyond 1915 (Wilson Fox 1923-7). Holy and Eye Wells at Colwall (Herefordshire) and Holy, Eye and St Anne's Wells at Malvern (Worcestershire), far from being suppressed, were instead incorporated within the spa establishments (Richardson 1935, 72; 1930b, 118-19).

Fashion was crucial in all this, and royalty determined fashion; no personage more so than Charles II, which, along with the tremendous impact he made on popular culture as 'the returning king', probably explains his association with so many wells. The King, tradition related, drank at Collinson's Well, Hutton in the Forest (Cumberland), before the Battle of Worcester, and hid at King's Well, Ellerton (Staffordshire), after it. He popularized taking the waters at Royal Spring, Longthorpe (Gloucestershire), and also at King's Well, Northaw (Hertfordshire), where visitors were so numerous that, during his stay, marquees had to be set up to accommodate them (Hutchinson 1794, i 512; Hope 1893, 160; Walters 1828, 80-81; VCH Herts, ii 358). Charles did more to promote hydrolatry in England, possibly, than any single person apart from St Anselm.

Wells became the subject of class-conflict as a result of enclosure. Public access to the springs had to be defended at Lady Wells, Birmingham

(Warwickshire) in 1818, and at Blackett's Well, Hampstead (Middlesex) in 1802. At Pillerton Horsey (Warwickshire), Leawell was reserved for the use of cattle when the common was enclosed in 1794; but when Lower Slaughter (Gloucestershire) was enclosed in 1731 the Act gave the Lord of the Manor the sole right to use the King's Well. On enclosure in Bolam (Durham) in 1786, the pattern of fields shows Dunn Well Road extended into the newly enclosed Dunwell Field to include the Well; and outside the walls of Durham in 1821 the parishioners of St Giles petitioned Lord Londonderry on the illegal diversion of water from 'Mair's Well of excellent water in a field called Magdalenes Close . . . a public well of great public utility and had been so from time immemorial' (Pearson 1901, 60–62; *VCH Middx*, iv 138; *VCH Warks*, v 133; *VCH Glos*, vi 129; Chapman 1958–65, 11; Meade 1970, 69 n.15). The author of the *Denham Tracts* was outraged by the diversion of Lady Well, Kirby Stephen, to supply Francis Birkbeck's brewery not long before 1840: 'The well has ever been looked upon as public property' (Hardy 1891, ii 34). On the other hand, the Lord of the Manor of Ashtead (Surrey) left a parcel of land out of the enclosure of the Common in 1676 so that the poor of the parish could still use Ashtead Well (Jackson;1977, 55). For Richard Gough in 1701, what was legal and what was moral were identical so far as water was concerned:

> Ast-well . . . is a great benefitt to them beecause of the goodnesse of the water. This well lyes in a peice of ground beelonging to Mr Robt Hayward who sometimes did offer to hinder people for fetching water there – butt I told him it was not onely an uncharitable thing to hinder people of that which God sends freely – butt it was a thing that wee claimed by prescription. (Gough 1981, 266)

The history of Eccleshill Holy Well (West Yorkshire) shows repeated conflict. When Thomas Burnley enclosed the Park in 1585 he granted some of the commons to Nicholas Kitching but ensured that he had the right to use the well and that a public way was opened to it. In 1704 the then Lord, John Stanhope, impeached Richard, Sarah and Mary White for diverting the water. The well had been enclosed by 1723 but was reopened that year because of a drought. By 1933 it was owned by Bradford Corporation, but it was 'choked with weeds and rubbish' (Preston 1933, 244–7).

The Common People

Here the territory is more hazardous. Map 12 shows dates when popular traditions are said to have lapsed, in accounts which are either contemporary or refer to 'living memory'. Naturally this map is misleading in some respects. It reflects the biases of research, both in terms of geographical spread and the over-influence of a few antiquarian surveys;* also, many past traditions, particularly of healing springs, are recorded with no hint of when they lapsed, and the number of continuously surviving traditions is very tiny (though my demand for *demonstrable* continuity may be over-strict!).

Yet there are some surprising features which cannot be explained by these objections. The full surveys of Wales reveal the lapse of traditions at, generally, an earlier date than those in much of England. Across two belts of land, from Pembrokeshire into Brecknockshire and most of the three northern counties, the dates we have range from the eighteenth century to 1844; while in parts of Yorkshire and most of the West Country traditions lingered into the twentieth century. We might ascribe this difference to the different styles of Nonconformity so influential in both areas, since in Cornwall, at least, Methodism appears to have slotted itself into the existing popular culture without much damage (below, pp.126–7). But it is north Somerset, a hotbed of Nonconformity since at least the Civil War when its villagers assembled on the hills to pray and drive out the Royalist Marquis of Hertford (Manning 1978, 182) which produces our earliest lapse-date in the area (c.1820): so the analysis is obviously not that simple. If we turn to analyse the figures with regard to urbanization, the pattern is a little clearer. The nine English urban sites which appear on the map produce an average lapse-date of 1842. There are also seven 'small town' sites whose equivalent average is 1880. The average of the forty-seven rural sites is, assuming the phrase 'twentieth century' to correspond to c.1940 (which is generous), slightly earlier at 1874.

Yet even in urban environments popular traditions could survive given the right conditions. In some parishes in Lambeth the belief that attendance at church on New Year's Eve was lucky was strong enough for the people to attempt to force incumbents to hold services against their will, and the churching of women was practised until the First World War. This was, paradoxically, combined with an alienation from the Church as a formal institution. As early as 1818 a priest in Sheffield was complaining that the working classes had contracted an 'inveterate habit' of non-attendance at church, and in the early 1900s the Vicar of St Mary the Less, Lambeth, declared that 'nobody goes to church, it has always been so . . . it is not dislike, it is not unbelief', it was simply habit, he thought (Cox 1982, 93,

---

* Thus in Leicestershire, John Nichols, writing in 1795, ascribed great importance in the process of decline to Enclosure, referring to it in the case of three wells (1795 ii 177, iv 897, iv 917). Nichols had a low opinion of enclosure and it is sometimes doubtful whether his detailed testimony should be trusted.

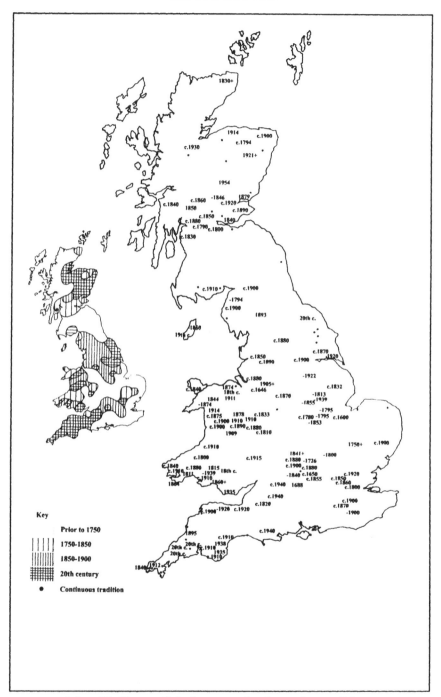

Map 12: Dates of the last records of popular traditions

102–3; Inglis 1963, 323–4). There is no escaping the fact that strictly religious observances were less strong in the towns than in the country-side, and possibly had been for a very long time; but churchgoing ought to be divided from the process of the decline of popular tradition with which it is usually bracketed.

There is no satisfactory explanation for the general trends of the map. Perhaps, for instance, advanced agriculture and enclosures might account for the total lack of lapse-dates in much of the South-East, East Anglia and Midlands, but this can hardly be the case for the North-East. If we drag in industry as an explanation this may help with the North-East, but what of the large belt of lapse-dates between 1850 and 1900 which covers Lancashire, West Yorkshire and much of the Black Country? We are left confused.

The answer may lie in the extreme localism of popular culture before the later nineteenth century. Whilst most large towns had a weak Anglican presence in the 1851 Census, for example, this was not the case for places such as Swansea, Merthyr Tydfil and Bath, for reasons which are unclear. In a study of the Civil War in the West Country, the effects of local culture have been found decisive in determining political allegiance. South-east Somerset was a hive of Royalism, apparently related to the prominence of customs such as Skimmington riding (connected to wells at Curry Mallett and Ashill) and maypoles; while Evercreech contained several times as many Royalists as Batcombe and Ditcheat despite being smaller than either (Underdown 1985, 203–4, 206). Methodism grew only slowly in villages where there was a church or resident gentleman; hence its strength in the belt of counties from Northumberland to Lincolnshire where there were few of either. The exact links between local culture and the survival of wells, though, are impossible to fathom without more intensive and historically conscious local study.

There is no reason, anyway, to believe that popular Nonconformity was necessarily injurious to the well-cult in many areas. North Cave (East Yorkshire) was an early centre of Quakerism, and in 1788 a meeting-house was built next to St Helen's Well, which soon became known as Quaker Well (*VCH E. Yorks*, iv 35; Smith 1923, 151–2). Baptists had good use for the wells. They baptized adults in pools at Dry Drayton (Cambridgeshire), and when Swan Wallis paid for the new Meeting House at Marston (Cambridgeshire) c.1799 he donated a parcel of land with a pool for baptisms. In the middle of the nineteenth century the Baptists of Peterchurch (Herefordshire) were making use of St Peter's Well (*VCH Cambs*, ix 88, viii 193; Watkins 1930, 184–5). But the most prominent denomination was Methodism. John Wesley himself drank from Lady Well, Dawley (Shropshire), and was cured of consumption at St Vincent's Spring, Bristol, in 1754. At Potterne (Wiltshire) a spring called Pitchers and Pans was used for Methodist baptisms, and on the first Sunday in May Wesleyan services were held in the old well-chapel at Madron (Cornwall), showing the Methodists' great ease in integrating with the indigenous sub-Catholic culture (Otter 1985, 13; Waite 1972, 13; *Wiltshire Magazine* 42, 390; Meyrick 1982, 93). There is no evidence as yet to support Otter's claim that pin wells are a reversion to pagan custom due to the repression of patterns by 'Methodist and evangelical preaching'. Both these groups showed little interest in, or knowledge of, the customs of ordinary people. Distribution also argues against it. There is only one known pin well in each of Derbyshire and West Yorkshire, but six in Glamorganshire, hardly a hotbed of Wesleyanism. Two of three Lancashire pin wells were mainly visited by Roman Catholics. Herefordshire, a county immune from Methodism, has three. The custom of pin-throwing was not exclusively 'pagan' in any case. The Pin Well of Lewes (Sussex) was well enough known and recognized to give its name to Pinewellestrete even in 1280 (Salzman 1934, ii 23).

Two denominations contributed to the rise of a well at Droylesden (Lancashire) to holy status. In 1781 there was only one Seventhorns Well. Two years later the Moravians opened up three wells to supply their settlement of Fairfield, and before long the name degenerated into Sentons. In 1849, long after the Moravians had left, a Roman Catholic mission opened nearby under the patronage of St Anne, and the following year the wells appear as 'St Anne's' too (Speake & Witty 1953, 29–30).

So far as we can tell from the map, with all the above reservations, the crucial period for the decline of the well-cult among the lower classes was c.1850 to c.1940; the time of, and succeeding, the phenomenon which has only been called, for want of a more precise title, the Great Change:

> Rather oddly, the historians have not settled on any name for the huge metamorphosis that took place in English rural society during the second half of the nineteenth century. perhaps this is because its manifestations are too vast, its causes likewise and its processes too long drawn-out, to be easily comprehended as a single event. (Fowles & Draper 1984, 15)

I quibble only with the word 'rural', for the Great Change affected towns too. To imagine otherwise links the decline of popular traditions with 'secularization', and if our figures above suggest anything, it is that there may be no such link. Besides, while the wells were in decline the Church was actually on the rise under the impact of Evangelical and Tractarian enthusiasm. Even in the poor, isolated Norfolk deaneries of Waxham and Repps there was a substantial revival in the 1820s and 30s, and the concern of such clerics as Bishop Magee of Peterborough about the conversion of the working classes led to a frenzy of church-building later in the century (Virgin 1988, 153–7; Inglis 1963, 23). By the end of the 1800s the Church was drawing more of the population into its services than at any time possibly since 1800; but the wells were still declining. 'Secularization' was not the issue. That had happened long before, so far as it had happened at all.

The phenomenon we are examining is the nationalization of culture. Its causes were manifold, its processes too interlinked to be drawn out in a logical sequence. All we have is a series of facts which chase one another. In 1836 railways carried a third of the population; in 1850 they bore three times the population. Between 1860 and 1900 the invention of the rotary printing press enabled an explosion in printed matter, notably newspapers, and a near-sixfold increase in the production of woodpulp. Local authority social programmes, such as the free milk and public health clinics established at Bradford in the 1880s, or the West Ham unemployment scheme of 1895, proved inadequate and the state was compelled to push itself once again into the localities. In Reading in the 1890s, voluntary organizations were in retreat under the impact of national corporations and commercial modes of operation. Reading Football Club, which rejected professional status in 1894, accepted it in 1895, and became a company two years later; the voluntarily funded Royal Berkshire Hospital suffered an extreme financial crisis; and from 1909 to 1913 branches of national trade unions in the town increased from thirteen to twenty-two (Mackenzie 1984, 17; Thane 1982, 46, 76–7; Harris 1972; Yeo 1976, 188–96, 213–15, 262–4). The process intensified with each round of social reform throughout the twentieth century, as the power and importance of the small and the local was lessened to the benefit of the central, the national, and the state.

Accompanying these tangible, if mysterious, changes was a subtle ideological one. Society lost its residual belief, slowly. That is, not only was the habit of churchgoing lost, but the habit of scepticism was becoming accepted. How far ordinary people had ever accepted orthodox Christian teaching is open to question (above pp.101–2), and no doubt since the Reformation the normal degree of faith was what the Bishop of Rochester in 1903 called 'diffusive Christianity': a vague belief in 'God' and a Pelagian view of the Gospel myth as a model of moral behaviour (Cox 1982, 93). But in the nineteenth century this sort of belief became official. The awful truth that the upper classes found it so difficult to come to terms with was that they themselves had ceased to believe decades before, and had come to see the Church primarily as a means of social control; the epitome of this attitude was Peel, the Prime Minister so anxious to preserve the Church who never attended worship himself. The slow rise of mechanistic science and its attendant modes of thought since,

Cupitt would argue, the time of Galileo (Cupitt 1984, 43–3), modes of thought which demanded evidence for opinions and beliefs, had made repression of Dissenters seem repugnant to thinking people even as far back as 1688; and by the 1850s there was a growing reluctance to repress *anything* – even Roman Catholicism.

A symbolic struggle was that following the publication of the liberal theological study *Essays and Reviews* in 1860. The long battle on the part of the conservatives finally resulted in the decision by the Judicial Committee of the Privy Council in 1864 that the Rev. H.B. Wilson, one of the Essayists, should be reinstated to his living from which his Bishop had suspended him, and, stunningly, that the doctrine of Hell formed no part of Anglican belief. Dr Pusey, who probably knew more about Anglican doctrine than the Privy Council, disagreed, and it seems indubitable that the Committee reached this decision not because Hell was not part of strict Anglican teaching but because they themselves could not bear to believe in it. In 1876 the Council overruled the Church Courts for supporting the Rev. F.S. Cook who had denied the Sacrament to a parishioner who did not believe in the Devil (Jarrett 1988, 46–9). The upper classes were losing even the residual belief that religion was a good thing for other people.

In this intellectual climate, how could the humble holy well survive? Recent folklore studies have painted a vivid picture of popular belief at the end of the nineteenth century and the social functions it performed. What strikes our attention first is the extreme localism of customs: thus Plough Monday was not observed in the pastoral Cotswolds, in contrast to the surrounding areas; these differences 'arise partly from the nature of local usage and partly from changes in the economic basis of the calendar itself'. The ancient rite of crying the neck at the end of the harvest was 'important to the labourers, not because of some ancient memory or survival of the worship of some pagan earth-mother, but because it reflected the co-operation between master and men and reinforced, at least for another year, the sense of community prevailing in the village' (Bushaway 1982, 35, 126).

In South Lindsey it is the divisions in this solidarity which are emphasized:

> Nature [was] still saturated with magical forces . . . they were psychologically still part of a pagan, animate natural world. For them nature was alive, and the Christian sacraments were dead . . . the origins of these contrasting outlooks lay in the growing divergence between elite and popular culture since the seventeenth century. (Obelkevich 1976, 302)

At Ormsby (Lincolnshire) in 1855, the four most regular communicants were Methodist labourers; but by the late 1880s there was even open scepticism of accepted folklore. An old gamekeeper doubted the power of the bishop to cure rheumatism by touch, not because he was a bishop, but because it was irrational: 'I puts my and on my at, now what good as my and done to my at? . . . The Bishop's ands can't do more good to my ed than my and did to my at' (ibid., 142–3, 273n). It takes little imagination to see how the processes we have outlined above affected this kind of residual popular belief. Rural areas, of course, had their own problems of social disruption attendant on technological changes which reduced the number of men required for a harvest working at ten acres a day from 130 in 1840 to 34 in 1870 and a mere three in 1940 (Bushaway 1982, 108). The decline of the countryside as a place of common work no doubt played a large role in the decline of popular customs and traditions of this sort.

The social functions of holy wells can hardly have altered since the middle ages; yet these functions were largely being provided by a whole new series of social mechanisms. Local communal solidarity was the casualty of the Great Change, and was nationalized into national politics and, later, the Welfare State, after the 1867 and 1885 Reform Acts. Church-organized youth groups, schools and scouts, trade unions and political parties provided new class- or age-based forms of social solidarity. And with the growth of scientific medicine, life was no longer so hazardous or so precarious that resort to the healing well was necessary.

> The water is still of the most pellucid clearness, sweet to the taste, though much neglected, full of fallen leaves and haunted by vermin . . . The present generation, however, have ceased to avail themselves of the medicinal properties of the waters, which have lost their virtue, or are eclipsed by the superior abilities of the Medical Practitioners to whose charge the health of Bampton is consigned. (Giles 1841, 66–8)

At Barmby (East Yorkshire), conflict between old and new was so pronounced that a local landowner filled in St Peter's Well, which had cured scurvy and eye complaints, for fear that it was harming his son's medical practice; this happened about 1820 (Smith 1923, 141–2). By the 1870s the reputation of the Holy Well of Stevington (Bedfordshire) had declined to the point at which locals used it as a sheep dip; a few centuries before the wells might have struck such transgressors dead, but their powers had been put to flight (Harvey 1872–8, 142).

In the towns the wells were fully tamed and brought under human control. The Swan's Well waterworks in Coventry had been founded in 1632; and the Corporation in 1780 established the City Waterworks which utilized St Catherine's Well, capable of producing 100,000 gallons per day before it dried up in 1847. Hull Corporation finally bought the Julian Springs (above, p.98) for £150 in 1794. Sir John Schorne's Well at North Marston (Buckinghamshire), once a place of considerable pilgrimage, was first used for the public supply in 1835, though it had been neglected for years before; and in 1853 the antiquary Thomas Beesley examined Holy Well, Tadmarton (Oxfordshire) with a view to its suitability for pumping to Banbury. In Tottenham, St Dunstan's Well was provided with a pump as part of the Muswell Estate Act's provisions for bringing water to the area in 1866 (*VCH Warks*, viii 392; *VCH E. Yorks*, i 371; Kelke 1859; Beesley 1853; *VCH Middx*, vi 168).

Those wells which were not wanted for these prosaic purposes were destroyed. At Portland (Dorset), Maiden Well was filled in after a typhoid outbreak in 1896; Merry Well was filled c.1903; and in 1914 the Council sealed up Fortune's Well, 'keen' as they were 'to tidy up the Island' (Morris 1987, 106–7, 120). The public of West Bromwich (Staffordshire) had to fight to keep Lyne Purl open after it was condemned in 1848; and St Clement's Well, London, was destroyed in the widening of the Strand in 1874 (*VCH Warks*, xvii 47; Foord 1910, 60–65). Indeed, of the 26 named wells in and around the City of London only three now survive: St Govor's Well, Clerk's Well, and a Holy Well in the King's Cross area. The pillage appears to be on the level of a third of the total in the less urbanized area of Dorset.

Yet out of this wasteland arose the conditions of salvation.

NINE

'This sick earth, this sick race of man': Wells and Suburban Angst

Folklore

The Folklore Society was founded in 1878. Its remit was not then, as it is now, 'the systematic comparative study of oral traditions and cultures', but actually to engage in an act of fairly desperate rescue work. Systematic folklore and folktale collection had more-or-less begun with the Grimms' work in Germany (we can overlook safely the earlier French Mother Goose collections which compare to the Grimms as Camden compares to Edwardian archaeology), but by the 1850s there was a sense of urgency to be found even in those areas of the British Isles most remote from modern influences. Sir George Webb wrote to J.F. Campbell, the pioneering collector of Gaelic folklore, in 1859, 'It is quite plain from these [tales] that a good deal is to be done before they die out. I hope the instinct of race will be strong enough to make some good Celt devote himself to gathering them before it is too late'; to which Campbell replied that 'I should rather like to save from perdition whatever may be valuable'. At the same time Alexander Carmichael was collecting the vast series of Highland poems and songs which he called the *Carmina Gadelica* (Thompson 1990, 91–2).

Important to note here is the element of wonderment at a lost world which these folklorists felt, even in the mind of a man such as Campbell, who had grown up with the Gaels.

> I cannot convey to anyone who has not experienced the extraordinary mass of stuff which is stored up in these old Highland minds. Men who cannot read a single letter or understand a word of any language but Gaelic, ragged old paupers men might pass off as drivelling idiots begin and sing long ballads which I know to be more than three hundred years old, and when they have done they begin another . . . When they have spun out Ossianic poetry they begin upon songs and then they begin upon stories. (ibid., 94).

132

It is vital to notice the shift in attitude in all this from the old antiquarian mode of thought (otherwise the argument doesn't work). No longer is the antiquarian interest in folk customs purely a matter of gentrified amusement; it now becomes a matter of preserving a vital human resource. The very title 'folklore' lent the subject a new dignity, yet emphasized how divorced it was from the people who actually did the studying. It was the 'lore' – a deliberately archaic term – of the 'folk', the pure, simple rural stock who remained closest to the origins of the race itself. Thus Alice Gomme defined folklore as 'a means of obtaining an insight into many of the beliefs and customs of our ancestors' (Gomme, 1894, i xvi). Earlier we drew parallels between the antiquarians' attitude to wells and their attitude to architecture (p.116–17); this parallel could be extended. Just as the view of Gothic architectural styles changed from artistic interest and fancy to moral and religious seriousness, so the study of folk custom underwent the same shift. No doubt urbanization was crucial in this process, by creating the image of a vast suburban monster chewing away the pure rural landscape. It was an image which must have dominated the consciousness even of such rural dwellers as J.F. Campbell.

In 1889 J.S. Udal had said of children's games that the process of collection 'must be done quickly', but by 1922 he was pessimistic:

> Such work cannot be done now. Our Board Schools have seen to that! Only very recently indeed there have been a few studied revivals in such matters. But the survivals – the genuine thing – no longer exist! (Udal 1922, preface)

Of course this also applied to wells. Henry Taylor hoped that his work

> may stimulate residents in North Lancashire to make systematic enquiries of old inhabitants before it is too late, especially in relation to the folklore and traditions associated with this subject, which are rapidly disappearing before the prosaic habits of modern life. (1902–4, iv, 8)

Only where wells were still a powerful aspect of local folklife was their survival not seen as a welcome accident adding to the meagre picturesqueness of the modern world:

> The object I have in view in the present publication, is simply, by holding up to the eye of the public the SUPERSTITIOUS AND DEGRADING PRACTICES herein described, and by thus bringing public attention to bear upon them in their true colours, clearly to demonstrate, that they are really the prolific sources of much of the IRRELIGION, IMMORALITY AND VICE which at present prevail to

such an awful extent through so many portions of our highly favoured land. (Hardy 1836, iii)

– wrote an extreme Protestant opponent of the well-cult in Ireland. Later observers were less hostile:

The national observances of Ireland have been obliterated by the unsparing hand of social progress, and the stern utilitarianism of modern times. Almost every adult still remembers the cherished customs and time-honoured institutions of his early days . . . In some districts [these] are still fondly cherished as dear momentos of the past. (Hogan 1873–4, 261–2)

It is odd that the folklorists maintained the view that they were uncovering a primeval rural past in the face of the very facts they were compiling. It is true that some of the 'survivals', if that is what they were, were astonishing. Udal found, for instance, elements in Dorset children's rhymes which sound oddly like debased Latin: 'Harum, scarum, Virgin Marum'; 'usque dandum, merry cum time' (Udal 1922, 392–3). But others showed folkloric elements of certain antiquity being attached to sites which were unquestionably modern by innumerable processes, a phenomenon we have looked at before (pp.35–6). Mother Pugsley, the widow of a soldier killed in the siege of Bristol in 1645, died in 1700 and was a popular local almsgiver. Her well swiftly gained a healing reputation, and its powers were said to derive from her tears. 'Diana's Well', East Witton (North Yorkshire), built by the earl of Aylesbury, was locally regarded as a pin well (above, p.119). Sir Benjamin Hall, First Commissioner of Public Works in London 1855–8, was ennobled as Lord Llanover. As his lands included the parish of St Govor in west Wales, he dubbed the public well he built in Kensington Gardens St Govor's Well; and within a few years an old woman was to be found next to it selling the waters (Nicholls & Taylor 1872, iii 152; Foord 1910, 171).

The increasing overlap between the 'low' culture of the lower classes and that of the upper classes, by all sorts of means, made it difficult to distinguish any 'pure' tradition. In Dorset a wishing ritual at Upwey well, itself a modern creation, involves making a cup of leaves, a motif borrowed from St Augustine's Well at Cerne Abbas and which in any case, appears to have derived from a novel. At Bradfield (Berkshire), the 'St Andrew's Well' mentioned in Hope's survey was 'sunk to obtain water for an ice factory' (Harte 1985, 6; Hope 1893, 3; VCH Berks, iii 395). And of course there is the famous instance of Glastonbury, where a whole series of legends has been concocted around an innocent spring.

The folklorists themselves, by asking locals to explain peculiar place-names, contributed to the growth of modern well-lore. Our Lady's Well,

Hempstead (Gloucestershire) was, according to the local people inter-viewed by Walters, 'where ancient ladies used to wash'. Local tradition associated Pecket Well, Wadsworth (West Yorkshire), with St Thomas Becket; and Whistlebitch Well, Delamere (Cheshire), derives from *twisel-bache*, a 'valley stream with a fork'. Walloper Well, Clitheroe (Lanca-shire), is recorded in 1617 and probably derives from *walla*, 'to boil up', but the explanation in 1920 referred to the supposed advice given to a wife-beater to 'wallop her well' (Walters 1928, 63–5; Smith 1961–3, iii 208; Dodgson 1970–81, iii 212; Weeks 1920, 61–3). The most extreme example of this confusion concerns Lady Wells. Confusion with secular ladies was always easy, and wells may have slipped readily from one category into another. At Dudley (Worcestershire) a seventeenth-century spa was known as Lady Ward's Saline Spa and Lady's Well, because it stood beside My Lady's Coppice which she had enclosed. Lady Anne Clifford, Countess Pembroke, had an enormous impact on the landscape of Westmorland. In 1664 she placed pillars on the borders of her estate which soon became known as Lady Pillars; she also rebuilt St Nicholas's Hospital in Carlisle and renamed it St Anne's! There is a strong and isolated cluster of Lady Wells in Westmorland, and some crossover is likely to have occurred (Map 9) (Richardson 1930b, 108–9; Smith 1967–8, ii 93, 17).

It was very, very easy for this sort of thing to occur. Tentative sugges-tions were repeated by other, less cautious authors and transformed into statements of fact. Thus at Finchampstead (Berkshire) was Dozell's Well 'which', said W. Lyon, 'we can reasonably suppose to be a corruption of "St Oswald's Well"' (Lyon 1895, 16–18). This corruption was successful, but others did not catch on so easily. People suggested that Synagogue Well, Frodsham (Cheshire) derived from 'St Agnes's Well', or that Kattswell or Cakeswell, Ewell (Surrey) was originally 'St Catherine's Well' (Beaumont 1881, 12–13; Willis 1969, 120). A further stage beyond this is the garbling of traditions. According to a popular 1950s account, St John's Well, Berkhamsted (Hertfordshire) was a pagan site, where St Hugh, as Bishop of Lincoln, had to intervene in order to stamp out the worship of 'nymphs and sprites' on whose account people danced round the well at night and dressed it with flowers. The Saint certainly did condemn the worship of the well, and 'St Hugh having forcefully decreed it, they knew to put it aside in future'. But there are no sprites recorded in the *Magna Vita Sancti Hugonis*, no nocturnal frolickings. Who started that story we do not know (Fry 1953–4, 106–7; Dimocke 1864, 348).

When folklorists start creating wells themselves, however, this is another matter. The well at Cranborne (Dorset) was Holewella, 'hollow well', in 1194 (Table 7), but on the basis of the proximity of a Roman villa it was rededicated. Eventually a stone block was deposited on the bank above the well: 'this stone was placed here in 1929 to mark the site of the ancient holy well a few feet from this spot'. Note also the prophetic Gypsey Springs, to be found at several places in East Yorkshire. William of Newborough knew of them in the middle ages, but when Camden toured the area he found nobody who knew anything of them. By the late nineteenth century, though, they had reappeared (Camden 1695, 741; Smith 1923, 68, 70, 77–8). We seem, then, to have a case of gentry antiquarianism and folklore study re-fertilizing 'popular' tradition.

And yet the idea of the holy well as an unpolluted survival not only persisted, it intensified. D. Mackenzie stated that 'I do not think it is going too far to look on "wishing wells" as having been originally holy wells at which barrenness could be cured' (1907, 222). Dom. Ethelbert Horne summed up the case admirably:

> When belief in the supernatural grew less, the request or prayer was called a wish, and pins were substituted for the sacrifice. Hence the wishing well appears to be nothing more than the the old holy well shorn of its appeal to the supernatural . . . The converts would need baptism, and so the well was made use of for the purpose, and probably its old heathen dedication was changed to a Christian one from that day onwards. (Horne 1923, 8–9)

But it was others who took the theory to the heights of romanticism. T.R. Potter believed that Maplewell, Charnwood (Leicestershire) derived from 'may pole well' and this inclined him to the opinion that 'on this spot the Druids were accustomed to celebrate the Bel-tein and, subsequently, the ancient foresters to offer honours to Flora' (Potter 1842, 93). According to the Rev. William Smith, Drewton (East Yorkshire) 'signifies the town of the Druids'. The Julian Springs, Anlaby/Cottingham, were 'pure and excellent founts' known by that name 'from Roman days'. At Kell Well, Swine (East Yorkshire), romance is unbound:

> Here the Druid may have chanted his incantations, the Roman kept his *fontinalia*, . . . the Norse certainly knew it and at it he may have worshipped. In the Middle Ages it would, without doubt, have been blessed by the priests in solemn procession. (Smith 1923, 7, 14, 115–17)

And so arose an assumption which graduated into a theory which became all-dominating. And at the root of that theory was romantic urban angst.

Hunting High and Low

The traditionally High wing of the Church of England had always smiled on the customs and amusements of the people; the late eighteenth-century Bishops Beilby Porteous and Samuel Horsely and Archbishop Manners-Sutton championed the retention of old holidays in the calendar, for example (Mather 1978, 275–6). But at first sight there was no necessary connection between holy wells and the rebirth of High Churchman-ship with the Oxford Movement of the 1830s and 1840s. Newman and Dr Pusey were always repelled even by any hint of ritualism which had orthodox theology behind it, let alone such eccentricities as holy wells. But this was not true of their disciples. The stress the Tractarians placed upon the Mass as the central event of the religious life demanded a greater emphasis on ritual; this expressed itself in the programme of the Cambridge Camden Society for the building and rebuilding of churches with a more prominent position for the altar (Yates 1983; Bentley 1978). Ritualism was an essential part of the developed Tractarian project.

Besides, most Tractarians were not academics like Newman and Pusey; they were ordinary parish priests and followed more the line of William Ward, whose book *The Ideal of a Christian Church* praised the forms of devotion of medieval Catholicism. The Rev. William Bennet of Knights-bridge was using chanting and vestments in the 1840s. Ritual was an aid to devotion, and many clerics were not picky about the objects around which their rituals were based. Father Richard Dolling was one of the more extreme brand of ritualist. As a child in Ireland he had conducted services for his sisters dressed in makeshift vestments, and after graduating from Salisbury Theological College went as curate to St Alban's, Holborn (Middlesex), where incense and a surpliced choir had been employed for years. When he gained his first charge at St Agatha's Mission church, Portsmouth, Dolling introduced all these elements as well as candles, bells and public processions accompanied by great clouds of incense. He

> had a clear sense that ritual was made for man, and not man for ritual. He hated all finicking and nervous worrying about correctness, and he sometimes, we think, made his ignorance about ceremonial details an excuse for introducing into a function some little action or notion of his own. (Osborne 1903, 109)

If ritualism could encompass almost any religious activity, why not holy wells? Many of the clerics who we know restored wells in this period – the Rev. R. Taylor of Bromfield (Cumberland) in the 1890s, for instance, or the Rector of Stowe (Staffordshire) in 1923 – may have been High Churchmen. One such was the Rev. William van Notten Pole, who restored the Cross Well at Condicote (Gloucestershire) in the 1860s. Pole graduated BA at Balliol College, Oxford in 1825 and was ordained in 1827 by the firm, old-fashioned High Churchman Bishop Monk of Gloucester. The patron of Condicote in 1868 was a Charles van Notten Pole, hence this was probably one of those long-standing High livings which descended virtually by hereditary tenure (Hope 1893, 74; Crockford's 1868, 526).

At Bisley (Gloucestershire) there is a host of wells of various kinds: the 'Poor Soul's Light' in the churchyard, the Seven Wells on the outskirts of the village, which to this day are dressed annually on Ascension Day, and an Eye Well on the hillside. Yet, as Partridge reminds us, the Seven Wells ritual 'is a modern fake dating from 1863'. This was an area of great ritualist penetration. the Vicar of Stow on the Wold was so fond of vestments that his parishioners called him 'the Pope's Washerwoman'; at Prestbury in 1878 the curate, John Edwards, was suspended for Catholic ritual practices, and services were disrupted by Evangelicals bussed in from Cheltenham. And the Vicar of Bisley just happened to be the Rev. Thomas Keble, who graduated BA at Corpus Christi, Oxford, in 1811, MA in 1815, and BD in 1824, and assumed his charge in 1827. His elder brother was the Rev. John Keble, Oxford's Professor of Poetry and one of the leading triumvirate of the Tractarians. Thomas himself wrote four of the *Tracts for the Times* and edited the *Homilies of St John Chrysostom*; he was also one of the first parish priests to introduce the daily celebration of the Eucharist (Partridge 1912, 335; *VCH Glos*, viii 79; Crockford's 1868, 381; *DNB*, 1184). The tradition was carried on by the Vicar's son Thomas, who received his BA at Magdalen, Oxford, in 1846, and was ordained by the uncompromising High Churchman Bishop Phillpotts of Exeter. Thomas junior became Vicar in 1873 (Crockford's 1890, 723).

St Clether's Well at St Clether (Cornwall) rises behind a chapel a quarter of a mile from the parish church, and for years both lay in ruins until in 1895 the Rev. Sabine Baring-Gould undertook to have them rebuilt. At the dedication service in 1898, a procession from the church was led by a cross-bearer and among the hymns sung were 'Exurgat Deus', 'Urbs Beata', and 'Nunc Dimittis'. A child was also baptized at the well and given the name of Clether (Bord 1985, 147). The famous Rev. J.S. Hawker of Morwenstow (Cornwall), who was received into the Church of Rome on his deathbed and who was wont to burst into a peculiar mixture of Latin and Cornish during services, fought a lawsuit against a local landowner to keep St John's Well in the vicarage garden (Meyrick 1982, 107). The Rev. Granville Phillimore of Crazies Hill (Berkshire) restored Rebra's Well and renamed it Rebecca's in 1870, placing a cross by the well; and his family and friends created a huge cross-topped Gothic water-fountain in Henley-on-Thames (Oxfordshire) to his honour in 1885 (Cleaver 1989; Davies 1989, 77). Other denominations could play a part too. A Holy Well in Christchurch (Dorset) owes its origin to being used for baptisms by the Roman Catholic chapel next door.

There is an obvious link with antiquarianism. The Cambridge Camden Society had been anxious to examine medieval documents in order to discover 'correct' forms of ritual, and there appears to have been a connection between the sort of cleric who was interested in history and the sort who was attracted to High Churchmanship. The Rev. J.T. Fowler was a canon of Durham who excavated the Galilee Well in 1896 (Fowler 1896–1905, 25–7) and restored it. He had attended Bishop Hatfield's Hall at Durham, where he became Vice-Principal in 1870, and he was made Librarian of Durham University in 1873. For the Surtees Society, of which he was Vice-President for a time, he edited the *Metrical Life of St Cuthbert* and, for the Yorkshire Archaeological Society, *Cistercian Statutes* and *Adamnani Vita Sancti Columbae* (Crockford's 1896, 481). At the other end of the country the Rev. R.J. Meade (BA Balliol, Oxford, 1815; MA 1818), Vicar of Castle Cary (Somerset) from 1845, contributed many lavish and loving histories of local religious houses to the *Proceedings of the Somerset Archaeological and Natural History Society*. He was an extreme High Church romantic: the Lady's Spring at Cary he claimed was 'probably "Our Ladye's"' – though where the 'Our' comes from is as mysterious as the origins of that final fake-antique 'e' (Crockford's 1868, 451; Meade 1856, 84).

To these romantic High Church antiquarians we owe another dubious extension of the cult of St Chad. Shodwell was a little hamlet near Bromborough (Cheshire) which first appears in the seventeenth century. It was the Curate of Eastham, the Rev. Francis Saunders, who first suggested it might derive from Chad Well, and by 1932 the well concerned was being excavated by the Bromborough Society and adopted as holy. The Rev. Palin felt that the name of Chadwell St Mary (Essex) 'reminds us that we are approaching holy ground' and that a well below the church was possibly 'such as' St Chad himself used. The St Chad's Well of Ilford (Essex) was originally Chadwell ('cold well'), also known as Brick Well or Wooden Well, a boundary mark and a healing spring with a reputation for helping with the ubiquitous eye complaints. The dedication arose, as the Rev. J.P. Shawcross tells us, only after the new St Chad's Church was consecrated in 1886 – on St Chad's Day, for good measure (Lowndes 1955, 58; Palin 1871, 89; Tasker 1901, 108–9; Shawcross 1904, 266–7).

Most notable of all these clerics was, perhaps, the Rev. John Edward Bazille-Corbin. A more acute 'victim' of Catholic romanticism it would be difficult to find. After graduating BA from Jesus College, Oxford, in 1911, he suffered a change in vocation and in 1920 switched from the Law to the Church. He attended Cuddesdon, the Highest of theological colleges, and proceeded to a curacy at East Blatchingdon, in the equally High See of Chichester. In 1922 he received the Rectory of Runwell (Essex): a photograph shows him decked out in the cassock and biretta of a Roman Catholic priest. He concocted an extraordinary series of legends which he then placed in his 'history' of the village: the tale of the Devil's Claw (to 'commemorate' which he inserted a skull-shaped flint into the church wall, beneath the legend 'Stipendia Peccati Mors'), the fable of the Prioress's Tomb, and the story of the conversion of the village by a pair of British evangelists, who rededicated the pagan holy well to Our Lady. This site grew, he claimed, into a 'Priory of Our Lady of the Running Well'. The 'evidence' for this was a record of a visit to the well paid in 1602 which was preserved in the parish register. This has now been 'lost', though Bazille-Corbin's history contains a 'letter' from the previous rector, in which the supposed text is given. Needless to say, apart from the un-challengeable presence of a pagan well, there is no proof for any of it (Crockford's 1953–4, 246; Collins 1983; Ekwall 1961, 397).

We would hardly expect the Low Church to show much interest in wells, but there was some of a didactic kind. At Bath was a Victorian fountain by the Abbey, adorned with a statue of Temperance and a plaque extolling the virtues of pure water over the demon drink. The message at the Cranwell Spring, Kelleythorpe (East Yorkshire) was the same; much in the manner of pious landowners who displayed Bible verses along their fences, Mr John Harker made a metal trough for the water inscribed with the legend 'O that men will put an enemy into their mouths to steal away their brains' (Smith 1923, 34–5). The public fountain at Newbury (Berkshire) is also decorated with Gospel quotations. Thus fresh water acquired something of a moral significance.

Heritage and Angst

Nationalized mass culture, the grind of capitalism (so thought), the soulless city – how to escape them?

> When we compare our modern, secular urban and industrial culture with what preceded it, we have an uneasy sense of loss, so that even today the majority of the human race still profess to have some degree of allegiance to the old faiths of the agricultural civilizations . . . faiths which are in some ways preposterously out of touch with modern knowledge and our present ways of life, yet which have something irreplaceably valuable that we cannot and dare not relinquish altogether. (Cupitt 1984, 182)

> It is very difficult to present the old rural past without creating this nostalgia, precisely because nowadays we have the bastardized versions of it thrown so continually at us . . . The rural masses were

undoubtedly culturally impoverished by the Great Change, but if that
had to be the price of escaping from the more literal and far more
terrible impoverishment of most labouring and living conditions, who
is to deny it – and who, seeing the price we still pay, not to regret it
also? (Fowles & Draper 1984, 17–18)

Why not run among the wells? You could repair your ruined heritage
or invent it anew. In 1843 Viscount Middleton commissioned Pugin to
design an new well-house in Gothic style for Bonfield Spring,
Peperharrow (Surrey) and the Corporation paid for a new Gothic well-
house to cover St Anne's Well, Nottingham, in 1856; local restorations
of Cornish wells took place in 1852 (St Neots), 1864 (St Cleer), 1927
(St Gennys), and 1936 (Cubert) (Whitaker 1912, 56; Morrell 1987, 10;
Meyrick 1982, 29, 35, 47, 138). As to invention, you could place a war-
memorial over a well, as the villagers of Leonard Stanley (Gloucestershire)
did – they also dressed the well each Armistice Day – and South Cave
(East Yorkshire) (Walters 1928, 38; Smith 1923, 153); or invent your own
well-dressing ceremony (Map 13). In recent years eleven new ceremonies
have been established in Derbyshire, and others have arisen at Whitchurch
Canonicorum (Dorset), Midgeley (West Yorkshire), Holywell and
Longstanton (Cambridgeshire). In the late 1800s a whole host of well-
dressing ceremonies were created at Hyde (Cheshire) to celebrate the
renovation of the wells and provision of a public water supply; six of the
wells were old, named ones. In Derbyshire the first revived ceremony was
at Belper in 1838, and many more followed. 'The day is usually observed
as a general holiday, with much feasting of friends and homely merriment,
finishing on the village green, or other rural jollity, that gives us, if but for
the nonce, a glimpse of "Merry England"' (Middleton 1932, 515; Rev.
G.S. Tyacke in Andrews 1892, 208–15).

The Churches continued to take an interest. The ancient well of
St Chad, Stowe (Staffordshire) was restored in 1923, and received
separate Anglican and Roman Catholic pilgrimages. In 1938 a Roman
Catholic pilgrimage to St Plegmund's Well, Plemstall (Cheshire) was
begun; and in 1942, at a time of war and crying, the Bishop of Dorchester
followed in the steps of St Birinus and led an open-air baptism at Bapsey
Pond, Taplow (Buckinghamshire), where, 1300 years before according to
local tradition, his saintly predecessor had baptized local pagan chieftains
(VCH Staffs, xiv 146–7; Richards 1947, 274; Fitch 1988, 62–7).

In his Presidential address to the Folklore Society in 1963, Peter Opie
remarked that 'it scarcely matters which spring, well, pool or fountain we
visit, we find the nation to be obsessed by the idea that it should lighten
its pocket whenever it sees contained water'. He came up with an
impressive list: a pool in Bridlington (East Yorkshire) illuminated gardens;

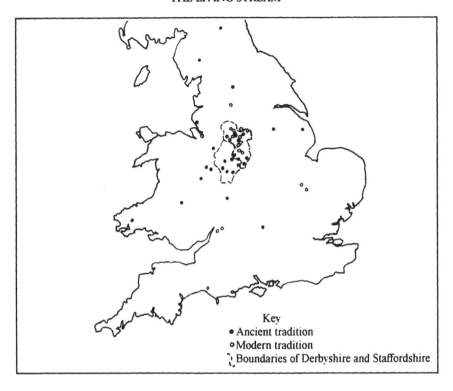

Key
● Ancient tradition
○ Modern tradition
⁝ Boundaries of Derbyshire and Staffordshire

Map 13: Well-dressing sites

a wishing well in Kingswear (Devon) which produced £100 per annum; the crocodile pool in London Zoo and a stream display in Harrods in April 1960 (Opie 1962–3, 511–12).

Most towns appear to have some sort of wishing well at present; the High Cross at Wells (Somerset), whose waters run from St Andrew's Well, is now called the Rotary Wishing Well after its latest restorers. But the phenomenon is indeed universal. In Wookey Hole (Somerset) the original Holy Well is in the now-flooded Fourth Chamber, but beside the path in the First Chamber along which tourists are now channelled is a shallow pool which has miraculously become a wishing well. Nearby, at Cheddar, St John's Well is a wishing well erected by locals to commemorate the village's great flood in 1968; all proceeds go to the St John Ambulance Fund, hence the dedication. For a folklorist, Theo Brown's reaction to this phenomenon was uncharitable.

'Wishing wells' are at best objects of sub-Christian superstition, that is, either frank paganism or, more likely, degraded sanctity. To attach

142

'luck' beliefs to a chlorinated town supply will hardly perform cures, edify holiday-makers, or make the recording of wells any simpler for my successors a hundred years hence. (Brown 1958, 60)

Nevertheless, the demand for an outlet to the inbred hydrolatrous instinct would not be stifled by such objections.

There is a more extreme form of holy well romanticism than the wishing well aspect, and its theoretical starting-point is Robert Graves's *White Goddess*, first published in 1946. In a dense – sometimes impenetrably dense – argument based on comparative analysis of Irish, Welsh and Classical mythology, Graves arrives at an idea of the past as a decay from an original, matriarchal society ruled by poets whose poetry was dedicated to the worship of a Great Goddess, to a patriarchal, rationalist society introduced by the Indo-Aryan hunters into Europe.

This is an Apollonian civilization . . . The age of religious revelation seems to be over . . . the White Goddess in her orgiastic character seems to have no chance of staging a comeback, until women themselves grow weary of decadent patriarchalism, and turn Bassarid again. (1961, 458)

The dichotomy is one between poetic, irrational 'lunar' knowledge, and rational, scientific 'sun' knowledge.

There are two other books to consider. The first is Margaret Murray's *The Witch Cult in Western Europe* (1921) which claimed that witchcraft was an organized pre-Christian religion which survived into the nineteenth century. Despite being wholly unconvincing on the reasonable grounds that there is no evidence for it (Hole 1980, 36–7), this idea has been astoundingly influential and most modern witches appear to believe it. It has also penetrated some feminist thought as a type-image of the persecution of female spirituality by male authority. Secondly we have John Michell's *View Over Atlantis* (1972) which revived the theory of ley lines and linked them with the other books by creating the idea of a pagan past in which human beings were sufficiently in touch with their environment to be able to construct alignments of sites which reflected 'power lines' within the earth.

It is not difficult to see how all this fits snugly into twentieth-century urban alienation: as the world grows more complex and more organized and more bewildering, how sweet it is to have a mythical simplicity to retreat to! It also fitted just as snugly into the established antiquarian and folkloric view of the origins of the holy well in pagan sites. It is worthwhile attempting to disentangle the various threads of the current attitudes governing the public view of holy wells, such as it is.

i. Celticism

Whereas the sort of paganism that so fascinated Hope and most early antiquaries was Classical, that which most occupies modern concerns is Celtic. Thanks to Graves – and the powerful image of 'Celtic twilight' – the Celts are seen as embodying the gentle, pure, natural religion that so contrasts with modern ways of living. Of course, this was not what he was aiming at:

> No poet can hope to understand the nature of poetry unless he has had a vision of the Naked King crucified to the lopped oak, and watched the dancers, red-eyed from the acrid smoke of the sacrificial fires, stamping out the measure of the dance. (1961, 448)

The lust for romantic violence has a history of its own, but gentle it is not. Few of Graves's invocators, though, seem to have read his book.

Most of the material evidence derives from Dr Ross's *Pagan Celtic Britain*, but material evidence plays little part in conditioning the image of the Celtic holy well. Monica Sjoo claims that St Non's Well, St Davids (Pembrokeshire) is dedicated to 'a form of Rhian/Non, the Great White Lunar and Sea-Mare Goddess of Wales'. A psychic investigation of visions in Saverley Green (Staffordshire) revealed a 'Well of the Sacred Blood' – a rather Christian-sounding concept – which had been holy 'in ancient Celtic times'. Even an orthodox archaeologist like Warwick Rodwell accepts the traditional link between wells and the Celts, as we have seen (above, p.1). On occasions this attitude can extend to other races in what can sound like disturbing generalizations. The Chinese, we are told, 'possess a natural tendency towards the receptive, Yin polarity which is seen in the Oriental disposition to introspection and the meditative nature of their culture, and in the collective group consciousness of the race' (Sjoo 1985, 34; Wise 1987, 26; Rodwell 1980, 39; Broadhurst 1988, 45).

ii. Irrationality

In his introduction to Broadhurst's book on Cornish wells, Colin Wilson outlines another debt to Graves, who had 'a profound insight into human history and human psychology. What Graves had understood was that . . . there is a totally different type of knowledge, and a totally different kind of knowing'. These different types – rational/irrational, solar/lunar – are then linked to neurological theories of the 'right' and 'left' brains, aspects of the brain which govern either rational or intuitive activities. 'In the course of creating civilization, we have suppressed these right-brain perceptions' (Broadhurst 1988, xix, xxi, xxiv). According to the Bords 'this link between humans, life, water and the earth was instinctively known by those people who lived before Water Boards came into being'

(1985, 1). The result of this attitude towards rationality is, first, that sloppy thinking is allowed to develop in regard to the history of holy wells, and secondly those branches of knowledge that do rely on rationality are so alienated that rectifying the mistakes becomes very difficult.

iii. Feminism

Despite the fact that both Graves's and Murray's theses are quite deeply sexist in the sense that they merely confirm traditional patriarchal stereotypes of women as intuitive, irrational creatures in touch with the elemental powers of Nature, they always seem to have appealed to that half of the feminist mind that aimed to stress the independent identity of the Essential Female, and to that part of the twentieth-century mind that felt keenly the losses of the Great Change. The mental outlook of the modern West was, it is said, 'a strong masculine and individualistic attitude'. This violated the traditional, natural order of the matrilineal Celts and other earlier civilizations, who recognized that Woman's position was more powerful than that of Man by virtue of her control over 'the essentials of life' – being, of course, 'menstruation, gestation, parturition and lactation'. A limited conception of a woman's role, perhaps (Broadhurst 1988, 45; Branston 1974, 190–99).

Sjoo's piece on St Non's Well is most informative in this respect. She ascribes the 'unconscious' inclusion of 'images of embryos and young life' in her painting to the influence of the well, which was 'clearly . . . an ancient sacred Goddess-site' as wells are 'the source of all life and healing'. She 'felt from the first that this place, and the whole coastline, had a wild and poetic aura of the Pagan Goddess'. She brings her friends, women peace-protestors, to the Well to bathe and pray, and concludes that 'this is a healing Birth-Well, a woman's-only sanctuary where women giving birth could be cared for by priestesses who were healers, oracles and midwives'.

As poetry and myth this is fine, but it will insist on impinging on the world of rational evidence too. In *The All Saints Ley Hunt* Ian Taylor states that 'it is not unknown for nuns to have adopted the role of guardians of the Sacred Waters, a position they may have taken over from earlier Pagan Goddess cults and local traditional witch covens (*Source* 4, 6). Thus all female figures remotely associated with wells – even the old ladies selling water in Kensington Gardens – become watered-down versions of the Great Goddess. For Barry Millard the 'spirit of the well' is recognized as 'another aspect of the Earth Mother' (*Source* 4, 17); and 'water symbolizes the Great Mother. Through her life is assured. The well or spring itself symbolizes the womb of the Great Mother' (Bord 1985, 144). Because Scarborough (North Yorkshire) has a well of Our Lady and a St Mary's Church and Chapel it is claimed that 'this whole area was sacred to the formative female powers'. 'Holy wells were sources of the feminine energy which smooths out the paths of the dragon . . . these places are in some way receptacles of the Cosmic breath, vessels of a strange, forgotten natural alchemy' (Whelan & Taylor 1989, 20; Broadhurst 1988, 45).

iv. Romanticism

And behind all the froth and foam is the crux of the matter: the aching alienation of the modern mind from the land itself. In the beginning

> There was no feeling of Man's separation from Nature that is the hallmark of our modern society . . . The inhabitants of the land . . . were all parts of the whole, dependent on each other for the harmonious continuity of the Earth . . . Nature was tamed for mutual benefit, not profaned to satiate greed and profit. (Broadhurst 1988, 4)

> The holy wells were . . . sparkling fountains of the surging life-force where human beings could, by various arcane methods, tap the very essence of life itself. (ibid., 46–7)

> It is believed by many that ancient peoples knew the art of tapping this energy for the benefit of mankind. It was almost like an electric cable . . . These currents were also associated with water. The Celtic saints are closely associated with their holy wells and churches were often built near the cell of a holy man or woman. (Rendell 1982, 9)

> As the materialist ethos palls in the minds of many people a new direction, perhaps a new cosmology, needs to be found which is profound, simple and natural . . . an acceptance of the numinous within ourselves and the material world. Where better place to begin than with the Holy Well – mysterious, peaceful, and timeless? (Whelan & Taylor 1989, 6)

Where indeed?

> Bride stands
> Silver and white
> Healing water in her hands.
> Heal this sick earth,
> This sick race of man,
> Blessed Bride. (Smith 1987)

This image appears to be having some effect. Not only has the rate of publications about holy wells shot up over the last decade or so, but there has also been a flurry of restorations; most prominently, the Melbourne Civic Society restored the Holy Well of King's Newton (Derbyshire) in 1985, and the Bishop of Salisbury rededicated St Whyte's Well,

Whitchurch Canonicorum (Dorset) after its restoration in 1986 (Usher 1986, 21; *Source* 3, 16). Nine hundred people visited the newly dressed well at Longstanton (Cambridgeshire) over the weekend flower festival in 1986 (Brown 1987).

And the ideas are sinking in as well. Church of England clergy, as anxious as anyone else to tap into the source of 'legitimacy' provided by the pagan past, scamper to claim pagan antecedents for their churches. The Beaminster (Dorset) church guide is proud of the mound beneath the church, 'which may be a pre-Christian sacred site', and the Rev. J. Wilcox of Holywell (Cambridgeshire) is equally proud of his Holy Well, which 'is probably the oldest landmark in the village, certainly pre-Christian', a brave statement indeed (Wilcox 1985, 11). Ley lines are now part of popular folklore. At Trent (Dorset) the inhabitants of Holywell House will tell you of a 'line of wells' from their own holy well to a well in Glastonbury, but there is no such thing.

To a degree it doesn't matter how true all this is, for it is useful. Firstly the mystical consensus draws attention to old wells; secondly it fulfils a deep psychological need. So long as rationality is not so far lost that historical errors cannot be corrected, there is no need to disagree with John Michell, who writes in a far less-quoted book than *View Over Atlantis*:

> There is now emerging a new myth of the Stone Age as a time when the interests of the living earth were closely studied and held sacred. That this myth largely *reflects* modern ecological concerns is undoubted . . . and all who share these concerns may welcome the new *theory of antiquity* which provides so *useful a model* for harmonious relations between this earth and the science of the future. (Michell 1972, 157 – italics added)

And yet . . . In 1982 Andy Collins spent a 'psychic quest' uncovering the site and nature of the Rev. Bazille-Corbin's 'Shrine of Our Lady of the Running Well' at Runwell (Essex). The well, on being rediscovered, was cleaned and restored and is currently visited each year on Boxing Day; in 1983 two hundred villagers took part in the procession, re-creating their communal identity anew by walking together and, so they might have thought, communing with their ancient pagan past (Bord 1985, 158). A *created* pagan past. Last laugh to the tricksters. And the historians.

147

ADDENDA

Christianity and Paganism, pp.1–2. In 745 St Boniface sent a report to the Vatican which was then discussed at the Synod of that year. This concerned a heretic named Aldebert who had formed what was to all intents and purposes a schismatical Church in the Low Countries and who was regarded by the people as a Saint. His churches and crosses were set up 'in the fields or near springs or wherever he had a mind' (Talbot 1954, 109–10). This is a most peculiar turn of phrase – we might expect roads or woods to be mentioned rather than springs – but it does not equip us to judge whether these were pagan wells.

Relevant to the conversion of wells on the Continent in the eighth century is the ornamental marble well-head of that date now in the Victoria and Albert Museum (accession number 1882:54), currently in Gallery 50. This hails from Murano, and is decorated with obviously Christian crosses.

Surveys, pp.4–6. A survey was planned for Lincolnshire by 'E.R.D.P.' in 1890–91. He argued that each parish probably had had a named well, and that names had to be recorded before they vanished from memory; but his appeal for information seems to have been met with silence, for nothing came of the project (*Lincs. Notes and Queries* ii (1890–91), 209). A proposed survey of Healing and Holy Wells of Bedfordshire in 1920 also had little visible consequence (*Pubs. of the Beds. Historical Record Soc.*, v (1920), 258).

Water Supply, p.99. The checking of the water supply was probably the origin of the annual Easter procession to St Anne's Well, Nottingham, held by civic dignitaries, accompanied by the town musicians and with a feast at the destination. Those who were charged with attending but failed to turn up were fined. The custom fell into abeyance in the Civil War (Morrell 1987, 7–8; Deering 1751, 125).

BIBLIOGRAPHY

This bibliography contains not only those works cited in the text, but also those used to compile general lists of wells for the distribution maps and so on, and those books which were used by Hope for his survey which I have been able to identify. As his work is usually the first stop for the well-enthusiast and his referencing system is idiosyncratic to say the least, this seemed a useful exercise.

ABRAM, W., 1877 *Parish of Blackburn, County of Lancashire*, Blackburn

ADAMS, J.C., 1951 *Hampton In Arden*, Birmingham

ADDISON, W., 1951 *English Spas*, London

ADELL, E., & J.D. Chambers, 1971 *The Story of Lincoln*, Wakefield

ALCOCK, L., 1971 *Arthur's Britain*, Harmondsworth

ALLIES, J., 1852 *On the Ancient British, Roman and Saxon Antiquities of Worcestershire*, Worcester

ANDERSON, A. & M., 1977 *Vanishing Spas*, Wimborne

ANDERSON, M. 1971 *History and Imagery in British Churches*, London

ANDREWS, H., 1915–22 'Rowney Priory', *East Herts. Arch. Soc. Trans.*

ANDREWS, W., 1892 *Bygone Derbyshire*, Derby

APPLEBY, N.W., 1910 'Folklore of the County of Durham', in H.R. Leighton ed., *Memorials of Old Durham*, London

ARMSTRONG, A., F. Mawer, F.M. Stenton & B. Dickens, 1950 *Place Names of Cumberland*, Cambridge

ARMAN, M., 1983 *A Short Historical Guide to the Ancient Town of Thaxted*, Thaxted

ARNOLD, T., 1880 *Memorials of St Edmund's Abbey*, London

ASTON, W., 1912 'Japanese Magic', *Folk-lore*

ATKINSON, J.C., 1861 *Forty Years in a Moorland Parish*, London

————, 1881, *The Whitby Cartulary*, Durham

AUBREY J., 1847 *The Natural History of Wiltshire*, ed. J. Britton, London

————, 1862 *Topographical Collections of John Aubrey*, ed. J. Jackson, London

————, 1881 *Remaines of Gentilisme and Judaisme*, ed. J. Britton, London

BAIGENT, F.C., 1891 *A Collection of Documents and Records relating to . . . Crondal*, London

BAILEY, C.J., 1982 *The Bride Valley*, Dorchester

BAINES, E., 1836 *History of the County Palatine and Duchy of Lancaster*, Lancaster

BAKER, E., 1929 'Weston Super Mare', *Procs. of Somerset Nat. Hist. and Arch. Soc.*

BAKER, M., 1988 *Folklore and Customs of Rural England*, London

BAKER, R., 1985 'Holy Wells and Magical Waters in Surrey', *Source 1*

BANKS, M., 1935 'Tangled Thread Mazes', *Folk-lore*

BARING-GOULD, S. & J. Fisher, 1907–13 *Lives of the British Saints*, London

BARKER, W.G.M.J., 1856 *Historical and Topographical Account of Wensleydale*, London

BARLEY, M.W., & R.P.C. Hanson, 1968 *Christianity in Britain 300–700*, Leicester

BARRETT, D.M., 1955–71 *Ecclesiastical Terriers of Warwickshire Parishes*, Oxford

BARTLETT, A.D., 1850 *Historical and Descriptive Account of Cumnore Place*, Oxford

BASCOMBE, K., 1973 'A Water Conduit Head at Wormley', *Herts. Archaeology X*

BEAUMONT, G.F., 1849 *Warrington in 1495*, Manchester

————, 1881 *An Account of the Ancient Town of Frodsham*, Warrington

————, 1890 *A History of Coggeshall*, Coggeshall

BECK, J., 1970 'The White Lady of Great Britain and Ireland', *Folklore*

BEDE, *Ecclesiastical History of the English People* – trans. L. Sherley-Price, London 1968; *Life of Cuthbert* – trans. J.F. Webb, London 1988

BEGG, E., 1985 *The Cult of the Black Virgin*, London

BENTLEY, R., 1978 *Ritualism and Politics in Victorian Britain*, Oxford

BERLYN, A., 1930 *Bishops Stortford and Its Story*

BIDDLE, M., 1969 'Interim Report on Old Minster, Winchester', *Antiq. Journ.*

BIGSBY, R., 1854 *Historical and Topographical Description of Repton*, London

BINNAL, P., 1940, 'Holy Wells in Derbyshire', *Derbys. Arch. and Nat. Hist. Soc. Journ.*

————, 1944–5, 'Some Theories Regarding Eye-Wells', *Folk-lore*

BIRCH, W. de G., 1881 *Memorials of St Guthlac*, Wisbech

BIRKBECK, J.D., 1976 *History of Bourne*, Bourne

BLACKBURN, T., 1975 *December's Child: A Book of Chumash Oral Narrative*, Berkeley

BLACKER, J., 1984 'The Exiled Warrior and the Hidden Village', *Folklore*

BLAIR, J., 1985, 'Identification of Secular Minsters in Domesday Book', in P. Sawyer ed., *Domesday Book Reconsidered*, Oxford

————, 1987, 'St Frideswide Reconsidered', *Oxoniensia*

————, 1988a, 'Eynsham as a Central Place in Anglo-Saxon Oxfordshire', *Eynsham Record*

————, 1988b, 'Minster Churches in the Landscape', in D. Hooke ed., *Anglo-Saxon Settlements*, Oxford

————, 1988c, *Minsters and Parish Churches*, Oxford

————, 1990, *Ecclesiastical Topography, Bampton Research Paper 3*, Bampton

BLAIR, P.H., 1977 *Anglo-Saxon England*, Cambridge

BLAKE, E.D., 1981 *The Cartulary of the Priory of St Denis, Southampton*, 1981

BOASE, F., 1887 *Historic Towns: Oxford*, London

BOND, C., & Tillar, K., 1987 *Blenheim, Landscape for a Palace*

BOND, F., 1914 *Dedications and Patron Saints of English Parish Churches*, London

BONNER, G., 1989 *St Cuthbert and His Community*, Woodbridge

BONNEY, D., 1979 'Early Boundaries and Estates in Southern England', in P. Sawyer ed., *English Medieval Settlement*, London

BONSER, W., 1926 'Dissimilarity of Ancient Irish Magic from that of the Anglo-Saxons', *Folk-lore*

BORD, J. & C., 1985 *Sacred Waters*, London

BOSTON, N., & Puddy, E., 1952 *Dereham, the Biography of a Country Town*, Dereham

BOWCOCK, E., 1923 *Shropshire Place Names*, Shrewsbury

BRAND, J., 1777 *Observations On Popular Antiquities*, Newcastle

————, 1789 *History and Antiquities of Newcastle*, London

————, 1812 *Observations on Popular Antiquities* ed. J. Ellis, London

BRANSTON, B., 1974 *The Lost Gods of England*, London

BRIGGS, K., 1974 *Folklore of the Cotswolds*, London

BRIGHTING, G., 1872 *Some Particulars Relating to the History and Antiquities of Carshalton*, London

BROADHURST, P., 1988 *Secret Shrines: In Search of the old Holy Wells of Cornwall*, Tintagel

BRODIE, W., 1886 *Legends and Superstitions of the County of Durham*, Sunderland

BROOK, R. & C., 1984 *Popular Religion in the Middle Ages*, London

BROOKES, C.C., 1929 *A History of Steeple Aston and Middle Aston*, Shipston on Stour

BROOKS, N., 1970 *The Early History of the Church at Canterbury*, Leicester

BROWN, B., & Loosey, J., 1982 *The Book of Portishead*, Buckingham

BROWN, J., & N. Guest, 1935 *A History of Thame*, Thame

BROWN, P., 1987 'Holy Well, St Michael's Churchyard, Longstanton', *Source* 7

BROWN, R., 1908 *Notes on the Early History of Barton on Humber*, London

BROWN, T., 1957–60, 1963, 1966, 1975, 'Holy and Notable Wells of Devon', *Trans. Devonshire Association* for those dates

————, 1958 'The Black Dog', *Folklore*

————, 1982 *Devon Ghosts*, Norwich

BROWN, W., ed., 1894 *The Cartulary of Guisborough*, Durham

BRUCE, J., 1968 *Manx Archaeological Survey IV*

BURGESS, W., 1876 *Historic Warwickshire*, London

BURKERT, W., 1985 *Greek Religion*, Oxford

BURNE, C.S., 1888 *Shropshire Folklore*

————, 1910 'Occult Powers of Healing in the Punjab', *Folk-lore*

BUSHAWAY, R., 1982 *By Rite: Custom, Ceremony and Community 1700–1880*, London

BUSHBY, G., 1928–33 'The Holy Springs of Waltham Abbey at Wormley', *East Herts. Arch. Soc. Trans.*

BUTCHER, R., 1660 *The Survey and Antiquitie of the Towne of Stamford*, London

BUTLER, L.A., 1986 'Church Dedications and the Cults of Anglo-Saxon Saints', in L.A. Butler & R. Morris eds., *The Anglo-Saxon Church*, London

CALDER, J.E., 1986 *History of Eggington*, London

CALVERLEY, W., 1894–5 'A Pre Norman Cross-Shaft at Heversham', *Trans. of the Cumb. & Westd. Arch. & Antiq. Soc.*

CAMDEN, W., 1695 *Britannia*, London

CAMERON, Cmdr., 1877 *Across Africa*

CAMERON, K., 1959 *Place Names of Derbyshire*, Cambridge

————, 1985, 1991 *Place Names of Lincolnshire I & II*, Cambridge

CANTERBURY Archaeological Trust, 1982 *Topographical Maps of Canterbury*, Canterbury

CAREY, J., 1983 'Irish Parallels to the Myth of Odin's Eye', *Folklore*

CARMINA BURANA, ed. C. Fischer, H. Kuhn, G. Bernt, Zurich & Munchen 1974

CARMICHAEL, A., 1988, E. de Waal ed., *The Celtic Vision*, London [Carmina Gadelica]

CAROE, W., & E. Gordon, 1893, *Sefton, a Description and Historical Account*, London

CATER, J., 1892 *Bisley Bits: Or, Records of a Surrey Corner*, London

CHAFY, W.K.W., 1901 *A Short History of Rous Lench*, Evesham

CHAPMAN, V., 1958–65 'The Fields of Bolam', *Trans. of the Arch. & Archit. Soc. of Northd. & Durham*

CHARLTON, L., 1779 *History of Whitby and Whitby Abbey*, York

CHENINGTON, A.C., 1968 *Shenington: Fiefs and Fields of a Buckinghamshire Village*, Cambridge

CHILDREY, J., 1661 *Britannica Baconica*, London

CHRISTY, M., & M. Thrush, 1910 *Mineral Waters and Medicinal Springs of Essex*, Stratford

CLACK, P., 1985 *The Book of Durham City*, Buckingham

CLARK, S., 1986 'The Conisbrough Holy Well', *Source 5*

CLARK, S., & P. Morgan, 1976 'Religion and Magic in Elizabethan Wales', *Journ. Eccl. Hist.*

CLARKE, J., 1787, *Survey of the Lakes of Cumberland, Westmorland and Lancashire*, London

CLARKE, D., & Stoyell, A., 1975 *Otford in Kent: A History*, Otford

CLARKE, K., 1962, *The Gothic Revival: An Essay in the History of Taste*, London

CLEAVER, A., 1985, 'A Marlow Well', *Source 1*

————, 1989, note on Rebra's Well, Crazies Hill

COATES, R., 1989 *Place Names of Hampshire*, London

COKER, J., 1732 *A Survey of Dorsetshire*, London

COLLEY MARCH, H., 1899 'Dorset Folklore Collected in 1897', *Folk-lore*

COLLINGWOOD, W., 1894–5 'Some Manx Names in Cumberland', *Trans. of the Cumb. & Westd. Arch. & Archit. Soc.*

————, 1932 *The Lake Counties*, London

COLLINS, A., 1983 *The Running Well Mystery*, Wickford

COLLINSON, J., 1791 *The History of Somersetshire*, Bath

COOK, A., 1905 'The European Sky God iii: the Italians', *Folk-lore*

COOKE, A.S., 1911 *Off the Beaten Track in Sussex*, Hove

COOPER, W., 1940 *History of Lillington*, Long Compton

COOPER, W.D., 1850 *History of Winchelsea*, Hastings

CORBETT, E., 1929, 'Scraps of English Folklore: Oxfordshire', *Folk-lore*

————, 1962, *A History of Spelsbury*, Banbury

CORDNER, W., 1940, 1942 'Some Old Wells in Antrim and Down', *Ulster Journ. of Arch.*

COX, J., 1875–9 *Notes on the Churches of Derbyshire*, Chesterfield

COX, J., 1982 *The English Churches in a Secular Society*, Oxford

CRANAGE, D.H.S., 1897 *An Architectural Account of the Churches of Shropshire*, Wellington

CRAMP, R.J., 1984 *Corpus of Anglo-Saxon Stone Sculpture I*, London

CROCKFORD'S Clerical Directory

CROOK, J.M., 1968 *The Greek Revival*, Feltham

CRYER, L.R., 1978 *A History of Rochford*, Chichester

CULLUM, J., 1893 *History and Antiquities of Hardwick and Hampstead*

CUNNINGTON, M.E., 1916 in *Wiltshire Magazine* vol. 35

CUPITT D., 1984 *The Sea of Faith*, London

CUTTS, E.L., 1888 *Historic Towns: Colchester*, London

DALE, M.K., 1950 *Court Roll of Chalgrave Manor*, Streatley

DAMES, M., 1902 'Balochi Folklore', *Folk-lore*

DANIELL, J.J., 1874 *History of Warminster*, Warminster

————, 1894 *History of Chippenham*, Chippenham

DANIELS, R., 1987 'Hartlepool', *Current Archaeology* (August)

DARBY, H., & Welldon Finn, J., 1967 *The Domesday Geography of South-western England*, Cambridge

DARLINGTON, R.R., 1948 *Cartulary of Dawley Abbey*, Kendal

DARWEN, N., 1988a, 'Becket's Well, Otford, Kent, *Source 9*

————, 1988b, 'Some Holy Wells in and Around Preston', *Source 8*

DAVIDSON, H., 1958–9 'Weyland the Smith', *Folklore*

DAVID-TYSSEN, J., 1872 'Parliamentary Surveys of the County of Sussex', *Sussex Arch. Colls.*

DAVIES, C.S., 1961 *A History of Macclesfield*, Manchester

DAVIES, P., 1989 *Troughs and Drinking Fountains*, London
DAVIES, J., 1918 'Breton Folklore', *Folk-lore*
DAVIS, K.R., 1982 *Britons and Saxons: the Chiltern Region*, Chichester
DEEDES, C., 1913 *Register or Memorial of Ewell*, London
DEERING, C., 1751 *Nottinghamia Vetus et Nova*, Nottingham
DEVEREUX, P., & Thompson, I., 1976 *The Ley-Hunter's Companion*, London
DEW, J., 1932 *Diocese of Hereford, Extracts from the Cathedral Registers*, Hereford
DICKENS, A.G., 1959 *Lollards and Protestants in the Diocese of York*, Hull
DICKINSON, W., 1819 *History and Antiquities of the Town of Southwell*, London
DICKONS, J., 1908 'Kirkgate Chapel, Bradford', *Bradford Antiquary*
DICTIONARY *of National Biography*
DIMOCKE, J., ed., 1864 *Magna Vita Sancti Hugonis*, London
DIXON, J., 1881 *Stories and Chronicles of the Craven Dales*, London
DOAN, J., 1980 'Five Breton Cantiques from Pardons', *Folklore*
DOBLE, G., 1942–3 'Hagiography and Folklore', *Folk-lore*
DODGSON, J., 1970–81 *Place Names of Cheshire*, Cambridge
DORSON, R., 1962 *Folklore of Japan*, Tokyo
DOVASTON, A., 1886 'Woolston Well', *Trans. of the Salop. Arch. and Nat. Hist. Soc.*
DREW, J.S., 1939 *Compton Near Winchester*, Winchester
DRINKWATER, C., 1910 'The Well of St Chad's College, Shrewsbury', *Trans. of the Salop. Arch. and Nat. Hist. Soc.*
DUIGNAN, W., 1902 *Notes on Staffordshire Placenames*, London
DUNCAN, L., 1893, 'Folklore Gleanings from County Leitrim', *Folk-lore*
DUNCAN, L.L., & Hussey, A., 1906–7, *Testimenta Cantiana*, London
DUNCAN, P., 1795, *History of Lewis and Brythelmstone*, Brighton
DUNLOP, G.D., 1940 *Pages from the History of Highclere*, Oxford
DYER, T., 1876 *British Popular Customs*, London
EARLES, A.R.T., 1922 *A Lecture on the History of Elstree*, London
EDDIUS STEPHANUS, *Life of Wilfrid*, ed., J.F. Webb, 1965
EDMUNDS, F., 1928 *The Wells and Springs of Sussex*, London
EDWARDS, E., 1866 *The Book of the Monastery of Hyde*, London
EKWALL, E., 1922 *The Place Names of Lancashire*, Manchester
————, 1961, *The Oxford Dictionary of English Placenames*, Oxford
ETTLINGER, E., 1942–3 'Documents of British Superstition in Oxford', *Folk-lore*
d'EVELYN, C., & Mills, A.J., eds., 1856 *The South English Legendary*, London
EVERITT, A., 1986 *Continuity and Colonization*, Leicester
FARMER, D.H., 1987 *The Oxford Dictionary of Saints*, Oxford
FARRER, W., 1898 *The Cartulary of Cockersand Abbey*, Manchester
FAUSET, A.H., 1931 *Folklore of Nova Scotia*, New York
FAWCETT, R., 1976 'The Story of Wilsden', *Bradford Antiquary*

FELL, C., 1984 *Women in Anglo-Saxon England*, London

FERNIE, E., 1983 *The Architecture of the Anglo-Saxons*, London

FIELD, J., 1972 *English Field-Names, a Dictionary*, Gloucester

FINBERG, H.P.R., 1962 *West Country Historical Studies*, London

FINNUCANE, R., 1977 *Miracles and Shrines*

FISHNICK, H., 1879 *History of the Parish of Garstang*, Manchester

FITCH, E., 1988 *Unknown Taplow*, Windsor

FLETCHER, A., 1981 *The Outbreak of the English Civil War*, London

FOORD, A., 1910 *Springs, Streams and Spas of London*, London

FOSTER, J., 1896–7 'Notes on the History of Exning, Cambs.', *Cambs. Antiq. Soc. Commns. and Reports*

FOWLER, J.K., 1911 *A History of Beaulieu Abbey*, London

FOWLER, J.T., 1878 *The Newminster Cartulary*, Durham

————, 1882 *Memorials of the Church of St Peter and St Wilfrid, Ripon*, Durham

————, 1896–1905 'The Galilee Well at Durham', *Trans. Archit. and Arch. Soc. of Northd. and Durham*

FOWLES, J., & Draper, J., 1984 *Thomas Hardy's England*, London

FOX, C., 1956 'The siting of the Monastery of St Mary and St Peter in Exeter', in D.B. Harden ed., *Dark Age Britain*, London

FRERE, S.S., 1976 'Sites Explored', *Britannia*

FRETTON, W.G., *Waters of the Arden*, Coventry

FRY, D., 1953–4, 'St John's Well', *Hertfordshire Countryside*, (Winter 1953–4)

FRY, K., 1888 *History of the Parishes of East and West Ham*, London

GALE, J., 1900 'Korean Beliefs', *Folk-lore*

GAMMON, F.S., 1934 *The Story of Keston in Kent*, London

GANTZEL, D.H., 1987 *Hazlemere*, High Wycombe

G.A.W., 1830 *The Well of Roan*, Richmond

GAYTHORPE, F., 1985 'A Hertfordshire Lady Well', *Source* 2

GEESON, C., c.1920 *A Short History of Kelloe and District*, Kelloe

GELLING, M., 1953–4 *Place Names of Oxfordshire*, Cambridge

————, 1973–4 *Place Names of Berkshire*, Cambridge

————, 1978 *Signposts to the Past*, London

————, 1979 'The Evidence of Place Names', in P. Sawyer ed., *English Medieval Settlement*, London

GELLING, M., & Foxall, H., 1990 *Place Names of Shropshire I*, Cambridge

GENT, 1730 *History of York*

GEOFFREY of Monmouth, *History of the Kings of Britain*, ed. L. Thorpe, 1966, Harmondsworth

GERVERS, M., ed., 1982 *Cartulary of the Knights of St John . . . Essex*, Oxford

GILES, J., 1848 *A History of the Town and Parish of Bampton*, Bampton

GLOVER, S., 1829 *History of the County of Derbyshire*, Derby

GODBER, J.C., 1963 *Cartulary of Newnham Priory*, Streatley

GODDARD, C.V., 1942 'Holy Wells', *Wiltshire Magazine*

GOMME, A.B., 1894 *Children's Singing Games*
GOOD, R., 1982 *The Lost Villages of Dorset*, Stanbridge
GOODCHILD & Kirk, 1954 'A Romano-British Temple at Islip', *Oxoniensia*
GOUGH, R., 1981 *History of Myddle*, ed. D. Hey, Harmondsworth
GOVER, J., A. Mawer & F.M. Stenton 1929–30, *Place Names of Sussex*, Cambridge
————, 1933 *Place Names of Northamptonshire*, Cambridge
————, 1934 *Place Names of Surrey*, Cambridge
————, 1936 *Place Names of Warwickshire*, Cambridge (with F. Houghton)
————, 1938 *Place Names of Hertfordshire*, Cambridge
————, 1940 *Place Names of Nottinghamshire*, Cambridge
————, 1942 *Place Names of Middlesex*, Cambridge (with S. Madge)
————, 1943 *Place Names of Wiltshire*, Cambridge
GRAEF, H., 1963–5 *Mary, a Study in Doctrine and Devotion*
GRAINGE, W., 1849 *The Vale of Mowbray*, London
GRAVES, J., 1808 *The History of Cleveland*, Carlisle
GRAVES, R., 1961 *The White Goddess*, London
GRAY, A., 1898 *The Priory of St Radegund*, Cambridge
————, 1925 *The Town of Cambridge*, Cambridge
GRAY, H. St J., 1908 *Report on the Excavations at Wick Barrow*, Taunton
GREEN, A.H., 1974 *Our Haunted Kingdom*, London
GREENWELL, W., ed., 1852 *Boldon Buke*, Durham
GREGOR, W., 1891 'The Guardian Spirits of Lakes and Wells', *Folk-lore*
GRESSWELL, W.P., 1903 *The Land of Quantock*, Taunton
GRIFFITHS, G., 1894 *A History of Tong*, Newport
GRINSELL, L.V., 1984 'Popular Names and Folklore of Prehistoric Sites in Menorca', *Folklore*
————, 1986 'The Christianization of Pagan Sites', *Landscape History*
GROVE, W., 1898 *History of Mansfield*, Nottingham
GRUNDY, G.B., 1919, 'Saxon Land Charters of Wiltshire', *Arch. Journ.*
————, 1935 *Saxon Land Charters of Somerset*, Taunton
GUEST, E., 1937 'Ballyvourney and Its Sheelanagig', *Folk-lore*
GURDON, E.C., 1893 *County Folklore: Suffolk*, London
GURNEY, F.C., 1920 'Yettingdon and the Tenth-Century Bounds of Chalgrave and Linslade', *Publications of the Bedfordshire Historical and Record Society*
HACKWOOD, F.W., 1906 *Annals of Willenhall*, Wolverhampton
————, 1915 *Oldbury and Round About*, Wolverhampton
HADDAN, A.W., & Stubbs, W., 1869–78 *Councils and Ecclesiastical Documents*, Oxford
HAGERTY, R., 1985 'The Buckinghamshire Saints Reconsidered: St Firmin of Crawley', *Records of Bucks.*
HAILSTONE, E., 1898 *History and Antiquities of the Parish of Bottisham*, Cambridge
HALL, G.R., 1880 'Notes on Modern Survivals of Ancient Well-Worship in North Tynedale', *Archaeologia Aeliana*, N.S.8

HALL, H., 1960 *Lindfield Past and Present*, Haywards Heath

HALL, T., 1661 *Flora Floralia; Or, the Downfall of May-Games*, London

HALL, C.P., & Ravensdale, J.R., eds., 1976 *The West Fields of Cambridge*, Cambridge

HALLEY, R., 1869 *Lancashire: Its Protestantism and Nonconformity*, Manchester

HALLIDAY, W., 1912 'Folklore Scraps from Greece and Asia Minor', *Folk-lore*

HAMILTON, P.J., 1927 'Puerto Rican Folklore', *Folk-lore*

HAMMERSON, M., 1978 'Excavations under Southwark Cathedral', *London Archaeologist* III

HANNA, K.A., 1989 *Cartularies of Southwick Priory*, Winchester

HARDY, J., ed., 1891 *The Denham Tracts*, London

HARDY, P., 1836 *The Holy Wells of Ireland*, Dublin

HARKE, F., 1990 'Warrior Graves? The Anglo-Saxon Weapon Burial Rite', *Past and Present*

HARRIS, J., 1972 *Unemployment and Politics*, Oxford

HARRIS, W., 1930–33, 'Excavation of the Romano-British Well at Thatcham Newton', *Trans. of the Newbury and Dist. Fd. Club*

HARRIS, M.D., & Huggins, J.E., 1924 *Unknown Warwickshire*, London

HART, W., ed., 1863 *History and Cartulary of the Abbey of St Peter, Gloucester*, London

HARTE, J., 1985, 'Dorset Holy Wells', *Source 1*

————, 1986 *Cuckoo Pounds and Singing Barrows*, Dorchester

HARTLAND, E., 1893 'Pin Wells and Rag Bushes', *Folk-lore*

HARTNETT, P.J., 1947 'Holy Wells of East Muskerry, County Cork', *Journ. of the Cork Hist. and Arch. Soc.*

HARVEY, W., 1872–3 *History of the Hundred of Willey*, London

HARWELL MILLENNIUM BOOK COMMITTEE, 1985 *Harwell, Village for a Thousand Years*, Harwell

HARWOOD, T., 1806 *History and Antiquities of the Church and City of Lichfield*, London

HASLAM, J., ed., 1984 *Anglo-Saxon Towns in Southern England*, London

HASSALL, W.O., 1949 *Cartulary of St Mary's Clerkenwell*, London

HASTED, E., 1797–1801 *History and Topographical Survey of Kent*, Canterbury

HAWKINS, *History of Middlesex*

HAYNES, T., 1987 'Well-wishing in St Albans', *Source 6*

HEARNE, T., 1914 *Remarks and Collections of Thomas Hearne*, ed. A. Salter, Oxford

HEIGHWAY, C., 1987 *Anglo-Saxon Gloucestershire*, Gloucester

HEWITSON, A., 1872 *Our Country Churches and Chapels*, Preston

HIGDEN, R., 1865–82 *Polychronicon*, ed. C.R. Babington & J.R. Lumby, London

HILL, C., 1963, 'Puritans and the Dark Corners of the Land', *Trans. of the Royal Hist. Soc.*

————, 1975 *The World Turned Upside Down*, Harmondsworth

HILL, J., 1948 *Medieval Lincoln*, Cambridge

HILL, R.M.T., ed., 1954, 1969 *Rolls and Register of Bishop Oliver Sutton*, Lincoln

HILL, S., 1907 *Bygone Stalybridge*, Stalybridge

HILLGARTH, J., 1986 *Christianity and Paganism*, Philadelphia

HINGESTON-RANDOLPH, H.C., ed., 1886–1915 *Register of Bishop Grandisson*, Exeter

HINRELLS, J., 1975 *Mithraic Studies*, Manchester

HINTON, D.A., 1987 'Minsters in Southeast Dorset', *Procs. of the Dorset Arch. and Nat. Hist. Soc.*

HOBBS, J.L., 1954 *Shrewsbury Place Names*, Shrewsbury

HOBSON, M., & Price, K., n.d. *Otmoor and Its Seven Towns*

HOCKEY, S.F., 1974 *The Beaulieu Cartulary*, Southampton

————, 1981 *The Cartulary of Carisbrooke Priory*, Carisbrooke

HODGSON, G.F., 1903 *The Borough of South Shields*, Newcastle

HODGSON, J., 1813 *Topographical and Historical Description of Northumberland*, London

HOGAN, J., 1873–4 'Patron Days and Holy Wells in Ossory', *Journ. of the Antiq. Assoc. of Ireland*

HOLE, C., 1940 *English Folklore*, London

————, 1966 *The Saint in Folklore*, London

————, 1980 *Witchcraft in Britain*, London

HOLLAND, E., 1927 'Some Notes on Weston-under-Penyard', *Transactions of the Woolhope Society*

HONE, W., 1826–7 *The Every Day Book*, London

————, 1831 *The Table Book*, London

HOLLAND, E., 1927 'Some Notes on Weston-Under Penyard', *Trans. of the Woolhope Soc.*

HOPE, R.C., 1893 *The Legendary Lore of the Holy Wells of England*, London

HOPE-TAYLOR, B., 1977 *Yeavering – An Anglo-British Centre of Early Northumbria*

HORACE, *Odes*

HORNE, E., 1923 *Somerset Holy Wells*, London

HORSBOROUGH, E.L.S., 1871 *Bromley, Kent*, London

HOWES, H., 1926, 'St Walstan, a Norfolk Popular Saint', *Folk-lore*

————, 1927, 'Gallegan Folklore', *Folk-lore*

'H.Tr', 1853 *Description of Cleveland*, London

HUBERT, J., 1977 'Sources Sacrees et Sources Saintes', *Memoriales Publiees par la Societe de l'Ecole des Chartes*, Geneva

HUDSON, A., 1988 *The Premature Reformation*, Oxford

HUGHES, J., 1988 'Caesar's Well, Wimbledon Common', *Source 9*

HUNNISET, R.F., 1961 *Bedfordshire Coroners' Rolls*, Streatley

HUNT, L., 1987 'Ancient Healing and Holy Wells of County Durham', *Source 7*

————, 1988, 'Some Ancient and Holy Wells of Devon', *Source 9*

HURST, D.E., 1868 *Horsham, Its History and Antiquities*

HURST, H., 1899 *Oxford Topography*, Oxford

HUTCHINS, J., 1861–70 *History and Antiquities of the County of Dorset*, Westminster

HUTCHINSON, W., 1794 *History of the County of Cumberland*, Carlisle

HUTTON, J., 1987 'The Local Impact of the Tudor Reformation', in C. Haigh ed., *The English Reformation Reconsidered*, London

HUTTON, W., 1783 *The History of Birmingham*, Birmingham

IGGLESDEN, C., 1927–8 *A Saunter Through Kent with Pen and Pencil*, Ashford

INGLIS, K.I., 1963 *The Church and the Working Classes in Victorian England*, London

IRVINE, P., 1989 'The Goddess at the Well'; 'Saints and Spas', *Dorset County Magazine* Apr & May 1989

JACKSON, A., ed., 1977 *Ashtead, A Village Transformed*, Leatherhead

JACKSON, C., 1877 *Yorkshire Diaries and Autobiographies*, Durham

————, 1916 *Place Names of Durham*, London

JACKSON, J.E., 1854 'Leland's Journey Through Wiltshire', *Wiltshire Arch. Magazine*

JACKSON, W., 1874–5 'The Richmonds of Highhead', *Trans. of the Cumbd. and Westd. Arch. and Antiq. Soc.*

————, 1876-7 'Whitehaven', *Trans. of the Cumbd. and Westd. Arch. and Antiq. Soc.*

JAMES, M., 1986 *Society, Politics and Culture*, Cambridge

JARRETT, D., 1988 *The Sleep of Reason*, London

JENKINS, J.G., ed., 1952 *Cartulary of Snelshall Priory*, Buckingham

————, 1962 *Cartulary of Missenden Abbey*, London

JOHNSTON, E., 1959 'A Roman Well at Exning', *Procs. of the Cambs. Arch. Soc.*

JOHNSTON, G.D., 1968–71 'Perambulation of the Parish of Ringmer', *Sussex Notes and Queries*

JONES, E., 1885, 'Historical Records of the Borough of Newport', *Trans. of the Salop Arch. and Nat. Hist. Soc.*

JONES, F., 1954 *Holy Wells of Wales*, Cardiff

JONES, G., 1986, 'Holy Wells and the Cult of St Helen', *Landscape History*

JONES, W., 1872, 'Customs of the Manor of Taunton Deane', *Procs. of the Somerset Arch. and Nat. Hist. Soc.*

JONES, W.H., 1882 'A Stroll Through Bradford On Avon', *Wiltshire Magazine*

JONES-BAKER, D., 1977 *Folklore of Hertfordshire*, London

JOPE, E.M., 1961 *Studies in Building History*

JORDAN, K., 1857 *Parochial History of Enstone*, Enstone

JUVENAL, *Satires*

KAYE, J.M., 1976 *Cartulary of God's House, Southampton*, Southampton

KEEF, D.C., 1939 'Some Downland Springs and Villages', *Sussex County Magazine*

KEENE, D., 1985 *Survey of Medieval Winchester*, Oxford

KELKE, W., 1859 'Master John Schorne, the Marston Saint', *Records of Bucks.*

KERMODE, P., 1909–18 *Manx Archaeological Survey I–V*

KELWAY, L.C., ed., 1908 *Memorials of Old Essex*, London

KNIGHTS, M., 1887 *Highways and Byways of Old Norwich*, Norwich

————, 1892 *Peeps at the Past, or Rambles Through Norfolk Antiquities*, London

KNOWLES, D., 1950 *The Religious Order in England*, Cambridge

————, 1951 'The Censured Opinions of Uthred of Baldon', *Procs. of the British Academy*

KNOWLES, D., & Hadcock, K., 1971 *Medieval Religious Houses of England and Wales*, London

KOEDER C., & Graves, F., 1905 'Recent Archaeological Discoveries at Alderley Edge', *Trans. of the Lancs. and Chesh. Antiq. Soc.*

KOKERITZ, H., 1940 *Place Names of the Isle of Wight*, Uppsala

KUPER, M., 1889–90 'Field Name Survivals in Dalston', *Trans. of the Cumbd. and Westd. Arch. and Antiq. Soc.*

LADURIE, E. le Roy, 1980 *Montaillou, Catholics and Cathars in a French Village*, Harmondsworth

LAMBERT, M.D., 1977 *Medieval Heretics*, London

LAMBERT, U., 1929 *Godstone: A Parish History*, Godstone

LAROUSSE Encyclopaedia of Mythology

LAUGHLIN, R.M., 1977 *Tales from Zinacantan*, Washington

LAWSON, R., 1898 *A History of Flixton, Urmston and Davyhulme*, Urmston

LEATHER, H., 1912 *Folklore of Herefordshire*, Hereford

LEGG, R., 1987 *Mysterious Dorset*, Milborne Port

LEGGATT, P. & H., 1987 *The Healing Wells, Cornish Cults and Customs*, Redruth

LEIGH, C., 1700 *Natural History of Lancashire, Cheshire and the Peak, Derbyshire*, Oxford

LEIGH, E., 1867 *Ballads and Legends of Cheshire*, London

LELAND, J., 1913 *Itinerary*, ed. J. Toulmin Smith, London

LETHBRIDGE, T.C., 1961 *Ghost and Ghoul*, London

LIVEING, H.G.D., 1966 *Records of Romsey Abbey*, Winchester

LLOYD, P., 1988 *Legends of Dorset*, St Teath

LOGAN, P., 1980 *The Holy Wells of Ireland*, Gerrards Cross

LONGSTAFF, W.G.D., 1854 *History and Antiquities of the Parish of Darlington*, Darlington

LOWNDES, W., 1955 *The Story of Bebington*, Bebington

LUCAN, *De Bello Civilis*

LUCAS, J., *Topographical Description of the Parish of Warton*, Kendal

LUKIS, W.C., ed., 1883 *Stukeley's Letters and Diaries*, Durham

LYON, W., 1895 *Chronicles of Finchampstead*, London

LYSON, D., 1806 *Magna Britannia*, London

MacCALL, H.B., 1910 *Richmondshire Churches*, London

MacCRAY, W.D., ed., 1863 *Chronicle of the Abbey of Evesham*, London

MacCULLOCH, E., 1903 *Folklore of Guernsey*

McINTIRE, W., 1944 'Holy Wells of Cumberland', *Trans. of the Cumbd. and Westd. Arch. and Antiq. Soc.*

McKAY, S.G., 1988 *Milborne Port in Somerset*

MacKENZIE, D., 1907 'Children and Wells', *Folk-lore*

MacKENZIE, J., 1984 *Propaganda and Empire*, Manchester

MacKINNON, D.D., 1930 *History of Speldhurst*, Speldhurst

MacLEOD, F., 1906 'History of Chirbury', *Trans. of the Salop Arch. and Nat. Hist. Soc.*

MacPHAIL, M., 1900 'Folklore of the Hebrides', *Folk-lore*

MANNING, B., 1978 *The English People and the English Revolution*, Harmondsworth

MANNING, O., & Bray, P., 1809 *History and Antiquities of the County of Surrey*, London

MARGRETT, E., 1906 'St Anne's Well and Chapel, Caversham', *Berks. Bucks. & Oxon. Arch. Journ.*

————, 1908 'The Old Conduit at Whitley, Reading', *Berks. Bucks and Oxon. Arch. Journ.*

MARSDEN, F., 1932 'Folklore of Upper Calderdale', *Folk-lore*

MARTIN, M., 1934 *A Description of the Western Isles of Scotland*, ed. J. MacLeod, Stirling

MARTIN, V., 1985 'Holy Wells in Kent', *Source 2*

MARTYROLOGY of Tallaght

MATHER, F., 1985 'Georgian Churchmanship Reconsidered', *Journ. of Eccl. Hist.*

MATTHEWS, C., 1989 *The Celtic Tradition*, Shaftesbury

MAWER, A., 1920 *Place Names of Northumberland and Durham*, Cambridge

MAWER, A., & Stenton, F.M., 1925 *Place Names of Buckinghamshire*, Cambridge

————, 1926 *Place Names of Bedfordshire and Huntingdonshire*, Cambridge

————, 1927 *Place Names of Worcestershire*, Cambridge (with F.S. Houghton)

MAXWELL-LYTE, H.C., 1909 *History of Dunster*, London

MAXWELL-LYTE, H.C., & Dawes, M.C.B., eds., 1934 *The Register of Thomas Bekynton*, Taunton

MAY, G., 1834 *History of Evesham*, Evesham

MEADE, D., 1968 'Hospital of St Giles at Kepier', *Trans. of the Archit. and Arch. Soc. of Northd. and Durham*

————, 1970 'The Medieval Parish of St Giles, Durham', *Trans. of the Archit. and Arch. Soc. of Northd. and Durham*

MEADE, J., 1856, 'Castle Cary', *Procs. of the Somerset Arch. and Nat. Hist. Soc.*

MEANEY, A.L., 1964 *A Gazetteer of Early Anglo-Saxon Burial Sites*, London

————, 1981 *Anglo-Saxon Amulets, Charms and Curing Stones*, Banbury

MEEKINGS, C.A.F., & Sherman, P., eds., 1906 *Fitzwells Cartulary*, Guildford

MERRIFIELD, R., 1987 *The Archaeology of Ritual and Magic*, London

MEYRICK, J., 1982 *A Pilgrim's Guide to the Holy Wells of Cornwall and their Saints*, Falmouth

MICHELL, J., 1982 *Megalithomania*, London

MIDDLETON, T., 1932 *History of Hyde and Neighbourhood*, Hyde

MILLS, A.D., 1977, 1980, 1989 *Place Names of Dorset I–III*, Cambridge

————, 1986 *Dorset Place Names*, Wimborne

MITCHELL, T.C., 1893 'St Alkelda of Middleham', *Yorkshire Archaeological Journal*

MONEY, W., 1892 *History of Speen*, Newbury

MONTELIUS, O., 1910 'The Sun God's Axe and Thor's Hammer', *Folk-lore*

MOORE, A., 1894 'Water and Well-worship in Man', *Folk-lore*

MORGAN, W., 1924 'A Few Folk and Other Stories', *Trans. of the Woolhope Club*

MORRELL, R.W., 1987, *St Ann's Well and Other Medicinal and Holy Wells of Nottingham*, Nottingham

————, 1988 *Nottinghamshire Holy Wells and Springs*, Nottingham

MORRIS, J., 1973 *The Age of Arthur*, London

MORRIS, R., 1989 *Churches in the Landscape*, London

MORRIS, R. & F., 1981 *Scottish Healing Wells*, Sandy

MORRIS, S., 1987 *A History of Portland*, Stanbridge

MORRIS, W., 1971 *Swindon, Reminiscences, Notes and Relics*, London

MORSE, A., 1925 'Scraps of English Folklore: Norfolk', *Folk-lore*

MORTIMER, R., 1979 *Leiston Abbey Cartulary and Butley Priory Charters*, Woodbridge

MUMBY, G.W., 1908 *Former Days at Turvey*, London

MURGOCI, A. & H., 1929 'The Devil in Roumanian Folklore', *Folk-lore*

MUSSET, L., 1975 *The Germanic Invasions*, London

MYLONAS, G., 1961 *Eleusis and the Eleusian Mysteries*, Princeton

MYRES, J.N.L., 1989 *The English Settlements*, Oxford

NASH, T.R., 1781–2 *Notes Towards a History of Worcestershire*, London

NATHAN, M., 1957 *Annals of West Coker*, Cambridge

NAYLOR, P.J., 1983 *Ancient Wells and Springs of Derbyshire*, Cromford

NEALE, J., 1957 *Elizabeth and Her Parliaments*, London

NEWCOMBE, P., 1795 *History of the Abbey of St Albans*, London

NEWMAN, L., & Wilson, E., 1952–3 'Folklore Survivals in the Southern Lake Counties and in Essex', *Folk-lore*

NIBBS, R.H., & Lower, M.A., 1872 *Churches of Sussex*, Brighton

NICHOLLS & Taylor, 1872 *Bristol Past and Present*, Bristol

NICHOLS, J., 1795 *History and Antiquities of the County of Leicester*, London

NICHOLSON, J., & Burn, W., 1777 *History and Antiquities of the Counties of Westmorland and Cumberland*, London

NORGATE, T.B., 1969 *A History of Taverham*, Taverham

OAKDEN, J., 1984 *Place Names of Staffordshire I*, Cambridge

OBELKEVICH, J., 1976 *Religion and Rural Society in South Lindsey 1825–75*, Oxford

OBOLENSKY, D., 1971 *The Byzantine Commonwealth*, London

O'COINDEALBAIN, S., 1946 'Holy Wells', *Journ. of the Cork Hist. and Arch. Soc.*

O'DANACHAIR, C., 1955, 'Holy Wells of Co. Limerick, *Journ. of the Roy. Soc. of Antiqs. of Ireland*

——, 1958, 'Holy Wells of North Co. Kerry', *Journ. of the Roy. Soc. of Antiqs. of Ireland*

——, 1960, 'Holy Wells of Corkaguiney, Co. Kerry', *Journ. of the Roy Soc. of Antiqs. of Ireland*

OPIE, P., 1962–3 'The Tentacles of Tradition', *Folklore*

ORMEROD, G., 1812 *History of the County Palatine of Cheshire*, London

ORMEROD, T., 1906 *Calderdale*, Burnley

ORTON, R.W., 1908 *Tattenhall*, Chester

OSBORNE, C., 1903 *Life of Father Dolling*, London

OSBORNE, G., 1987 *Dorset Curiosities*, Stanbridge

O'TOOLE, E., 1933 'Holy Wells of County Carlow', *Bealoideas*

OTTER, L., 1985–8 'Notes Towards a Survey of Shropshire Wells', *Source 3–8*

OVID, *Ars Amatoris*

OWEN, D.M., 1984 *The Making of King's Lynn*, London

OXLEY, J.E., 1965 *The Reformation in Essex*, Manchester

PADEL, E., 1985 *Cornish Place-name Elements*, Cambridge

PAFFORD, J., 1954 'Spas and Mineral Springs of Wiltshire', *Wiltshire Magazine*

PAGE, W., 1915 'Some Remarks on the Churches of the Domesday Survey', *Archaeologia*

PALIN, W., 1871 *Stifford and Its Neighbourhood*, Stifford

PALMER, R., 1992 *The Folklore of Hereford and Worcester*, Almley

PALMER, W.M., 1939 *A History of the Parish of Borough Green*, Cambridge

PAPE, T., 1938 *Newcastle Under Lyme in Tudor and Early Stuart Times*, Manchester

PARIS, M., 1874 *Chronica Majora*, ed. Luard, H.R., London

PARKE, H.J., 1967 *Oracles of Zeus*, Oxford

——, 1985 *Oracles of Apollo in Asia Minor*, Beckenham

PARKE, H.J., & Wormell, D., 1956 *The Delphic Oracle*, Oxford

PARKINSON, T., 1888 *Yorkshire Legends and Traditions*, London

PARSONS, C., 1933 'The Association of the White Lady with Well', *Folk-lore*

PARSONS, W., 1895 in *Wiltshire Magazine*

PARTRIDGE, J., 1774 *History of Nantwich*, Shrewsbury
PARTRIDGE, J.B., 1912 'Cotswold Place lore and Customs', *Folk-lore*
PATCHELL, P. & E., 1987 'The Wells of Old Warwickshire', *Source 6*
PATTERSON, T., 1949 'The Cult of the Well in Co. Armagh', *Ulster Arch. Journ.*
PATON, C., 1941 'Manx Calendar Customs', *Folk-lore*
PATON, W., 1907 'Folklore, Nursery lore etc., from the Aegean Islands', *Folk-lore*
PEACOCK, M., 1896a 'Executed Criminals and Folk Medicine', *Folk-lore*
————, 1896b 'The Hood game at Haxey, Lincolnshire', *Folk-lore*
PEARCE, S., 1973 'Celtic Dedications in the Southwest', *Trans. of the Devonshire Assoc.*
————, 1978 *The Kingdom of Dumnonia*, Padstow
PEARSON, H., 1901 'Birmingham Wells and Springs', *Trans. of the Birmingham Arch. Soc.*
PECK, F., 1727 *Academia Tertia Anglicana, or The Antiquities of Stamford*, London
PENN, K., 1980 *Historic Towns in Dorset*, Dorchester
PENNICK, N., 1985 'Holy and Notable Wells of the Cambridge District', *Source 1*
PERFECT, C.T., 1917 *Ye Olde Village of Hornchurch*, Colchester
PERSIUS, *Satires*, ed. J.R. Jenkinson, 1980 Warminster
PHELPS, W., 1836 *Antiquities of Somerset*, London
PHYTHIAN-ADAMS, C., 1972 'Ceremony and the Citizen, the Communal Year at Coventry' in P. Clark & P. S Slack eds., *Crisis and Order in English Towns*, London
————, 1975 *Local History and Folklore: A New Framework*, London
PILE, J., 1986 'The Homewell, Havant', *Source 5*
PITFIELD, F.P., 1981 *Dorset Parish Churches A–D*, Milborne Port
PLINY, *Natural History*
PLOT, R., 1686 *The Natural History of Staffordshire*, Oxford
————, 1705 *The Natural History of Oxfordshire*, Oxford
POCOCKE, R., 1888 *Travels Through England of Dr Richard Pococke*, ed. J.J. Cartwright, London
POLWHELE, R., 1803 *Antiquities of Cornwall*, Falmouth
POOLE, A., 1968 'A Romano-British Well at Welwyn', *Herts. Arch.*
PORTEOUS, C., 1973 *The Well-Dressing Guide*, Derby
PORTER, E., 1969 *Cambridgeshire Customs and Folklore*, London
POTTER, C., 1985a 'The River of Wells', *Source 1*
POTTER, C., 1985b 'Holy Wells of Leicestershire and Rutland', *Source 1*
POTTER, T., 1842 *The History of Charnwood Forest*
POTTS, T., 1892 *Sunderland: A History of the Town*, Sunderland
POUND, N.J.G., 1942–3 'Holy Wells and Climatic Change', *Folk-lore*
POWELL, T., 1661 *Tom of All Trades, or the Plain Pathway to Preferment*, London
POWICKE, F., & Cheney, D., 1964 *Councils and Synods II*, Cambridge

PRESTON, A., 1941 'The Caswell, Ock Street, Abingdon', *Berks. Arch. Journ.*

PRESTON, W., 1933, 'Some Local Holy Wells', *Bradford Antiquary*

PROCEEDINGS of the Society of Antiquaries of Newcastle, Second series, 1896, 1902

PROCKTER, A., & Taylor, R., 1979 *The A–Z of Elizabethan London,* London

PROTHEROE, A., 1925 'Scraps of English Folklore: Derbyshire', *Folk-lore*

PRYME, A. de la, 1870 *Diary of Abraham de la Pryme,* ed. C. Jackson, Durham

PURTON, R., 1987 'Further Notes on the History of the Parish of Chetton', *Trans. of the Salop. Arch. and Nat. Hist. Soc.*

QUIN, W.F., 1981 *A History of Braintree and Bocking,* Lavenham

QUINE, D.A., 1982 *St Kilda Revisited,* Frome

RAHTZ, C., 1964, 'Excavations at Chalice Well, Glastonbury', *Procs. of the Somerset Arch. and Nat. Hist. Soc.*

————, 1979 'The End of Roman Temples in the West of Britain' (with L. Watts), in P.J. Casey ed., *The End of Roman Britain,* Banbury

RAHTZ, P., Harden, D.P., Dunning, G., & Radford, R., 1957 'Three post-Roman Finds from the Temple at Pagans Hill', *Medieval Archaeology*

RAINE, A., 1955 *Medieval York,* London

RAINE, J., ed., 1837 *Charters of the Priory of Finchale,* London

————, 1863a *The Black Book of Hexham,* Durham

————, 1863b *The Priory of Hexham,* Durham

RANCE, A., 1986 *Southampton, an Illustrated History,* Portsmouth

RANSFORD, R., ed., 1989 *Early Charters of . . . Waltham Abbey,* Woodbridge

RATCLIFF, O., 1900 *History and Antiquities of Newport Pagnell Hundred,* Olney

RATTUE, J., 1986–8 'Some Wells in the South and West', *Source 5–9*

————, 1990 'Ancient, Holy and Healing Wells of Oxfordshire', *Oxoniensia*

————, 1993a 'An Inventory of Ancient Wells in Dorset', *Procs. of the Dorset Nat. Hist. & Arch. Soc.*

————, 1993b 'An Inventory of Named Wells in Leicestershire', *Trans. of the Leics. Arch. & Hist. Soc.*

RAWLINS, R.R., 1823 'On the Ancient Custom of Decorating Wells', *Gentleman's Magazine* (1823, ii)

READER'S DIGEST 1973, Folklore, Myths and Legends of Britain, London

REANEY, P.J., 1935 *Place Names of Essex,* Cambridge

————, 1943 *Place Names of Cambridgeshire and the Isle of Ely,* Cambridge

REGINALD OF DURHAM, 1835 *Libellus de Admirandi Beati Cuthberti,* London

————, 1847 *Libellus de Vita et Miraculis Sancti Godrici,* Durham

RENDELL, J.,1982 *Cornish Churches,* St Teath

RICE, M.A., 1939 *Abbots Bromley,* Shrewsbury

RICHARDS, R., 1947 *Old Cheshire Churches,* London

RICHARDSON, L.R., 1925 'Horwood Spa', *Procs. of the Somerset Arch. and Nat. Hist. Soc.*

————, 1928a *Wells and Springs of Somerset*, London

————, 1928b *Wells and Springs of Warwickshire*, London

————, 1930a *Wells and Springs of Gloucestershire*, London

————, 1930b *Wells and Springs of Worcestershire*, London

————, 1931 *Wells and Springs of Leicestershire*, London

————, 1935 *Wells and Springs of Herefordshire*, London

RIDEN, P., & Blair, J., 1980 *History of Chesterfield V*, Chesterfield

ROBLIN, M., 1976 'Fontaines Sacrées et Nécropoles Antiques', *Revue d'Histoire de l'Eglise de France*

RODWELL, W., 1980 'Wells, the Cathedral and City', *Current Archaeology* August

————, 1981 *The Archaeology of English Churches*, London

————, 1982 'From Mausoleum to Minster: The Early Development of Wells Cathedral' in S. Pearce ed., *The Early Church in Western Britain and Ireland*, Banbury

RODWELL, W., & Rodwell, R., 1982 'St Peter's Church, Barton on Humber', *Antiq. Journ.*

ROGER OF HOVEDEN, 1870 *Chronica*, ed. W. Stubbs, London

ROLLASON, D., 1988 *Saints and Relics in Anglo-Saxon England*, Oxford

ROSE, H., 1925 'Some Indian Folklore in the Lay of Ahra', *Folk-lore*

ROSS, A., 1967 *Pagan Celtic Britain*, London

————, 1986 *The Pagan Celts*, London

ROUSE, W., 1896 'Folklore First-Fruits from Lesbos', *Folk-lore*

ROYAL COMMISSION on Historic Monuments, vols. for Essex and Oxford

RUDKIN, E., 1938 'The Black Dog', *Folk-lore*

————, 1954–5 'Lincolnshire Folklore', *Folk-lore*

RUSSELL, J. & S., 1801 *The History of Guildford*

SALTER, H.A., 1907 *The Eynsham Cartulary*, Oxford

————, 1912 *Records of Medieval Oxford*, Oxford

————, 1937 *Medieval Oxford*, Oxford

SALZMAN, L.F., ed., 1934 *Cartulary of the Priory of St Pancras of Lewes*, Sussex Record Society

SANDRED K., & Lindstrom, D., 1989 *Place Names of Norfolk I*, Nottingham

SAWYER P., 1979, see BONNEY

————, 1982 *Kings and Vikings*, London

SAYCE, A., 1900 'Cairene Folklore', *Folk-lore*

SCARISBRICK, J., 1984 *The Reformation and the English People*, Oxford

SCHMITT, J., 1983 *The Holy Greyhound*, Cambridge

SCHOLES, J.C., 1892 *History of Bolton*, Bolton

SCHOOL OF EDUCATION, 1989 *Redding 1540–1640*, Reading

SESSIONS, F., 1898 'Syrian Folklore Notes Gathered on Mount Lebanon', *Folk-lore*

SHARP, C., 1851 *A History of Hartlepool*, Hartlepool

SHAW, R.C., 1949 *Kirkham in Amounderness*, Preston

SHAW, S., 1798–1801 *History and Antiquities of Staffordshire*, London

SHAW, W.F., 1870 *Liber Estriae, or Memorials of the Parish of Eastry*, London

SHAW, —, 1815 *History of Verulam and St Albans*

SHAWCROSS, J.P., 1904 *History of Dagenham*, London

SHEAHAN, T., & Whellan, T., 1856 *History and Topography of the City of York, the Ainsty Wapentake and the East Riding of Yorkshire*, East Riding

SHORE, T., 1891 'Springs and Streams of Hampshire', *Procs. of the Hants. Fd. Club*

SIMPSON, J., 1987 *European Mythology*, London

SIMPSON, R., 1852 *History and Antiquities of Lancaster*, Lancaster

SINGLETON, A., 1904 'Dairy Folklore and Other Notes from Meath and Tipperary', *Folk-lore*

SJOO, M., 1985 'St Non's Well', *Source 1*

SMITH, A., 1978 'St Augustine in History and Tradition', *Folklore*

SMITH, A.H., 1928 *Place Names of the North Riding of Yorkshire*, Cambridge

————, 1937 *Place Names of the East Riding of Yorkshire*, Cambridge

————, 1961–3 *Place Names of the West Riding of Yorkshire*, Cambridge

————, 1964a *Place Names of Gloucestershire*, Cambridge

————, 1967–8 *Place Names of Westmorland*, Cambridge

SMITH, B., & Ralph, E., 1972 *A History of Bristol and Gloucester*, Beaconsfield

SMITH, B.S., 1964b *History of Malvern*, Leicester

SMITH, G., 1988 *Bentworth, the Making of a Hampshire Village*, 1988

SMITH, J., 1987 'Bride's Well, Melvost Borve', *Source 7*

SMITH, R., 1986 *The Well of Our Lady*, Lewisham

SMITH, R.L., ed., 1932 *Lancaster Registers V*, London

SMITH, W., 1923 *Ancient Springs and Streams of the East Riding of Yorkshire*, London

SMITH, W.C., 1902 *Dunstable, Its History and Surroundings*, London

SMYTH, J., 1892 *History of the Hundred of Berkeley*, Gloucester

SOUTHERN, R.W., 1987 *The Making of the Middle Ages*, London

SOX, D., 1985 *Relics and Shrines*, London

SPARKS, M., ed., 1980 *The Parish of St Martin and St Paul*, Canterbury

SPEAKE, R., & Witty, F.R., 1953 *A History of Droylesden*, Stockport

SPEIGHT, H., 1912 'Ancient Streets and Lanes of Bradford', *Bradford Antiquary*

SPENCER, K.G., 1989 *An Outline History of Habergham Eaves*, Burnley

SPOER, H., 1907 'The Powers of Evil in Jerusalem', *Folk-lore*

STANLEY, A., 1868 *A History of the Memorials of Westminster Abbey*, London

STENTON, F.M., 1989 *Anglo-Saxon England*, Oxford

STEPHENS, W.B., ed., 1970 *History of Congleton*, Manchester

STEPHENSON, J., ed., 1858 *Chronicle of St Albans*, London

STEPHENSON, W., 1877-8 'On the Discovery of a Well in Beverley Minster', *Yorks. Arch. Journ.*

STOKES, A., 1933 *A History of East Ham*, Stratford

STOKES, H.P., 1926 *A History of the Wilbraham Parishes*, Cambridge

STONE, L., 1965 *The Crisis of the Aristocracy*, Oxford

STOUT, E.J., 1936 *Folklore from Iowa*, New York

STRATTON, C., 1902 'An English Manor in the Time of Elizabeth', *Wiltshire Magazine*

SUMMERNELL, M., et al., *The Book of Wendover*, Buckingham

SUMMERS, J.W., 1858 *History and Antiquities of Sunderland*, Sunderland

SUMMERS, M., 1925 *The History of Witchcraft*, London

SWALE, W.E., 1969 *Grange Over Sands: the Story of a Gentle Township*, Grange

SWANTON, E.W., ed., 1984 *Bygone Haslemere*, London

SYER, G.V., 1981 *St Candida and Holy Cross*, Whitchurch Canonicorum

SYKES, E., 1900 'Persian Folklore', *Folk-lore*

TACITUS, *Annales; Germania*

TALBOT, C.H., ed., 1954 *The Anglo-Saxon Missionaries in Germany*

TASKER, G.E., 1901 *Ilford Past and Present*, Ilford

TATE, G., 1866 *History of the Borough, Castle and Barony of Alnwick*, Alnwick

TAYLOR, H., 1906 *The Ancient Crosses and Holy Wells of Lancashire*, Manchester (first edn. published 1902-4 in four portions)

TAYLOR PAGE, J., 1990 *Cumbrian Holy Wells*, Wigan

————, 1990-91 'Cumbrian Earth Mysteries', *Northern Earth Mysteries*, 44-5

TEBBUTT, C., 1962-3 'St Patrick's Well, Oran, Eire', *Folklore*

TEVERSHAM, T.F., 1942 *A History of Parish of Sawston*, Sawston

THANE, P., 1982 *Foundation of the Welfare State*, Harlow

THOMAS, C.E., 1985 *The Exploration of a Drowned Landscape*, London

THOMAS, K.V., 1978 *Religion and the Decline of Magic*, London

THOMAS OF BURTON, 1866 *Chronicle of Melsa*, ed. E.A. Bond, London

THOMAS OF WALSINGHAM, 1869 *Gesta Abbatum Monasterii Sancti Albani*, ed., H.T. Riley, London

THOMPSON, B., 1911-15 'Peculiarities of Waters and Wells', *Journ. of the Northants. Nat. Hist. Soc. and Fd. Club*

THOMPSON, F., 1990 'John Francis Campbell', *Folklore*

THOMPSON, G.H., 1888a, in *Monthly Chronicle of North Country Lore and Legend*

THOMPSON, J., 1888b 'The Capping Well', *Monthly Chronicle of North Country Lore and Legend*

THOMPSON, J.S., 1990 *Hundreds, Manors, Parishes and the Church*, Bedford

THOMSON, T.R., 1961 *Materials for a History of Cricklade*, Oxford

THOMSON, —, 1935, *History of Hayes*, London

THUNDER, J., 1885-6 'Holy Wells of Meath', *Journ. of the Antiq. Assoc. of Ireland*

TIDDEMAN, R., 1910 *The Water Supply of Oxfordshire*, London
TODD, M., 1987 *The Southwest to A.D.1000*, London
TONGUE, R., 1967 *Somerset Folklore*, London
TOULSON, S., 1987 *The Celtic Alternative*, London
TRANSACTIONS *of the Cumberland and Westmorland Antiquarian and Archaeological Society*, 1887–8; 1891–2
TREDWELL, M.D., 1982 *Links Across the Centuries . . . Eaton By Tarporley*, Eaton
TUFNELL, B., 1924 'Czecho-Slovak Folklore', *Folk-lore*
TURTON, R., 1912–13 'Roseberry Topping', *Yorks. Arch. Journ.*
TURVILLE-PETRE, E.O., 1964 *Myth and Religion in the North*, London
TYACKE, N., 1987 *Anti-Calvinists*, Oxford
TYMMS, S., 1859 'Woolpit Church', *Procs. of the Suffolk Arch. Institute*
UDAL, J., 1922 *Dorsetshire Folklore*, Dorchester
UNDERDOWN, D., 1985 *Revel, Riot and Rebellion*, Oxford
URRY, W., 1967 *Canterbury Under the Angevin Kings*, London
USHER, H., 1986 'The Holy Well of King's Newton', *Source 4*
VALENTINE, M., 1985a 'Buckinghamshire Wells', *Source 2*
———, 1985b *Holy Wells of Northamptonshire*, Northampton
VAN BUREN, E., 1925 'Archaeologists in Antiquity', *Folk-lore*
VERMASEREN, M., 1963 *Mithras the Secret God*, London
VICTORIA COUNTY HISTORIES
VINCE, J., 1978 *Wells and Water Supply*, Aylesbury
VIRGIN, P., 1988 *The Church in an Age of Negligence*, Cambridge
VITRE, J. de, 1931 in *Berks. Bucks. and Oxon. Arch. Journ.*
VUKANOVIC, T., 1985 'Neolithic Blind Statues and Balkan Folklore of the Blind', *Folklore*
WAITE, V., 1972 'The Bristol Hotwell', in P. McGrath ed., *Bristol in the Eighteenth Century*, Bristol
WAKEMAN, W., 1879–82 'On Certain Wells Situate in the Northwest of Ireland', *Journ. of the Antiqs. Assoc. of Ireland*
WALKER, D., 1976, *A History of the Church in Wales*, Penarth
WALKER, J., 1944–7a 'Robin Hood Identified', *Yorks. Arch. Journ.*
———, 1944–7b 'The Battle of Winwaed', *Yorks. Arch. Journ.*
WALKER, V.W., & Gray, D., 1940 *Newstead Priory Cartulary*, Nottingham
WALLACE-HADRILL, J., 1985 *The Barbarian West*, Oxford
WALLENBERG, J., 1934 *Place Names of Kent*, Uppsala
WALLER, J., 1875 'The Hole-Bourne', *Trans. of the London and Midd'x. Arch. Soc.*
WALTER OF COVENTRY, 1874 *Memoriales*, ed. W. Stubbs, London
WALTERS, C., 1898 'Holy Wells', in W. Andrews ed., *The Church Treasury*
WALTERS, R.C.S., 1928 *Ancient Wells, Springs and Holy Wells of Gloucestershire*, Bristol
———, 1953–60 'Notes on Buckinghamshire Wells', *Records of Bucks.*
WANKLYN, C., 1927 *Lyme Regis: A Retrospective*, London
WATLAM, I., 1920 *Oswestry*, Oswestry

WATKINS, A., 1930 in *Transactions of the Woolhope Society*

WEBB, E.A., et al., 1899 *The History of Chislehurst*, London

WEEKS, W., 1920 'Further Legendary Stories and Folklore of the Clitheroe District', *Trans. of the Lancs. and Chesh. Antiq. Soc.*

WELFORD, R., ed., c.1881 *Newcastle and Gateshead in the Fourteenth and Fifteenth Centuries*, London

WESTERMARCH, E., 1905 'Midsummer Customs in Morocco', *Folk-lore*

WESTROPPE, T., 1910, 1911, 'Folklore Survey of County Clare', *Folk-lore*

——————, 1912 'Co. Clare Folklore and Myths', *Folk-lore*

——————, 1923 'Folklore on the Coasts of Connacht', *Folk-lore*

WHELAN, E., 1985–8 'Holy Wells in Yorkshire', *Source 3–9*

WHELAN, E., & I.Taylor, 1989 *Yorkshire Holy Wells and Sacred Springs*, York

WHITAKER, 1823 *A History of Richmondshire*, London

WHITAKER, T.D., 1878 *History and Antiquities of the Deanery of Craven*, London & Leeds

WHITAKER, W., 1908 *The Water Supply of Kent*, London

——————, 1910 *The Water Supply of Hampshire and the Isle of Wight*, London

——————, 1912 *The Water Supply of Surrey*, London

——————, 1916 *The Water Supply of Essex*, London

——————, 1921a *The Water Supply of Buckinghamshire and Hertfordshire*, London

——————, 1921b *The Water Supply of Norfolk*, London

——————, 1922 *The Water Supply of Cambridgeshire, Huntingdonshire and Rutland*, London

——————, 1925 *The Water Supply of Wiltshire*, London

——————, 1926 *Wells and Springs of Dorset*, London

WHITAKER, W., & Reid, C., 1889 *The Water Supply of Sussex*, London

WHITE, W., 1863 *History, Gazetteer and Directory of Leicestershire and Rutland*, Sheffield

WHITELOCK, D., Brett, M., & Brook, C., 1981 *Councils and Synods I*, Cambridge

WHITING, R., 1988 *The Blind Devotion of the People*, Cambridge

WHITLOCK, R., 1976 *The Folklore of Wiltshire*, London

——————, 1979 *In Search of Lost Gods*, Oxford

WHITNEY, A.W., & Bullock, C.C., 1925 *Folklore from Maryland*, New York

WICKHAM, C., 1981 *A History of Medieval Italy*

WIDNALL, S.P., 1875 *History of Grantchester*, Granchester

WILCOCK, J., 1976 *A Guide to Occult Britain*, London

WILD, J., 1871 *History of Castle Bytham*, Stamford

——————, 1901 *Tentney, Lincolnshire: A History*, Grimsby

WILKERSON, J.R., 1974 *John Norden's Survey of Barley*, Cambridge

WILLIAM OF MALMESBURY, 1870 *Gesta Pontificum Anglorum*, ed. N.E.S.A. Hamilton, London

WILLIAMS, P., 1987 *Bromyard, Minster, Manor and Town*, Bringsty

WILLIAMSON, G.C., & Kelly, B., 1929 *The Church of St Edward the Confessor*, Guildford

WILLIS, C.S., 1969 *A Short History of Ewell and Nonsuch*, Epsom

WILSON, J., 1889–90 'Baptismal Fonts', *Trans. of the Cumbd. and Westd. Antiq. and Arch. Soc.*

WILSON, P., 1966–7 'The Romano-British and Welsh Churches: Continuity or Discontinuity?', *Welsh Hist. Revue*

WILSON, R., 1991 *Holy Wells and Spas of South Yorkshire*, Sheffield

WILSON FOX, Mrs., 1923–7 'Notes on Northaw and District', *East Herts. Arch. Soc.*

WILTSHIRE, K., 1975 *Wiltshire Folklore*, Compton Chamberlayne

WIMBOLT, S.E., & Annett, S., 1941 'Wayside Springs in the Weald', *Sussex County Magazine*

WINNIFRITH, J., 1984 'The Medieval Church of Ebony and Its Successors', *Archaeologia Cantiana*

WISE, C., 1987 'The Well of the Sacred Blood', *Source 7*

WOOD, A., 1889 *A Survey of the Antiquities of the City of Oxford*, Oxford

WOODWARD, H., 1904 *The Water Supply of Lincolnshire*, London

WOODWARD, H., & Thompson, B., 1909 *The Water Supply of Bedfordshire and Northamptonshire*, London

WOOLLEY, W., 1981 *History of Derbyshire*, ed. C. Glover & P. Riden, Chesterfield

WORCESTRE, William, 1981 *Itinerary*, ed. J. Harvey, Oxford

WORDSWORTH, C., 1941 'Holy Wells of Wiltshire', in *Wilts. Notes and Queries*

WRIGHT, 1982 *Frant, Story of a Wealden Parish*, Frant

WRIGHTSON, K., 1982 *English Society 1580–1680*, London

YATES, N., 1983 *The Oxford Movement and Anglican Ritualism*, Historical Association

YEO, S., 1976 *Religion and Voluntary Organizations in Crisis*, London

YOUNG, G., 1817 *History of Whitby*, Whitby

INDEX OF WELLS IN ENGLISH COUNTIES

GENERAL INDEX

Printed and bound by CPI Group (UK) Ltd, Croydon, CR0 4YY

25/03/2025

14647332-0001